Scott Foresman

Assessment Handbook

Grades 2-3

Glenview, Illinois • Boston, Massachusetts • Chandler, Arizona • Upper Saddle River, New Jersey

ISBN-13: 978-0-328-48543-7
ISBN-10:   0-328-48543-8

4 5 6 7 8 9 10 V016 18 17 16 15 14 13 12 11 10
CC1

Contents

Scott Foresman *Reading Street* Assessment

Some Questions and Answers

This *Assessment Handbook* will be a resource throughout the school year. The handbook presents an overview of the Scott Foresman *Reading Street* assessment program, and it provides numerous resources that you may use to best fit your assessment, instruction, and learning goals. In addition, the *Assessment Handbook* may be regarded as a professional development resource. Inside you will find:

- guidance for using a variety of diagnostic, entry-level, progress-monitoring, summative, and classroom-based assessments;

- suggestions for using writing to strengthen learning and to assess learning;

- proven methods and models for assessing, evaluating, and grading student work;

- steps for designing quality assessments in all content areas; and

- instructional strategies for preparing children for state-required assessments.

Scott Foresman *Reading Street* assessments reflect current theories of teaching language and literacy and are aligned with solid classroom teaching practices. Formal and classroom-based assessments, combined with "assessable moments" during instruction, become a continuous cycle in which one is always informing and supporting the other, resulting in a seamless learning program for students.

Following are some commonly asked questions about the Scott Foresman *Reading Street* assessment program.

How was the Scott Foresman *Reading Street* assessment program developed?

The assessment components of Scott Foresman *Reading Street* were developed by a specialized testing organization, Questar Assessment, Incorporated. Scott Foresman authorial and editorial staff guided these development activities, specifying the purposes to be served by each component and their general coverage. In addition, Scott Foresman editorial teams critiqued and approved the test specifications and prototype test items for each program element that were developed by Questar. Finally, Scott Foresman reviewed and provided editorial feedback on all test content. However, the development of all materials was the responsibility of Questar Assessment staff.

Questar Assessment's development team, formerly Beck Evaluation & Testing Associates, Incorporated (BETA), is one of the country's most experienced assessment-development corporations. Over the past twenty years, Questar's test development team has provided standardized test content for a broad range of state and federal agencies in addition to most leading test and textbook publishers. Questar has played key roles in developing large-scale, high-stakes testing programs in over twenty-five states. Questar staff regularly assist state Departments of Education and federal agencies on matters of test development, implementation, and psychometrics, providing such consultation to over thirty-six state Departments of Education. Over the past decade, Questar has developed over 82,000 test items for use in large-scale assessment programs. Most of these programs include the assessment of elementary reading and other language-arts skills.

All test items developed by Questar are written by experienced assessment-development professionals, all with extensive experience in creating test questions in the appropriate content areas and for the targeted grade levels. The development activities in support of Scott Foresman *Reading Street* were directed by Questar senior staff members, and all test items were written specifically for Scott Foresman *Reading Street*.

How will your program help prepare children for required state and national standardized tests?

In many ways! The Student Editions, Teacher's Editions, and Reader's and Writer's Notebooks are all carefully crafted to teach the knowledge, skills, and strategies students need in order to meet or exceed the standards in all their reading and writing tasks. Many Reader's and Writer's Notebook pages contain items that reflect common standardized test formats, allowing students repeated opportunities to become familiar with question patterns. In addition, the formal entry-level, progress-monitoring, and summative assessments are comprised of literal, inferential, and critical-analysis questions based on the question-answer framework used in instruction and are similar to question types on high-stakes tests used in school districts. Tips on instructional strategies designed to prepare students for state-required assessments are described in Chapter 1 of this handbook and in Chapter 6, where they are tailored for English language learners. With the preparation provided by Scott Foresman *Reading Street* materials, students will have experience with a variety of test-taking situations and learn a variety of test-taking skills.

How do I find out where students are at the beginning of the year?

Finding a starting point for each student can be difficult. Scott Foresman *Reading Street* makes it easier by providing test options and parent and learner surveys to help you get to know students' skills, abilities, and interests.

Entry-level assessments provide information about where to begin instruction for individual learners. The more you know about your students at the beginning of the year, the better equipped you are to maximize their learning experiences to ensure that they achieve continuous growth in writing, speaking, reading, and listening skills. The group-administered *Reading Street* Baseline Group Test gives you information about the instructional needs of your class and points you to program features that help you meet those needs. The Group Reading Assessment and Diagnostic Evaluation (GRADE) is a norm-referenced formal assessment that helps you to determine students' prerequisite skills and knowledge. The Developmental Reading Assessment (DRA) enables you to make a quick analysis of a student's independent reading level. Student surveys, such as the questionnaire Myself as a Reader and Writer, familiarize you with each student's reading attitudes and interests, while parent surveys, such as My Child as a Learner, give you insights into their literacy habits and behaviors when they are not in school. Chapter 2 of this handbook describes all of the entry-level formal and informal classroom-based assessment techniques and tools available to you through Scott Foresman *Reading Street*. All entry-level and diagnostic assessment information helps you determine which content standards have been mastered, resulting in appropriate placement and planning for each student in your class.

How do I know that students are being tested on the right skills?

Scott Foresman *Reading Street* is founded on a carefully crafted scope and sequence of skills, based on the most current research and accepted practices in reading instruction, and systematically aligned with state language arts and reading standards.

This scope and sequence is the basis for both the instructional plan and for the depth and breadth of the Scott Foresman *Reading Street* assessment program. Target skills and strategies are taught in each lesson and then assessed in the Weekly Test. Each target skill is also assessed in the Unit Benchmark Test after it has been taught and reviewed multiple times. This systematic alignment of instruction and assessment ensures that students are being tested on what they are being taught, in the way they are being taught.

What is the best way to assess my students? How does your program provide what I need?

Accurate and ongoing assessment enables teachers to monitor students' progress toward achieving the standards, to evaluate classroom instruction, and to help students monitor their own learning. An effective assessment system incorporates a variety of assessment methods—both formal and informal—to help teachers meet those varied purposes.

Scott Foresman *Reading Street* provides a full complement of materials to meet your assessment requirements. For a formal assessment of unit skills and selections, you will find several different tests from which to choose. For classroom-based assessment, the *Assessment Handbook* contains surveys, observation forms, and reporting forms, as well as questioning and observation techniques you can adapt for your classroom needs. These informal strategies will assist you in making student self-assessment, peer assessment, portfolios, and grading more efficient. Also, the Teacher's Editions provide tools for you to make both immediate and long-term decisions about the instructional needs of your students.

How does your program support assessment of my English language learners?

Scott Foresman *Reading Street* recognizes the unique challenges and rewards of teaching and assessing the progress of English language learners. Chapter 6 of the *Assessment Handbook* discusses research-based methods of assessing the strengths and needs of English language learners in your classroom. Scott Foresman *Reading Street* classroom-based assessments reflect those methods as they help teachers monitor progress in the basic reading and expression skills of alphabetic understanding, decoding, sight vocabulary, and grammar, along with measurement of the more complex skills of fluency, comprehension, and vocabulary. The chapter provides guidance on instructional strategies designed to prepare English language learners for standardized tests, including high-stakes tests, as well as advice on appropriate use of accommodations for Scott Foresman *Reading Street* formal assessments.

Will your program help me when I have to assign grades?

Because we know that grading is a major concern for many teachers, we devote an entire chapter (7) to record keeping and grading. We recognize that you will be using the *Reading Street* tools to assess students' literacy skills and strategies at the beginning of the year and monitor progress throughout the year. You will be collecting large amounts of information about your students. Access to this data informs sound decision-making relating to the focus of the curriculum, effectiveness of instruction, meaningful feedback to students and parents, and improved achievement, but it is often difficult to manage.

In Chapter 7, you will find guidance for keeping accurate, informative records and sharing details with students, parents, and others. Advice for implementing student portfolios and grading is also provided; you will review how to design scoring rubrics, evaluate student participation in class discussions and group activities, grade oral presentations, and assess individual or group writing.

Add to this the many formal testing opportunities, which are an integral part of the program, and you have an assessment program that gives you the information you need to meet your assessment requirements.

Program Assessment Overview

A variety of assessment instruments, used with fiction and nonfiction selections, allow you to

- determine students' strengths and needs
- monitor students' progress
- measure students' skill and strategy proficiencies
- evaluate the effectiveness of instruction

from the beginning of the school year to the end!

Baseline Group Tests

Weekly Tests

Fresh Reads for Fluency and Comprehension

Unit Benchmark Tests

End-of-Year Benchmark Test

Assessment Handbook

Technology

Online
ASSESSMENT
ReadingStreet.com

Beginning of the Year

Entry-Level Assessments

Baseline Group Test

- Is administered as a placement test to your entire class
- Provides options for group and individual administration
- Identifies your below-level students requiring strategic intervention
- Identifies your on-level students
- Identifies your above-level students requiring challenge
- Helps you use Scott Foresman *Reading Street* features and components to focus instruction on students' needs
- Establishes baseline data

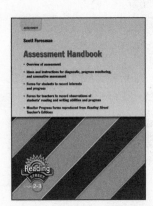

Assessment Handbook for Grades 2–3

Informal, classroom-based assessment tools and techniques, including:

- Student and parent surveys
- Reading, writing, and oral-language teacher checklists
- Learner inventories and profiles

During the Year

Progress-Monitoring Assessments

Teacher's Edition and *First Stop*

- Ongoing assessment
- Success Predictor boxes
- Guiding Comprehension questions
- Reading fluency assessment
- Think Critically
- Look Back and Write model answers
- Writing Scoring Rubrics
- Spelling tests
- Weekly assessment for phonics and word analysis, vocabulary words, and comprehension

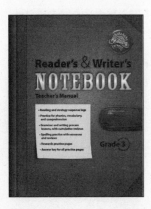

Reader's and Writer's Notebook

- Provides practice pages for phonics, vocabulary, spelling, and comprehension skills
- Grammar and writing process practice and cumulative reviews
- Reading and writing logs
- Helps you identify students needing more instruction

Weekly Tests

- Are multiple-choice tests administered on Day 5 of every week
- Measure students' understanding of each week's introduced vocabulary words, phonics/word analysis skills, and comprehension skills
- Help identify students who have mastered each week's words and skills and students who may need intervention

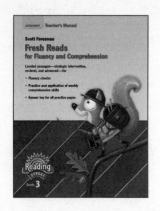

Fresh Reads for Fluency and Comprehension

- Are multiple-choice and constructed-response tests administered throughout the year, each week after students have been taught the comprehension skill lesson

- Give students opportunities to practice the target and review comprehension skills of the week with new selections matched to their instructional reading levels

- Provide checks of oral reading fluency

Unit Benchmark Tests

- Are multiple-choice and constructed-response tests administered throughout the year, at the end of each six-week unit

- Measure students' abilities to apply target comprehension skills and other literacy skills taught during each unit

- Help you make instructional decisions for each student

- Provide feedback about the effectiveness of your instruction and help you plan instruction for the next unit

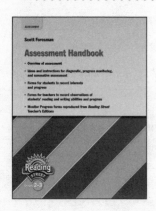

Assessment Handbook for Grades 2–3

Informal, classroom-based assessment tools and techniques, including:

- Questioning strategies
- Teacher observation forms
- Fluency checks
- Retelling and summarizing forms
- Work habits and skills conference records
- Parent observation form
- Self, peer, and group assessment forms
- Student portfolios
- Reading and writing logs and responses

Technology

- Online assessment and data management with diagnostic prescriptions

- Exam View: Test generator with alignment to statewide and district-wide standards and prescriptions

End of the Year

Summative Assessments

End-of-Year Benchmark Test

- Is a cumulative test administered at the end of each grade

- Provides three reading selections

- Tests comprehension skills, vocabulary strategies, phonics skills, written conventions (grammar, usage, and mechanics skills), and writing

- Combines multiple-choice and constructed response questions

- Provides an integrated approach to assessment

. . . .

Assessment Handbook for Grades 2–3

Informal, classroom-based assessment tools and techniques, including:

- Summary reports, forms, and checklists

- Student portfolios

- Cumulative folder forms

- Reading and writing logs

- Reading and writing assessment forms

- Guidance with grading

. . . .

Technology

- Online assessment and data management with diagnostic prescriptions

- Exam View: Test generator with alignment to statewide and district-wide standards and prescriptions

Chapter 1

Assessment Literacy

Overview

Classroom teachers make an extraordinary number of decisions every hour of the school day. Four important decisions are:

1. What are the critical understandings and skills that I want students to know and be able to do upon completion of this lesson/unit/grade?

2. How will I know if the students have reached these expectations?

3. What will I do to support those who have not met these standards?

4. What will I do to support those who already have exceeded the standards?

The critical understandings and skills are the **learning targets,** usually based on school, district, and state curriculum standards. The second question is the focus of this introductory section of the handbook: ***How will I know? What evidence must I collect?*** Scott Foresman *Reading Street* Teacher's Editions and other program resources provide ongoing guidance for implementing intervention techniques for struggling readers and extending and enriching the curriculum for advanced learners. *Reading Street* also offers valuable resources, strategies, and tools for collecting evidence of achievement and encourages educators to be wise about the subject of **assessment**—what it is, when to use it, how to do it, and why it is so important.

What Is Assessment Literacy?

Now, more than ever before, it is important for all teachers and administrators to be "literate" about educational assessment and evaluation. Why? Research tells us that the use of meaningful classroom assessment strategies and tools, such as questioning, observational methods, and student self-assessment, empowers educators, guides instruction, and improves learning.

Further, we cannot ignore that increased demands for accountability at the state and national levels, e.g., *Reading First, No Child Left Behind (NCLB),* and *Adequate Yearly Progress (AYP),* etc., have produced an unprecedented proliferation of testing, and students' test performance has become the accountability yardstick by which the effectiveness of schools, districts, states, and even teaching is measured and judged.

To be informed consumers and creators of assessment, individuals must:

- understand the power of assessment in promoting student achievement;

- become knowledgeable about the functions, strengths, and limitations of formal and informal assessment;

- maintain a balance of summative and formative assessments in their classrooms and schools;

- embrace standards of quality as they evaluate and create assessments; and

- use sound assessment practices to design and administer quality classroom-based assessments.

What Is Assessment?

The Latin root of the word "assess" means "to sit beside." This is a much gentler notion of this concept than most of us have, although "sitting beside" a student to confer about the development of a story in progress, to conduct a fluency check, or to observe a group discussion are valuable assessment techniques. What is assessment? *Assessment is simply the gathering and interpretation of evidence about student learning.* There are many methods for collecting information to determine if students have mastered the knowledge and skills, or the learning targets. We can use a variety of formal and informal or classroom-based measures to collect that evidence.

Summative and Formative Assessment

Summative assessments are formal assessment measures, most often regarded as tests or tasks presented to students in order to obtain conclusive evidence about their performance. Tasks are designed to provide samples of individual achievement and are administered, scored, and interpreted according to mostly prescribed conditions. These activities are regarded as **summative** because they come at the *end* of an instructional process and are used to determine placement or assign grades. Examples might be chapter tests, unit projects, culminating performances, and final examinations. (Airasian, 2000)

Standardized tests are summative assessments designed to be administered to large numbers of test-takers. The tests are administered at the same time each year, and testing conditions, such as precise directions, time allowances, and security procedures, are tightly controlled. Test questions are written, reviewed, and revised following tryouts by a representative sample of the population for which the instrument is designed.

Examples of standardized tests are commercially published tests, as well as state assessments, which are now used annually to measure student achievement of standards for reporting and accountability purposes, in compliance with federal *NCLB* legislation and other mandates. These tests are often called "high-stakes," because scores are made very public, and schools and districts are subject to sanctions and embarrassment if they do not make annual *AYP* goals. (Popham, 2004)

Dr. Richard Stiggins distinguishes between assessment *of* learning and assessment *for* learning. Assessments *of* learning are generally formal, summative assessments administered at the end of an instructional period. They answer the question, "How much have students learned as of a particular point in time?" (Stiggins, 2002)

Formative assessment is the process of systematically and continuously collecting evidence about students' learning and monitoring their progress. It is classroom-based assessment *for* learning that helps us *dig deeper* in order to ascertain exactly *how* individual students are making progress toward achievement of the learning targets. These assessments are called **formative** because they are influential in "forming" the process under way and are intended to guide and inform instruction.

Reading Street offers a variety of formal and informal formative assessment techniques. While informal assessment tasks may not be the same type or depth for all students, and may not be recorded in a prescribed, standardized manner, they are not "informal" in the sense of "casual" or "random." Instead, use of informal assessments is the thoughtfully planned, intentional monitoring of learning embedded within the instructional process, rather than the evaluation of learning at the conclusion of the process.

Examples of formative assessment tools are teachers' questions, observations, checklists, portfolios, homework, student self-assessment, and teacher-student conferences, as well as weekly and unit tests.

Balancing Formative and Summative Assessment

Annually administered tests provide general feedback about students' performance related to broad content standards, or achievement targets. These tests are not designed to offer the immediate and ongoing information about achievement that teachers need to make critical instructional decisions. Even once-a-unit classroom tests do not provide sufficient information to improve teaching and increase learning. (Stiggins, 2004)

> "Balance continuous classroom assessment in support of learning with periodic assessments verifying learning."
> (Stiggins, 2004)

To establish and maintain productive, learning-centered classroom environments, teachers rely on a balance of informal assessments *for* learning and formal assessments *of* learning to guide their instruction. They use an array of formative and summative measures *derived from* and/or *aligned with* the content standards and based on their assessment purposes.

Why and when do we monitor progress with formative assessment?

- To diagnose students' strengths and needs

- To elicit prior knowledge for a concept or topic

- To provide frequent feedback to students that is descriptive and helpful, rather than judgmental, as in grades

- To motivate learners to increase effort as they experience incremental successes

- To build students' confidence in themselves as learners

- To help students take responsibility for their learning as they monitor their progress and adjust their goals

- To plan, modify, and regulate the pace of instruction to meet the needs of all students

- To communicate with parents and caregivers (e.g., learning expectations, students' progress in meeting learning targets, and methods of providing support at home)

Why do we obtain evidence with summative assessment?

- To report achievement of the content standards, the learning targets

- To document growth over time (e.g., unit-to-unit, year-to-year)

- To assign grades appropriately at the end of a unit, for a report card, etc.

- To validate judgments and decisions about student achievement

- To recommend students for promotion and placement in special programs

- To gauge program effectiveness, note strengths, and identify gaps

- To examine comparative data across schools and districts in order to make programmatic decisions (e.g., establish school improvement priorities, improve curriculum alignment, establish a need for intervention programs, additional resources, etc.)

- To satisfy state and federal accountability mandates, such as AYP

- To inform the public (e.g., taxpayers, business leaders, and legislators)

Evaluating Assessments for Quality

Most textbooks and instructional programs, including Scott Foresman *Reading Street*, have accompanying assessments for teachers to use. The formal and informal measures within *Reading Street* reflect the highest standards of quality and seamlessly align with the instructional program, yet teachers may wish to occasionally construct their own tests and performance assessments for other content areas and interdisciplinary studies. In order to implement fair and sound assessment, teachers are encouraged to consider the following standards for evaluating the quality of commercial assessments and designing their own classroom assessments to augment or replace the textbook measures.

> "…educators need to become sufficiently assessment literate so they can understand and, if necessary, help improve any accountability system that relies on unsuitable achievement tests."
>
> (Popham, 2004)

Know Your Learning Targets

Statewide and district-wide curriculum standards embody the content knowledge and skills we want our students to have, and they are the basis for all of our testing.

- "Unpack" the content standards to identify the underlying knowledge, concepts, processes, skills, and dispositions (e.g., attitudes, values, habits of mind) that become the **learning targets.**

- Translate the targets into student-friendly language.

- Post the targets in the classroom for all to see.

- Discuss the targets with the students at the beginning of the instructional process (e.g., lesson, unit, marking period).

- Review them throughout the process so that students have clear, reachable targets to hit.

Determine the Match

Teachers must carefully scrutinize each test item to ensure that the assessment has **content validity**. To what extent does the assessment measure what it is used to measure? Does the content of the test or task represent a balanced and adequate sampling of the targeted knowledge and skills as they are taught in the classroom? In other words, a recall exercise in which students are to match vocabulary words with their definitions would not be a valid assessment of a vocabulary standard requiring students to use structural analysis and context clues to determine word meanings. Test questions and tasks should be "instructionally sensitive"; that is, they should clearly reflect the learning targets and require students to perform the behaviors as you have taught them.

Consider the Number of Tested Standards

An effective assessment measures only a modest number of important learning targets and measures them well, so that teachers and students are not overwhelmed by the length and complexity of the activity. (Popham, 2004) Assessments are meant to sample components of the learning that takes place in the classroom, so an appropriate test or task must also contain a sufficient number of items related to each sampled learning target. In this way, teachers can be confident that the results will identify target skill areas that have been thoroughly taught and those that need improvement.

Strive for Reliability and Fairness

Reliability: How trustworthy is this assessment? Can I rely on the scores? Will this assessment give me the same results about the same learning targets every time?

Scoring of selected-response tests is considered quite reliable, and two teachers scoring the same set of multiple-choice tests will probably get the same results, barring a small chance of human error.

Although constructed-response assessments may measure more meaningful learning targets, they are considered less reliable because extensive training is needed in order to achieve consistency in scoring. To increase reliability, many states and school districts develop scoring rubrics and train scorers in a thorough, systematic way. Panels of raters score a large number of papers and discuss their scores until they're consistent in their ratings. Some papers are chosen as anchor papers because the raters believe they exemplify score points on the rubric. These papers are then used to guide subsequent scoring sessions, and reliability is improved. This activity can be replicated at the building level as teachers of the same grade level collaborate to design and score performance assessments, such as end-of-unit projects and presentations.

Fairness: Do all students, including those with diverse cultural and linguistic backgrounds, have an equal chance to demonstrate what they know and can do? Have all of them had the same opportunity to learn the content? Are the directions clear? Is the environment comfortable?

Fairness in assessment is compromised when teachers assess knowledge and skills that have not been taught or use assessment formats that do not reflect *how* the learning targets have been taught (e.g., asking for opinions and reasons when the emphasis has been on recall of facts).

Designing Quality Classroom Assessments

Teachers can construct multi-purpose classroom assessments that reflect the standards of quality—validity, reliability, and fairness. Purposes include diagnosing students' strengths and needs; planning, monitoring progress, and adjusting instruction; and providing feedback to students, parents, and others regarding progress and proficiency. The following design questions are intended to guide educators as they plan and build their own assessments:

1. **What learning target(s) based on the statewide and district-wide curriculum standards will you assess?**

2. **For which formative or summative purpose(s) is this assessment being administered?**

   - To detect strengths and needs

   - To motivate learners

   - To assign grades

   - To check progress

   - To group for instruction

   - To collect additional evidence

   - To evaluate instruction

   - Other

3. **Who will use the results of this assessment?**

   - Students

   - Teacher(s)

   - Parent

   - Principal

   - Community

   - Other

4. **What format will the assessment take?**

   It is important to select the format that most appropriately matches the target. For example, you wouldn't create a multiple-choice test to assess students' *use* of action verbs in their writing. Rather, you would assign a constructed-response activity asking them to incorporate action verbs in their text.

   Conversely, you wouldn't use a constructed-response format to assess students' identification of states and their capitals. An activity requiring them to match states and capitals would suffice for this purpose—assessing recall. Constructed responses are valuable because they help us seek insights into students' reasoning behind their answers or evidence that they can apply what they have learned. Possible assessment formats and examples of activities are listed in the table on page 23.

5. What criteria will you use to evaluate performance?

- How will you know it when you see it?

- What does hitting the target look like? What are the qualities?

- Is there one right answer or several possible answers?

- What will you accept as evidence that students have hit the target; that is, that they have acquired the knowledge and skills identified in the content standards?

6. What type of feedback will be provided to guide improvement?

How will results be communicated? How will you tell the story behind the numbers? Will you use a letter grade, a rubric score, written descriptive comments, a checklist, a point on a continuum of learning (such as an oral language behaviors' continuum), or another way?

The most valuable feedback is very specific and descriptive of how the performance hits (or does not hit) the target. Give concrete suggestions rather than vague comments or encouragement, such as "Nice work!" or "You can do better next time!" Share clear examples of successful work with students, and have them compare their work with the model. Allow students opportunities to revise their performances.

Transforming learning expectations into assessment tasks, assigning criteria, designing scoring procedures, and preparing feedback are challenging and time-consuming activities when they are attempted alone. It is a rewarding and collegial experience to collaborate with peers in articulating expectations, designing common assessments, analyzing student work, and selecting anchor/model performances. When educators work together to become assessment-literate, they empower each other with the ability to improve assessment practices and accountability systems in their school districts and states. More importantly, they increase learning for students.

Assessment Design Options

Possible Format	Examples of Tasks	Suggested Scoring/Feedback
Selected-Response	• Multiple-choice • Matching • True-false	One right answer; cut scores and percentages
Short Constructed-Response (written/oral)	• Fill-in-the-blank • Sentence completion • Graphic organizer • Brief response to prompt	One (or few) right answers; cut scores and percentages
Extended Constructed Response (written/oral)	• Prompt-based narrative, descriptive, expository, and persuasive writing • Retellings • Position with support • Summaries	More than one right answer; scoring with checklists, descriptive criteria, standards, continuum, rubrics, comparative models
Performances	• Oral presentation • Demonstration • Discussion • Role play	More than one right answer; scoring with checklists, descriptive criteria, standards, continuum, rubrics, peer and self-evaluation, comparative models
Products	• Science project • Visual display • Model • Video • Poem, story, play • Log/journal • Portfolio	More than one right answer; scoring with checklists, descriptive criteria, standards, continuum, rubrics, comparative models
Processes	• Strategy applications (e.g., think-alouds, questioning) • Teacher-student conferences • Peer and group assessments • Student self-assessments • Interviews • Inventories • Observations • Book club participation • Surveys of reading or writing behaviors • Portfolio entry slips • Response logs • Reading/writing lists	No one right answer; it is not necessary to score; collect as additional evidence; provide descriptive feedback to students

What Is the Scott Foresman *Reading Street* Assessment System?

All assessments in the program reflect current theories of teaching language and literacy and are aligned with solid classroom teaching practices. Scott Foresman *Reading Street* offers a "seamless assessment system" at each grade. The formative and summative assessments, combined with "assessable moments" during instruction, become a continuous cycle where one is always informing the other, resulting in a seamless learning program for the students.

Fundamental to this cycle are clear, grade-appropriate, and important learning targets that are aligned with statewide and district-wide reading and language arts curriculum standards.

> To prepare students for standardized tests, teachers should teach "the key ideas and processes contained in content standards in rich and engaging ways; by collecting evidence of student understanding of that content through robust local assessments, rather than one-shot standardized testing; and by using engaging and effective instructional strategies that help students explore core concepts through inquiry and problem solving."
>
> (McTighe, Seif, & Wiggins, 2004)

- At the beginning of each school year, the cycle begins with the administration of entry-level assessments used for screening and diagnosis. They will help you establish a starting point for students and determine the amount of instructional support students will need in order to hit the targets. Informal tools will provide additional information about students' learning styles, confidence, and interests that will help you in designing effective instructional plans.

- During the school year, literacy achievement is checked daily and weekly through formative, progress-monitoring assessments—informal, such as teacher observations, running records, retellings, and conferencing, as well as formal assessments. For example, the Scott Foresman *Reading Street* Weekly Tests assess students' understanding of the skills taught during the week, and the Fresh Reads for Fluency and Comprehension give students opportunities to practice comprehension and build fluency with new selections matched to their instructional levels.

- The Unit Benchmark Tests and the End-of-Year Benchmark Test are formative and summative assessments designed to assess students' understanding of the targeted skills, strategies, and critical thinking skills taught throughout the unit and the school year.

What Are the Assessment Targets?

Reading

What are the reading targets? *Reading Street* emphasizes the reading skills that are described by the National Reading Panel. These reading skills are essential as students learn to become independent, strategic readers and writers.

Phonemic awareness is the ability to identify the separate sounds, or *phonemes*, that make up spoken words and to alter and arrange sounds to create new words. It is a subset of phonological awareness, a broad term meaning the awareness of sounds in spoken language. Knowledge of phonemic awareness allows students to hear separate sounds, recognize a sound's position in a word, manipulate sounds, and understand the role sounds play in language. In Scott Foresman *Reading Street*, phonemic awareness instructional and assessment activities include isolating, blending, segmenting, deleting, adding, and substituting phonemes.

Phonics is the study of how letters represent sounds in *written* language, unlike phonemic awareness, which is strictly *oral*. Phonics instruction and assessment in *Reading Street* include:

- **Print awareness** Understanding the relationship between oral and written language, that written language carries meaning, and that print is read from left to right.

- **Alphabetic knowledge** Knowledge of the shapes, names, and sounds of letters.

- **Alphabetic principle** Understanding that there is a systematic relationship between sounds (phonemes) and letters (graphemes).

- **Decoding** The process of analyzing letter-sound patterns in words to ascertain meaning.

- **Knowledge of high-frequency words** Sometimes called "sight words," these are the words that appear most often in our written language. Because students need to know these words when they read stories and write sentences, the words are introduced before students have learned many letter-sound patterns. Many high-frequency words cannot be decoded easily because of irregular and uncommon letter-sound patterns. Others do conform to phonics rules but must be taught as whole words because students have not yet learned the letter-sound relationships within them.

Oral reading fluency is the ability to effortlessly, quickly, and accurately decode letters, words, sentences, and passages. Fluent readers are able to group words into meaningful grammatical units and read with proper expression. Fluency is an essential component of comprehension and is assessed regularly in Scott Foresman *Reading Street*.

Vocabulary acquisition and development contribute significantly to overall text comprehension. While extensive reading experiences with varied text types and opportunities for classroom discussion are known to increase word knowledge, *Reading Street* explicitly teaches and assesses vocabulary skills through the study of context clues, word structure, and dictionary/glossary use.

- Context clues from the words or phrases surrounding an unknown word help readers identify its meaning. Some words have multiple meanings and can only be understood through the context in which they are used. Context clues include synonyms, antonyms, definitions, explanations, descriptions, and examples that appear within the text surrounding an unfamiliar word.

- The study of word structure is the analysis of word-meaning elements to make meaning of the word as a whole. Such meaningful elements include word roots, prefixes, suffixes, and compound words. Syllabication generalizations and inflected endings, which change the tense, case, or singular-plural form of words, but do not affect meaning or part of speech, are also taught and assessed.

> "Having a strong vocabulary is not only a school goal, it is a characteristic that allows us to participate actively in our world, and it is viewed by those we meet as the hallmark of an educated person."
> (Blachowicz, 2005)

- Understanding what dictionaries/glossaries are and why, when, and how to use them helps to increase students' vocabularies. They become familiar with the organization and format of dictionaries and glossaries and are guided and assessed in their use of the components of an entry, including syllabication, pronunciation, part of speech, etymology, and definition.

Reading comprehension, the overarching goal of reading, is the active process of constructing meaning from text. It is a complex process in which readers apply their prior knowledge and experiences, use their understandings about text (types, structures, features, etc.), and intentionally employ an array of before-, during-, and after-reading strategies and skills, in order to attain meaning. Effective readers combine their own experiences with their interpretation of the author's intent as they work to make sense of ideas in text.

In Scott Foresman *Reading Street*, students' use of targeted comprehension strategies and skills (e.g., identification of main idea, details, author's point of view and purpose, sequence, and inferences) is monitored continuously on the Weekly Tests and Fresh Reads for Fluency and Comprehension. Students read a variety of engaging, culturally- and age-appropriate narrative and expository texts and respond to appropriate multiple-choice questions designed to assess how they use the comprehension skills in constructing meaning. There are three types of comprehension questions that correspond to the *In the Book* and *In My Head* categories of questions in the instructional program.

- **Literal** questions, which focus on ideas explicitly stated in the text, although *not necessarily* verbatim. In response to these items, students *recognize* and *identify* information which might be found in a single sentence or in two or more sentences of contiguous text.

- **Inferential** questions, which are based on the theme, key concepts, and major ideas of the passage and often require students to *interpret* information from across parts of the text and to *connect* knowledge from the text with their own general background knowledge.

- **Critical-analysis** questions, which are also inferential in nature and focus on important ideas in the selection. Yet they differ from inferential questions in that readers are required to stand apart from the text and *analyze*, *synthesize*, and/or *evaluate* the quality, effectiveness, relevance, and consistency of the message, rhetorical features (tone, style, voice, etc.), author or character motivation, and the author's purpose or credibility. (The Grade 2 assessments contain few of these advanced-level questions.)

Throughout the program, students are scaffolded and guided as they move from literal understanding, to inferential comprehension, and to critical analysis of text.

Writing

Targeted skills are based on the writing strategies and writing applications strands of state language arts standards. Skills include:

- Focus on the topic
- Writing coherent sentences
- Writing a single paragraph with a topic sentence
- Organizational structure with effective beginning, middle, and end
- Demonstrating understanding of purpose
- Use of supporting facts, details, and examples
- Interesting word choice and sentence variety
- Narrative, descriptive, and expository compositions
- Friendly and formal letters
- Understanding of the structure and organization of reference materials
- Evaluation and revision of writing
- Penmanship

The Unit Benchmark Tests and End-of-Year Benchmark Test require responses to narrative, descriptive, expository, and friendly-letter writing prompts.

Other informal writing assessments in *Reading Street* include:

- Myself as a Reader and Writer is a questionnaire in which students can reflect on their own reading and writing habits at the beginning of the school year.

- Written retellings demonstrate students' abilities to understand narrative and expository text elements and to recall and record information in writing.

- Teacher-student conferences provide insights about students' writing behaviors and strategies.

- Student portfolios, containing draft and final copies of work, give evidence of students' growth and progress in writing.

- Writing logs allow students to monitor their writing growth over time.

- About My Writing is a form in which students can reflect on their writing progress at various points during the school year.

- Writing Strategy Assessments help teachers synthesize information about students' writing progress and use of writing strategies.

Writing Conventions

Skills include:

- Sentence structure

- Grammar, including singular/plural constructions, contractions, subject-verb agreement, parts of speech, etc.

- Punctuation, capitalization, and spelling

Skills are assessed in the Unit and End-of-Year Benchmark Tests. The writing scoring rubrics assess sentence structure, fluency, and variety, as well as control of writing conventions.

Speaking and Listening

Skills include:

- Listening comprehension

- Organization and delivery of oral communication

- Analysis and evaluation of oral and media communication

- Recitation, retellings, relating personal experiences, and providing descriptions

Informal assessments that allow you to document students' oral language development throughout the year are oral retellings, teacher-student conference records, ongoing teacher observation, and student portfolios. Student self-assessments are opportunities for students to monitor and evaluate their growth in speaking and listening and to set goals for improvement.

Research/Study Skills

Skills include:

- Understanding and using graphic sources, such as charts, maps, diagrams, graphs, etc.

- Understanding and using reference sources, such as dictionaries, encyclopedias, library databases, etc.

- Understanding and using the research process

Skills are assessed informally by having students demonstrate the ability to perform a task involving the use of the skill.

What instructional strategies will help to prepare students for formal assessments and high-stakes tests?

- Use the Scott Foresman *Reading Street* program to continually monitor student progress and refine instruction to reflect your students' needs.

- Use the administration of the formal progress-monitoring and summative assessments as a way to teach test-taking skills.

- Literal, inferential, and critical-analysis questions on the Weekly, Unit, and End-of-Year Benchmark Tests are based on the question-answer framework used in instruction and are similar to question types on high-stakes assessments. Daily practice in answering literal, inferential, and critical-analysis questions will improve student achievement on high-stakes standardized tests.

- Download and examine released items from standardized assessments, reviewing the various item constructions and test vocabulary. Model and discuss the thinking steps involved in responding to multiple-choice and constructed-response items, as well as writing prompts.

- Familiarize your students with the formal language of test directions. Instruct them to listen to, restate, follow, and write test directions.

- Pre-teach the "language of tests" encountered in directions and test items, including

  - Question words: *who, what, which, where, when, why,* and *how*

  - Emphasis words: *not, except, most likely, probably, major, both, neither, either, most,* and *least*

  - Action words: *explain, describe, discuss, persuade,* and *support with evidence*

- Encourage students to be careful readers and to check their own work.

- Provide repeated opportunities for practicing all of the techniques above.

References

Airasian, P. W. *Classroom Assessment: Concepts and Applications*. New York: McGraw-Hill, 2000.

Blachowicz, C. L. Z. "Vocabulary Essentials: From Research to Practice for Improved Instruction." *Research-Based Vocabulary Instruction*. Glenview, IL: Scott Foresman, 2005.

Heritage, M. "Formative Assessment: What Do Teachers Need to Know and Do?" *Phi Delta Kappan*, vol. 89, no. 2 (2007), pp. 140–145.

McTighe, J., E. Seif, and G. Wiggins. "You Can Teach for Meaning." *Educational Leadership*, vol. 62, no. 1 (September 2004), pp. 26–30.

National Reading Panel. "Teaching Children to Read: An Evidence-Based Assessment of the Scientific Research Literature on Reading and Its Implications for Reading Instruction." *Reports of the Subgroups*. National Institute for Literacy, National Institute of Child Health and Human Development, 2000.

Popham, W. J. "Instructional Insensitivity of Tests: Accountability's Dire Drawback." *Phi Delta Kappan*, vol. 89, no. 2 (October 2007), pp. 146–150, 155.

Popham, W. J. "Tawdry Tests and AYP." *Educational Leadership*, vol. 62, no. 2 (October 2004), pp. 85–86.

Stiggins, R. J. "Assessment Crisis: The Absence of Assessment for Learning." *Kappan Professional Journal*. http://www.pdkintl.org/kappan/k020sti.htm (accessed May 8, 2005).

Stiggins, R. J. "New Assessment Beliefs for a New School Mission." *Phi Delta Kappan*, vol. 86, no. 1 (September 2004), 22–27.

Vaughn, S., and S. Linan-Thompson. *Research-Based Methods of Reading Instruction, Grades K–3*. Alexandria, VA: Association for Supervision and Curriculum Development, 2004.

Chapter 2 Entry-Level Assessment: What to Do at the Beginning of the Year

Overview

By second grade, entry-level assessment becomes complicated by several factors, including the quantity and variety of prerequisite knowledge and skills that students are expected to have achieved by this point in their education. Entry-level assessments determine foci for initial instruction as well as interventions that might be needed for individual students. There are many formal and informal assessment tools that provide the type of information needed to make decisions about where to begin instruction for individual learners.

What is the purpose of using entry-level assessments?

Entry-level assessments are used for screening and diagnosis. The results of entry-level assessment tests are reported by specific knowledge and skill areas and can be used to:

- help you get to know your students and find a starting point for good instructional decisions;

- help you gather information about students' knowledge and skills in reading, writing, speaking, and listening at the beginning of the year; and

- gather information about students' learning needs, such as English language learners, students with disabilities, struggling readers, and advanced learners.

What do I want to learn from entry-level assessments?

Learning where to begin instruction is the primary goal of entry-level assessments. The more you know about your students at the beginning of the year, the better equipped you are to provide learning experiences that achieve continuous growth in writing, speaking, reading, and listening skills. Entry-level assessments identify students who are already proficient and need challenge, as well as those who need additional support and literacy intervention, in areas such as:

- Phonemic awareness
- Phonics and word reading
- Oral reading fluency
- Reading comprehension
- Vocabulary
- Writing

What types of assessments should be used at the beginning of the year?

Use a variety of assessment practices early in the year to screen and diagnose students' achievement of writing, speaking, reading, and listening skills. Both formal and informal assessments will help you diagnose your students' prerequisite knowledge and skills, as well as gain a personal understanding of your students.

FORMAL ASSESSMENTS

- Formal entry-level assessments provide detailed analyses of students' performance in specific domains. They make available information about the degree to which students have acquired the knowledge and skills and identify areas in which additional instruction is needed for particular students.

- Formal entry-level assessments can be used to:

  - assess instructional needs of individual students;

  - focus instruction to meet targeted needs of all of the students in your classroom; and

  - determine what needs to be pretaught or retaught to individual students or groups of students.

INFORMAL ASSESSMENTS

- Informal entry-level assessments provide additional information about areas where instructional support is needed. They also provide useful background information, including knowledge about students' learning styles, confidence, and interests that will help you in designing effective instructional plans.

- Informal assessments, such as conferencing with students and administering developmentally-appropriate inventories, surveys, and checklists at the beginning of the school year will help you:

  - identify students' interests and attitudes about literacy;

  - assess instructional and motivational needs of individual students;

  - assess instructional needs of the class as a whole;

  - learn specifics about students with particular needs; and

  - make focused instructional decisions.

When do I gather the information?

The best time to administer entry-level assessments is during the first few weeks of the school year. However, it is important to avoid overwhelming students with too much assessment at one time. Plan carefully and spread a variety of assessment tasks throughout the first month of school. Prioritize the tools and tasks in relation to their importance to beginning instructional planning.

What techniques and tools are available?

FORMAL ENTRY-LEVEL ASSESSMENT TOOLS AND TECHNIQUES

- **Baseline Group Test** (See pages 38–39.)
  This Scott Foresman Reading Street test, one at each grade level, has both a written multiple-choice format and one-on-one teacher–student oral subtests for phonemic awareness and fluency in grades 2 and 3. It enables you to establish baseline data for determining the level of instructional support students need and placing them into instructional groups.

- **Group Reading Assessment and Diagnostic Evaluation (GRADE)** (See pages 35–36.)
  A group-administered, norm-referenced, diagnostic reading assessment for grades PreK–Adult that provides information about the skills students have mastered and the skill areas in which they need mastery or intervention.

- **Developmental Reading Assessment® Second Edition (DRA2)** (See page 37.)
  This is a set of individually administered criterion-referenced reading assessments for students in kindergarten through grade 8. The DRA2 is used to identify students' independent reading levels in terms of accuracy, fluency, and comprehension.

INFORMAL ENTRY-LEVEL ASSESSMENT TOOLS AND TECHNIQUES

- **Getting to Know You Conference** (See page 40.)
  An individual conversation with a student that explores his or her learning interests, strengths, challenges, and goals

- **Myself as a Reader and Writer** (See page 41.)
  An informal questionnaire that gives students an opportunity to identify the reading genres and topics that are of interest to them

- **Reading and Me** (See pages 42–43.)
  A survey to assess students' attitudes and confidence about their reading

- **How Do I Learn?** (See page 44.)
  A survey to identify students' learning styles and preferences

- **Reading Behaviors Checklist** (See page 45.)
  A checklist for recording observations about students' reading skills (e.g., letter and word knowledge, oral fluency, understanding of story structure)

- **Writing Behaviors Checklist** (See page 46.)
  A checklist for recording observations about students' writing skills (e.g., basic writing conventions, word choice, ability to record ideas)

- **Oral Language Behaviors Checklist** (See page 47.)
  A checklist for recording observations about students' oral language (e.g., verbal expression, listening skills, conventional grammar, retelling)

- **Profile of English Language Learners** (See page 48.)
  A checklist that identifies the strengths and needs of English language learners

- **My Child as a Learner** (See page 49.)
  A survey that tells information about students' literacy behaviors at home

Want to learn more about entry-level assessment?

If you are interested in learning more about research that discusses the use of entry-level assessment tools and practices, you will find the following resources interesting.

References

Allinder, R. M.; M. Rose; L. S. Fuchs; and D. Fuchs. "Issues in Curriculum-Based Assessment." In *Critical Issues in Special Education: Access, Diversity, and Accountability.* Eds. A. M. Sorrells, H. J. Rieth, and P. T. Sindelar. Boston: Allyn and Bacon, 2004.

Buly, M. R., and S. W. Valencia. "Below the Bar: Profiles of Students Who Fail State Reading Tests." *Educational Evaluation and Policy Analysis*, vol. 24 (2002), pp. 219–239.

Chard, D.; S. McDonagh; S. Lee; and V. Reece. "Assessing Word Recognition." In *Classroom Literacy Assessment: Making Sense of What Students Know and Do.* Eds. J. R. Paratore and R. L. McCormack. New York: Guilford Press. pp. 85–100.

Cunningham, P. M. "The Multisyllabic Word Dilemma: Helping Students Build Meaning, Spell, and Read 'Big' Words." *Reading and Writing Quarterly*, vol. 14 (1998), pp. 189–218.

Ehri, L. C. "Development of the Ability to Read Words: Update." In *Theoretical Models and Processes of Reading*, 3rd ed. Eds. R. B. Ruddell, M. R. Ruddell, and H. Singer. Newark, DE: International Reading Association.

Helman, L. A. "Using Literacy Assessment Results to Improve Teaching for English-Language Learners." *The Reading Teacher*, vol. 58, no. 7 (April 2005), pp. 668–677.

Johnston, P. H., and R. Roger. "Early Literacy Development: The Case for Informed Assessment." In *Handbook of Early Reading Research*. Eds. S. B. Neuman and D. K. Dickinson. New York: Guilford Press, 2001, pp. 377–389.

Kame'enui, E. J.; R. H. Good; and B. A. Harn. "Beginning Reading Failure and the Quantification of Risk: Reading Behavior as the Supreme Index." In *Focus on Behavior Analysis in Education: Achievements, Challenges, and Opportunities.* Eds. W. L. Heward, et al. Upper River, N.J.: Pearson/Merrill/Prentice Hall, 2005.

McMillan, James H. "Essential Assessment Concepts for Teachers and Administrators." In *Experts in Assessment* series. Eds. T. R. Guskey and R. J. Marzano. Thousand Oaks, CA: Corwin Press, Inc., 2001.

Group Reading Assessment and Diagnostic Evaluation (GRADE)

What is it?

GRADE is an accurate, in-depth, and easy-to-use entry-level assessment for pre-kindergarten children through young adult, postsecondary students. It is a normative diagnostic reading assessment that determines developmentally which skills students have mastered and where they need instruction or intervention. GRADE is a research-based assessment that can be group-administered. It was standardized and normed using the most up-to-date methodology.

Why would I use it?

You will want to use GRADE for many reasons.

- It helps you screen your students and determine the strengths and weaknesses of individuals or groups of students in relation to specific skills.

- It helps you determine your students' prerequisite skills and knowledge.

- It allows you to save time through whole-group administration as opposed to individual student administration.

- You can score the assessment and analyze results using information in the teacher manual or scoring and reporting software.

- Students who appear to have significantly above- or below-grade-level reading performance can be given an out-of-level test form.

- Parallel forms offer the opportunity to test up to four times a year.

- Results are linked to specific follow-up instruction and interventions.

- Using GRADE assessment to focus instruction will improve student achievement and help deliver Adequate Yearly Progress gains.

| **What does it test?** | In second and third grades, GRADE assesses essential elements of reading, including: |
| | |

What does it test?

In second and third grades, GRADE assesses essential elements of reading, including:

- Vocabulary
- Oral language
- Comprehension

Administering earlier levels of GRADE to students in grades 2 and 3 will assess their knowledge of phonemic awareness and phonics.

When do I use it?

When GRADE is used as an entry-level assessment, it should be administered by the end of the first month of school. GRADE can be used up to four times a year, with the recommendation that three months be allowed between testing sessions.

How do I use it?

- Give the appropriate grade-level assessment or an out-of-level assessment if you determine the student will perform below or above grade level.

- Analyze students' results using normative tables for converting raw scores to standard scores, stanines, percentiles, normal curve equivalents, grade equivalents, and growth-scale values.

- Use results to plan focused instruction for individuals or groups of students.

- Use activities and exercises that are correlated with the assessment results from the *GRADE Resource Library* and *Head for Success* to plan interventions for students with special learning needs.

Developmental Reading Assessment® Second Edition (DRA2)

What is it?

- The DRA2 is a set of individually-administered criterion-referenced reading assessments for students in kindergarten through grade 8. Modeled after an informal reading inventory, the DRA2 is designed to be administered, scored, and interpreted by a classroom teacher. The DRA2 for grades 2 and 3 identifies a student's independent reading level based on the student's accuracy, fluency, and comprehension.

Why would I use it?

You will want to use the DRA2 for many reasons, including:

- To identify your students' strengths and weaknesses
- To evaluate the phonological awareness and phonics skills of students in grades 1 through 5
- To help you prepare students to meet classroom and testing expectations
- To provide information about your students' reading achievement levels for Adequate Yearly Progress

What does it test?

The DRA2 assesses essential elements of reading and language arts, including:

- Independent reading level
- Reading engagement
- Oral reading fluency (rate and accuracy)
- Reading comprehension

When do I use it?

The DRA2 can be given twice a year (fall and spring) to provide you with information to guide instruction. It can also be administered at mid-year to identify the needs or skills of students who are challenged readers, to monitor progress, and to provide more instructional guidance.

How do I use it?

- The student completes a reading survey (orally for younger and less proficient students and in writing for levels 28 and up).
- You have an individual reading conference with each student involving the student's reading a text orally.
- As the student reads aloud, you use a text-specific observation guide to record reading behaviors and errors.
- You convert the total number of oral-reading errors to an accuracy score and calculate the student's reading fluency as words correct per minute (WCPM).

2 • Entry Level

Copyright © by Pearson Education, Inc., or its affiliates. All Rights Reserved.

37

Baseline Group Test

What is it?

- A placement test given at the beginning of the school year to establish a baseline for each student

Why would I choose it?

- To identify students who are on grade level, those who need intervention, and those who could benefit from more challenge
- To recognize how best to shape the curriculum to fit the needs of all students

What does it test?

- In grade 2, phonemic awareness, phonics, high-frequency words, vocabulary words, and reading comprehension skills are tested. Also included are a graded oral vocabulary test and a passage for testing fluency and/or doing a running record (both optional).
- In grade 3, phonemic awareness, phonics, vocabulary words, and reading comprehension skills are tested. Also included are a graded oral vocabulary test and a passage for testing fluency and/or doing a running record (both optional).

When do I use it?

- At the beginning of the school year, to establish baselines for students and to place them in groups according to their level of ability
- Throughout the year as needed to assess progress and determine instructional requirements of new students

How do I use it?

- The test is designed to be group administered
- Each test includes a table specifying how many correct responses indicate the various levels of mastery (Strategic Intervention, On-Level, or Advanced)

How do I use the results?

- The teacher manual includes charts with percentage scores, an evaluation chart, and an interpretation key that will allow you to place each student in an appropriate instructional group

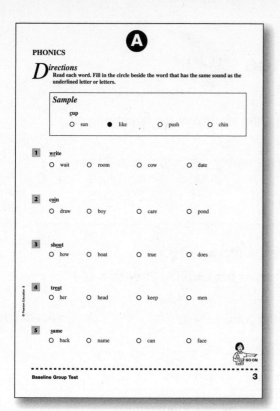

PHONICS

D*irections*
Read each word. Fill in the circle beside the word that has the same sound as the underlined letter or letters.

> **Sample**
>
> c̲up
>
> ○ sun   ● like   ○ push   ○ chin

1 wr̲ite
○ wait   ○ room   ○ cow   ○ date

2 c̲o̲in
○ draw   ○ boy   ○ care   ○ pond

3 sh̲out
○ how   ○ boat   ○ true   ○ does

4 tr̲e̲at
○ her   ○ head   ○ keep   ○ men

5 s̲ame
○ back   ○ name   ○ can   ○ face

Baseline Group Test   **3**

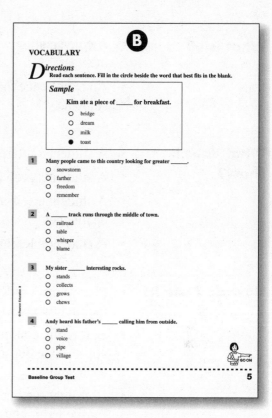

VOCABULARY

D*irections*
Read each sentence. Fill in the circle beside the word that best fits in the blank.

> **Sample**
>
> Kim ate a piece of _____ for breakfast.
>
> ○ bridge
> ○ dream
> ○ milk
> ● toast

1 Many people came to this country looking for greater _____.
○ snowstorm
○ farther
○ freedom
○ remember

2 A _____ track runs through the middle of town.
○ railroad
○ table
○ whisper
○ blame

3 My sister _____ interesting rocks.
○ stands
○ collects
○ grows
○ chews

4 Andy heard his father's _____ calling him from outside.
○ stand
○ voice
○ pipe
○ village

Baseline Group Test   **5**

A Students are tested in phonics knowledge as well as vocabulary and comprehension.

B Vocabulary words are tested in context.

C Students read several passages and answer comprehension questions about them.

Samples are from Grade 3 Baseline Group Test.

READING COMPREHENSION

D*irections*
Read each selection and answer the questions that follow. Fill in the circle beside the best answer to each question.

Ready for Blast-Off

Mom watched eagerly as the workers wheeled the new refrigerator into the kitchen. Katie and her brother Rory were excited too. The refrigerator came in a giant cardboard box. "What should we do with such a big box?" asked Katie.

Rory had an idea. "Let's make it into a spaceship!"

The children cut round windows and a door in the box. They drew buttons, levers, and knobs that would control the spaceship. When they were done, they crawled inside.

"Ready for blast-off!" shouted Rory, and Katie pushed a red button.

The children felt the box shudder, shake, and rise into the air. They peeked through the windows and saw dark sky and shiny stars. "We're really going to the moon!" Katie cried.

When the box landed with a bump, Rory and Katie crawled out. They explored the moon's craters and mountains. Everything was dark, dusty, and rocky.

"Let's stay here all night," suggested Rory.

"No, let's go home," replied Katie. "Mom will wonder where we are."

Rory followed her back to the box, still wishing they could stay longer. Katie pushed the red button again, and they were home just as Mom called them in for supper.

1 How did Katie and Rory feel about going to the moon?
○ bored
○ excited
○ relieved
○ disappointed

2 What part of this story could not really happen?
○ Two children decorate a big box.
○ A family gets a new refrigerator.
○ A mother calls her children for supper.
○ Two children go to the moon in a box.

3 Why did Katie want to go back home?
○ She didn't want her mother to worry.
○ She was hungry.
○ She was frightened.
○ She had homework to do.

4 Which of the following is the most likely reason the author wrote this story?
○ to describe the size of a refrigerator box
○ to give information about the moon
○ to explain how to make a rocket ship
○ to tell an entertaining story about two children

5 What did the children do after they explored the moon?
○ They watched workers deliver a refrigerator.
○ They drew buttons and levers on a box.
○ They went back home for supper.
○ They went to sleep in the box.

8   Baseline Group Test

Baseline Group Test   **9**

Getting to Know You Conference

What is it?

- A conversation with each individual student at the beginning of the year
- An experience that personalizes learning for both you and your students

What does it show?

- A student's interests
- A student's preference for different literacy experiences
- A student's self-assessment of his or her learning strengths and challenges
- A student's learning goals for the coming year

How do I use it?

- Plan to meet individually with each student for five minutes during the first two weeks of school.
- Before the conference, prepare a list of developmentally appropriate questions to select from as you conference with each student.
- Highlight the questions that you think might be the most relevant for the particular student being interviewed.
- Questions might include:
  - What was the best story you or your teacher read last year? What did you like about it?
  - What do you like to read about?
  - During choice time at school, what would you rather do: read, write, or draw? What do you usually read, write, or draw?
  - What did you do last year that you liked the best? What did you like about it?
  - What did you do last year that you liked the least? What didn't you like about it?
  - What do we do in school that is easy for you?
  - What is the hardest thing we do in school?
  - When you don't know how to do something, what do you do? How do you get help?
  - What would you like to do better this year?
- Keep notes of the conference and add them to the student's portfolio or cumulative folder.

Interest Inventory
Myself as a Reader and Writer

What is it?

- An informal questionnaire that gives students an opportunity to tell you about their reading and writing interests

- A tool that helps students reflect on their reading and writing habits

What does it show?

- Genres and topics that are of interest to students

How do I use it?

- Have students complete the form early in the school year. (Read the form aloud to students who need help.)

- As an extension, ask students to exchange forms and find classmates with similar interests.

- Place the completed form in each student's portfolio as additional information about the student.

- Consider using the inventory during parent conferences.

2 • Entry Level

A Checklist format is easy for students to complete and for you to interpret.

B Form probes students' interests in specific topics as well as genres.

Form for reproduction is on page 134.

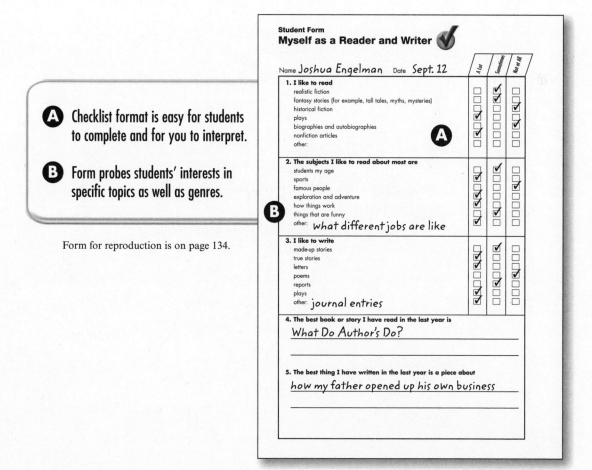

Survey
Reading and Me

What is it?

- An in-depth survey to gauge students' feelings about and confidence in their reading

What does it show?

- How students assess various aspects of their behavior as readers
- How students think they read various kinds of materials
- The value students place on reading

How do I use it?

- Administer the survey early in the school year.
- Evaluate students' responses in the four categories that are described on page 43.
- Place the completed form in each student's portfolios as additional information about the student.

Student Form
Reading and Me ✔

Name _Joshua Engelman_   Date _9/30_

Mark the box next to the answer that tells how you feel.

1. How often do you like to read?
- [ ] All of the time
- [ ] Sometimes
- [x] Not too often
- [ ] Never

2. When I read I
- [ ] always try my best.
- [x] try my best most of the time.
- [ ] don't try very hard.
- [ ] often give up.

(A)

3. In general, when I read I
- [ ] really enjoy it.
- [ ] think it's OK.
- [x] don't like it very much.
- [ ] dislike it a lot.

4. I think reading is
- [ ] my favorite thing to do.
- [ ] one of my favorite things to do.
- [x] not one of my favorite things to do.
- [ ] my least favorite thing to do.

5. I read
- [ ] a lot better than my classmates.
- [ ] a little better than my classmates.
- [x] about the same as my classmates.
- [ ] worse than my classmates.

6. When I am reading by myself, I understand
- [ ] most of what I read.
- [x] some of what I read.
- [ ] not much of what I read.
- [ ] very little of what I read.

7. I am
- [ ] a great reader.
- [ ] a good reader.
- [x] an OK reader.
- [ ] a poor reader.

(B)

8. I care what other kids think about my reading.
- [ ] Never
- [ ] Not too often
- [ ] Sometimes
- [x] Always

9. I think that reading is
- [ ] very easy.
- [ ] kind of easy.
- [x] kind of hard.
- [ ] very hard.

10. When I read in school I usuall[y]
- [ ] feel good about it.
- [x] feel OK about it.
- [ ] feel not too good about it.
- [ ] feel terrible about it.

Student Form
Reading and Me (continued) ✔

Name _____   Date _____

Mark the box next to the answer that tells how you feel.

11. I talk with my friends about the things that I read
- [ ] all of the time.
- [ ] sometimes.
- [x] not too often.
- [ ] never.

12. People who read a lot are
- [ ] very interesting.
- [x] kind of interesting.
- [ ] not very interesting.
- [ ] pretty boring.

(C)

13. I think that reading in school is
- [ ] very important.
- [ ] important.
- [x] somewhat important.
- [ ] not too important.

14. I think that reading at home is
- [ ] very important.
- [ ] important.
- [ ] somewhat important.
- [x] not too important.

15. I like getting a book for a present.
- [ ] All the time
- [ ] Sometimes
- [x] Not very often
- [ ] Never

16. I read newspapers
- [ ] very well.
- [x] pretty well.
- [ ] not too well.
- [ ] not well at all.

17. I read schoolbooks
- [ ] very well.
- [ ] pretty well.
- [x] not too well.
- [ ] not well at all.

(D)

18. I read comics
- [x] very well.
- [ ] pretty well.
- [ ] not too well.
- [ ] not well at all.

19. I read magazines
- [ ] very well.
- [ ] pretty well.
- [x] not too well.
- [ ] not well at all.

20. I read storybooks or novels
- [ ] very well.
- [x] pretty well.
- [ ] not too well.
- [ ] not well at all.

(A) Items 1–4 probe students' motivation as readers.

(B) Items 5–10 get at students' feelings about their reading and how they measure themselves against other readers.

(C) Items 11–15 probe the value that students put on reading.

(D) Items 16–20 have students assess their abilities at reading different kinds of materials.

Forms for reproduction are on pages 135–136.

Survey
How Do I Learn?

What is it?
- A form to help you recognize students with particular learning styles or preferences

What does it show?

The survey can help you begin to identify:

- students who learn best through sight or mental images (visual/spatial learners);
- students who learn best through body positions and movements (kinesthetic learners); and
- students who learn best through interactions or negotiations with others (interpersonal learners).

How do I use it?
- Have students complete the form early in the school year. (Read the form aloud to students who may have difficulty reading it on their own.)
- Use the explanations below to help you begin to identify students with particular learning preferences.

A An (a) response to questions 1 and 2 helps to identify students with strong visual/spatial or interpersonal preferences, respectively.

B Consistent responses to questions 3–5 point out
(a) visual/spatial learners;
(b) kinesthetic learners;
(c) interpersonal learners.

Form for reproduction is on page 141.

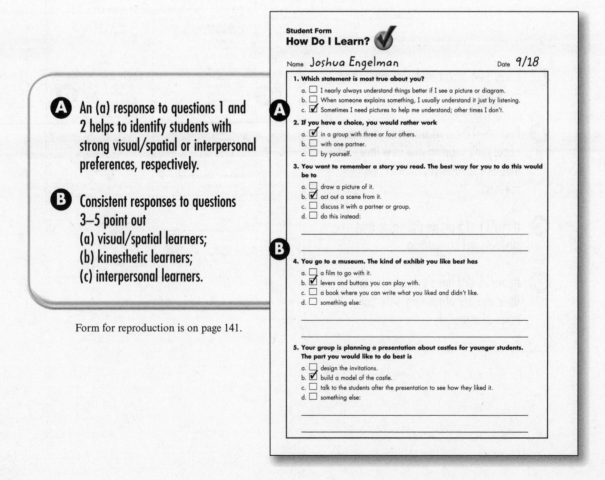

Student Form
How Do I Learn?

Name _Joshua Engelman_   Date _9/18_

1. Which statement is most true about you?
a. ☐ I nearly always understand things better if I see a picture or diagram.
b. ☐ When someone explains something, I usually understand it just by listening.
c. ☑ Sometimes I need pictures to help me understand; other times I don't.

2. If you have a choice, you would rather work
a. ☑ in a group with three or four others.
b. ☐ with one partner.
c. ☐ by yourself.

3. You want to remember a story you read. The best way for you to do this would be to
a. ☐ draw a picture of it.
b. ☑ act out a scene from it.
c. ☐ discuss it with a partner or group.
d. ☐ do this instead:

4. You go to a museum. The kind of exhibit you like best has
a. ☐ a film to go with it.
b. ☑ levers and buttons you can play with.
c. ☐ a book where you can write what you liked and didn't like.
d. ☐ something else:

5. Your group is planning a presentation about castles for younger students. The part you would like to do best is
a. ☐ design the invitations.
b. ☑ build a model of the castle.
c. ☐ talk to the students after the presentation to see how they liked it.
d. ☐ something else:

Teacher Form
Reading Behaviors Checklist

What is it?
- A form to record your observations of students' reading behaviors at the beginning of and throughout the year

What does it show?
- Students' awareness of print and word concepts
- Students' knowledge of phonological awareness and phonics

How do I use it?
- Complete this form as you observe students interacting with print materials.
- Use your observations to assess students' needs and to make instructional decisions.
- Place the completed form in each student's portfolio as additional information about the student.

A Checklist format is quick to complete and easy to interpret.

B Checklist includes all important aspects of a student's early reading behaviors.

C "Not Applicable" column makes checklist adaptable to different grade levels.

Form for reproduction is on page 137.

2 • Entry Level

Teacher Form
Reading Behaviors Checklist

Student Kristen Cleaver   Date 9/16

Behavior	Yes	No	Not Applicable
Recognizes letters of the alphabet	✓		
Recognizes name in print	✓		
Recognizes some environmental print, such as signs and logos	✓		
Knows the difference between letters and words	✓		
Knows the difference between capital and lowercase letters	✓		
Understands function of capitalization and punctuation	✓		
Recognizes that book parts such as cover, title page, and table of contents offer information		✓	
Recognizes that words are represented in writing by specific sequences of letters	✓		
Recognizes words that rhyme	✓		
Distinguishes rhyming and nonrhyming words	✓		
Knows sound-letter correspondences	✓		
Identifies and isolates initial sounds in words	✓		
Identifies and isolates final sounds in words	✓		
Blends sounds to make spoken words	✓		
Segments one-syllable/two-syllable spoken words into individual phonemes	✓		
Reads consonant blends and digraphs			✓
Reads and understands endings such as -es, -ed, -ing			✓
Reads vowels and vowel diphthongs			✓
Reads and understands possessives			✓
Reads and understands compound words			✓
Reads simple sentences	✓		
Reads simple stories		✓	
Understands simple story structure	✓		
Other:			

45

Teacher Form
Writing Behaviors Checklist

What is it?
- A form to record your observations of students' writing behaviors at the beginning of and throughout the year

What does it show?
- Students' awareness of basic writing concepts
- Students' ability to communicate through writing

How do I use it?
- Complete this form as you observe students drawing and/or writing.
- Use your observations to assess students' needs and to make instructional decisions.
- Place the completed form in each student's portfolio as additional information about the student.

A Checklist format is quick to complete and easy to interpret.

B Checklist includes all important aspects of a student's early writing behaviors.

C "Not Applicable" column makes checklist adaptable to different grade levels.

Form for reproduction is on page 138.

Teacher Form
Writing Behaviors Checklist

Student **Kristen Cleaver**   Date **9/28**

Behavior	Yes	No	Not Applicable
Produces detailed and relevant drawings	✓		
Dictates messages for others to write	✓		
Writes using scribble, drawing, or letterlike forms	✓		
Distinguishes between writing and drawing	✓		
Writes own name and other important words	✓		
Writes all letters of the alphabet, capital and lowercase		✓	
Writes labels or captions for illustrations and possessions	✓		
Writes messages that move from left to right and top to bottom		✓	
Uses phonological knowledge to map sounds to letters when writing		✓	
Holds pencil and positions paper correctly	✓		
Uses basic capitalization and punctuation		✓	
Writes messages that can be understood by others		✓	
Shows understanding of sequence in writing		✓	
Stays on topic when writing			✓
Expresses original ideas	✓		
Elaborates with details			✓
Has an identifiable voice			✓
Chooses precise and vivid words		✓	
Takes risks with vocabulary			✓
Uses descriptive words	✓		
Writes in different forms			✓
Writes for different audiences and purposes			✓
Writes to record ideas and reflections	✓		
Other: Writes using rhyming words	✓		

Teacher Form
Oral Language Behaviors Checklist

What is it?

- A form to record your observations of students' speaking and listening behaviors at the beginning of and throughout the year

What does it show?

- Students' facility with oral language
- Students' ease at speaking and listening in various situations and for various purposes

How do I use it?

- Complete this form as you observe students speaking and listening, both individually and in groups.
- Use your observations to assess students' needs and to make instructional decisions.
- Place the completed form in each student's portfolio as additional information about the student.

A Checklist format is quick to complete and easy to interpret.

B Checklist includes all important aspects of a student's early oral language behaviors.

Form for reproduction is on page 139.

Teacher Form
Oral Language Behaviors Checklist

Student Kristen Cleaver   **A**   Date 9/26

Behavior	Yes	No	Example
Follows simple oral directions	✓		
Follows directions of several steps		✓	got confused making a book page
Listens to stories read aloud	✓		
Participates actively when predictable rhymes and songs are read aloud	✓		
Understands and retells spoken messages	✓		
Gives precise directions		✓	couldn't explain how to get to office
Expresses ideas clearly	✓		
Responds appropriately to questions	✓		
Knows and uses many words	✓		
Participates in conversations and discussions	✓		
Listens in small-group situations	✓		
Listens in whole-group situations	✓		
Stays on topic in discussions		✓	led TV discussion away from topic
Uses language conventions appropriately	✓		
Listens to others courteously, without interrupting	✓		
Can retell simple stories in sequence			forgot order in "Three Bears"
Recalls details from stories	✓		
Reads orally with appropriate fluency	✓		
Listens and speaks for various purposes	✓		
Adapts speaking to audience		✓	
Listens critically to oral readings, discussions, and messages	✓		
Connects cultural experiences and prior knowledge through speaking and listening	✓		
Other:			

47

Survey
Profile of English Language Learners

What is it?

- A form to help identify the strengths and needs of students whose first language is not English

What does it show?

- An English language learner's proficiency with speaking, reading, and writing English

How do I use it?

- Identify students whose English proficiency you are uncertain about.

- Use the criteria on the form to assess students' abilities in the various language areas, noting specific examples.

- Use the form as a rough guideline of where students are in their English language development and where they may need help.

What do I do next?

Scott Foresman *Reading Street* offers your English language learners

- standards-based instruction at all levels of language acquisition—Beginning, Early Intermediate, Intermediate, Early Advanced, and Advanced

- the English Language Learners Handbook with instructional material and comprehensive guidance for teachers and effective, efficient, and explicit instruction for English language learners. Building on the *Reading Street* literacy instruction, the guide uses components such as ELL Posters, ELL Readers, and English Language Support (blackline masters).

(A) Checklist format is easy to interpret.

(B) Space is provided for you to note your own responses.

Form for reproduction is on page 140.

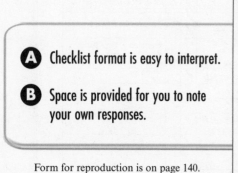

Teacher Form
Profile of English Language Learners

Student: Tomás Alvarez

Trait	Mostly	Unevenly	Rarely	Date/Comment
Speaks and/or understands a few basic words	✓			
Speaks fluently but makes frequent errors			✓	10/16 seems to know more words than he is comfortable using
Uses names of many objects		✓		
Uses and understands basic everyday vocabulary		✓		
Asks and answers simple questions			✓	10/16 reluctant to ask for help
Follows simple directions		✓		
Takes part in discussions			✓	10/16 good at communicating through art
Conveys ideas or stories through drawings	✓			
Needs pictures to comprehend simple text		✓		
Recognizes basic sound/letter relationships in words		✓		
Follows text being read aloud		✓		
Joins in choral reading	✓			10/16 likes to join in with the class
Retells predictable text		✓		

Survey
My Child as a Learner

| **What is it?** | • A survey to help you get to know your students better from their families' perspectives |
| | • An opportunity to establish a positive relationship with your students' families from the start |

| **What does it show?** | • Students' behaviors that families observe at home |
| | • A family's view of a student as a learner |

How do I use it?	• Send the survey home at the beginning of the school year with a cover letter explaining the value of family input.
	• Place the completed form in each student's portfolio as additional information about the student.
	• Discuss it during parent conferences.

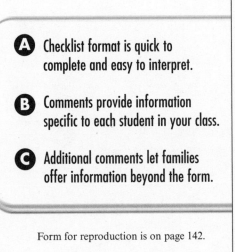

A Checklist format is quick to complete and easy to interpret.

B Comments provide information specific to each student in your class.

C Additional comments let families offer information beyond the form.

Form for reproduction is on page 142.

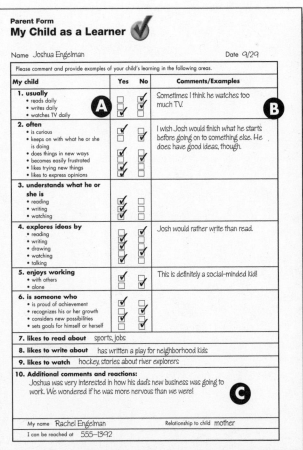

49

Chapter 3

Progress-Monitoring Assessments: What to Do During the Year

Overview

Assessments designed to monitor student progress take many forms, including weekly tests, unit tests, checklists and rubrics used in self-assessment, and teacher-managed activities, such as collecting and analyzing work samples and observing students while engaged in literacy tasks. Progress monitoring involves using a variety of formal and classroom-based assessment formats that are characterized by timely feedback aligned with instructional goals. After using entry-level assessments to determine where to begin instruction for individuals and groups of students, it becomes equally important to monitor the progress that your students make throughout the year and the effectiveness of your instruction. The assessments labeled progress-monitoring tools in this handbook provide ongoing feedback on the progress your students make toward achievement of the skills and knowledge described in the strands and domains of national and state reading and language arts standards.

What are the benefits of progress-monitoring?

- It helps you determine if all students are progressing as expected and helps you focus instruction for individuals and groups of students, as opposed to teaching to the middle performance level in your classes.

- It allows you to determine students' progress in meeting or exceeding national and state reading and language arts standards based on a regular process of observing, monitoring, and judging the quality of their work.

- You can guide student learning better if you have an up-to-date understanding of your students' current performance levels, wasting no time on skills students have already mastered and focusing instead on the areas that need additional attention.

- Frequent use of progress-monitoring assessments gives *all* your students a more equitable opportunity to demonstrate their skills because high standards are most reliably achieved in small, consistent increases that occur over time.

- Because many progress-monitoring assessments are curriculum-embedded and aligned to instruction, they provide feedback on the effectiveness of your instruction.

What are the purposes of progress-monitoring?

- To identify mastery of national and state reading and language arts standards both at the individual student level and at the class level

- To determine when differentiation of instruction is required for individuals or groups of students

- To provide a basis for focused instructional decision-making

- To help you modify or emphasize parts of your curriculum and instruction to reflect the results of progress-monitoring assessments

- To determine report card grades and/or communicate progress to parents

- To encourage student self-assessment and evaluation by helping students learn how to make judgments about the quality of their own work

- To evaluate instructional approaches

- To promote continuous improvement

What are some typical classroom-based activities that might be used to monitor progress?

- Class discussions

- Oral reports, oral readings, dramatizations, and retellings

- Drawings, sculpture, and other artwork

- Graphic organizers

- Collaborative activities and projects

- Student response logs

- Student reflective essays

When do I use progress-monitoring assessment activities?

Use these activities throughout the school year to measure students' growth and development. Make assessment part of your classroom culture, an established classroom routine, and a natural step in learning.

> "…quality is the result of regular inspections (assessments) *along the way*, followed by needed adjustments based on the information gleaned from the inspections."
> (McTighe, 1997)

Who should engage in progress-monitoring?

Although you are the primary initiator of progress-monitoring assessments, your students should be given opportunities to engage in ongoing self-monitoring. There are many benefits to involving students in their own progress-monitoring. When your students participate in self-assessment practices, they are more likely to develop metacognitive awareness and exhibit self-regulating skills. This means they will become consciously aware of their learning and actively set goals designed to increase their performances. Engaging in self-assessment leads to the development of positive attitudes toward learning. Furthermore, self-assessment emphasizes application of the knowledge and skills identified in statewide and district-wide reading and language arts standards and promotes higher-order thinking and the development of reasoning skills.

- **How can you help students become better self-assessors?**

  - Model self-monitoring by sharing your thoughts with students as you evaluate and reflect on a project you are doing, such as putting up a bulletin board, writing a note to another teacher, or drafting directions for an assignment you are going to give them.

  - Make the criteria on which students are assessed public so that they can use this information to self-assess.

  - Schedule regular times for self-assessment.

  - Give students opportunities to draft criteria for assessing their own work.

  - Provide opportunities for students to engage in activities that encourage thinking, writing, and talking about their performances.

- **What kinds of activities support self-assessment?**

  - Writing and Reading Conferences with you

  - Writing and Reading Conferences with classmates

  - Reflection journals and cognitive logs

  - Portfolio reviews

  - Use of self-assessment checklists and rubrics

  - Student-led parent-teacher conferences

3 • Progress Monitoring

What techniques and tools are available?

FORMAL ASSESSMENT TOOLS AND TECHNIQUES FOR MONITORING PROGRESS

- **Weekly Tests** (See pages 58–59.)

    These multiple-choice tests measure students' understanding of each week's vocabulary, phonics/word analysis skills, and comprehension skills as applied to a new passage.

- **Fresh Reads for Fluency and Comprehension** (See pages 60–61.)

    These multiple-choice and constructed-response tests allow students to practice comprehension skills with a new selection matched to their instructional reading level. They also provide a check of reading fluency.

- **Unit Benchmark Tests** (See pages 62–63.)

    These tests are designed to measure your students' abilities to apply target comprehension skills and other literacy skills taught in each unit.

INFORMAL ASSESSMENT TOOLS AND TECHNIQUES FOR MONITORING PROGRESS

- **Questioning Strategies** (See pages 64–65.)

    Skillful questioning is an important assessment technique. Your ability to frame and ask powerful questions is an effective way to monitor the learning progress of your students.

- **Ongoing Teacher Observation** (See page 66.)

    Observation of your students allows you to monitor their performance in the context of classroom activities and provide helpful feedback while students are in the process of learning, rather than after-the-fact.

- **Fluency Check** (See pages 67–68.)

    This assessment technique is an individually-administered procedure for recording and analyzing your students' reading rates and reading behaviors.

    > "Any decision of consequence deserves more than one piece of evidence."
    >
    > (Pearson, 1998)

- **Retelling and Summarizing** (See pages 69–70.)

    These oral or written recountings of narrative or expository text in your students' own words serve as indicators of what they can remember after reading or listening to a text.

- **Work Habits Conference Record** (See page 71.)

    This record sheet can be used when conferencing with students and provides a way to monitor your students' understanding of task completion and time management behaviors.

- **Skills Conference Record** (See page 72.)

    This checklist allows you to capture information about your students' reading, writing, speaking, and listening behaviors, strategies, and proficiencies.

- **Observing English Language Learners** (See page 73.)

    This form allows you to record ongoing observations about your English language learners' progress in developing reading skills.

- **Observing My Child's Reading** (See page 74.)

    This form allows parents to comment on behaviors they notice as their child reads aloud to them.

- **Student Self-Assessment** (See page 75.)

    This form provides your students with an opportunity to assess themselves as readers, writers, and learners.

> "Research on accomplished readers demonstrates that they are planful and aware and capable of online monitoring of their reading."
> (Afflerbach, 2001)

- **Peer Assessment** (See page 76.)

    This form affords your students an opportunity to assess a peer's work and apply what they are learning about the quality of effective reading, writing, and speaking.

- **Group Assessment** (See page 77.)

    This form allows students to assess their collaborative efforts during group work as well as those of other group members.

- **Student Portfolios** (See pages 78–79.)

    Maintaining a portfolio is a process that allows your students to use work samples to document and reflect on their growth in reading, writing, speaking, and listening. See Chapter 7 for descriptions of the Portfolio Guide and the Portfolio Selection Slips.

- **Reading Log** (See page 80.)

    This form allows students to keep track of the literature they have read, as well as rate the quality of the selections.

- **About My Reading** (See page 81.)

    This form encourages your students to describe and evaluate their own reading progress.

- **Writing Log** (See page 82.)

    This form helps students keep track of and reflect on the pieces they have written.

- **About My Writing** (See page 83.)

    This form encourages your students to describe and evaluate their own writing progress.

Want to learn more about progress-monitoring assessment?

If you would like to learn more about how to use progress-monitoring assessment practices in your classroom, you will find the following resources interesting.

References

Afflerbach, P. *Understanding and Using Reading Assessment K–12*. Newark, NJ: International Reading Association, 2007.

Afflerbach, P. "Teaching Reading Self-Assessment Strategies." In *Comprehension Instruction: Research-Based Best Practices*. Eds. C. Block and M. Pressley. New York: The Guilford Press, 2001, pp. 96–111.

Bailey, J. M., and T. R. Guskey. "Implementing Student-Led Conferences." In *Experts in Assessment* series. Eds. T.R. Guskey and R.J. Marzano. Thousand Oaks, CA: Corwin Press, Inc., 2001.

Danielson, C., and L. Abrutyn. *An Introduction to Using Portfolios in the Classroom*. Alexandria, VA: ASCD, 1997.

Gambrell, L. B., P. S. Koskinen, and B. A. Kapinus. "Retelling and the Reading Comprehension of Proficient and Less-Proficient Readers." *Journal of Educational Research*, vol. 84 (1991), pp. 356–363.

Gambrell, L. B., W. Pfeiffer, and R. Wilson. "The Effects of Retelling Upon Reading Comprehension and Recall of Text Information." *Journal of Educational Research*, vol. 78 (1985), pp. 216–220.

Good, R. H., D. C. Simmons, and S. Smith. "Effective Academic Interventions in the United States: Evaluating and Enhancing the Acquisition of Early Reading Skills." *School Psychology Review*, vol. 27, no. 1 (1998), pp. 45–56.

Hasbrouck, J. E., and G. Tindal. "Curriculum-Based Oral Reading Fluency Norms for Students in Grades 2 through 5." *Teaching Exceptional Children*, vol. 24 (1992), pp. 41–44.

Keene, E. O., and S. Zimmermann. *Mosaic of Thought*. Portsmouth, NH: Heinemann, 1997.

Marzano, R. J., D. Pickering, and J. E. Pollock. *Classroom Instruction That Works: Research-Based Strategies for Increasing Student Achievement*. Alexandria, VA: ASCD, 2001.

Marzano, R. J., et.al. *Handbook for Classroom Instruction That Works*. Alexandria, VA: ASCD, 2001.

McMillan, J. H. "Essential Assessment Concepts for Teachers and Administrators." In *Experts in Assessment* series. Eds. T. R. Guskey and R. J. Marzano. Thousand Oaks, CA: Corwin Press, Inc., 2001.

McTighe, J. "What Happens Between Assessments?" *Educational Leadership*, Vol. 54, no. 4 (1997), pp. 6–12.

Morrow, L. M. "Effects of Structural Guidance in Story Retelling on Children's Dictation of Original Stories." *Journal of Reading Behavior*, vol. 18, no. 2 (1986), pp. 135–152.

Moss, B. "Teaching Expository Text Structures Through Information Trade Book Retellings." *The Reading Teacher*, vol. 57, no. 8 (May 2004), pp. 710–718.

Pappas, C. C. "Fostering Full Access to Literacy by Including Information Books." *Language Arts*, vol. 68, no. 6 (October 1991), pp. 449–462.

Raphael, T. E. "Teaching Question Answer Relationships, Revisited." *The Reading Teacher*, vol. 39, no. 6 (February 1986), pp. 516–522.

Wixson, K. K., and M. N. Yochum. "Research on Literacy Policy and Professional Development: National, State, District, and Teacher Contexts." *Elementary School Journal*, vol. 105, no. 2 (November 2004), pp. 219–242.

Wood, K. D.; D. B. Taylor; B. Drye; and M. J. Brigman. "Assessing Students' Understanding of Informational Text in Intermediate- and Middle-Level Classrooms." In *Classroom Literacy Assessment: Making Sense of What Students Know and Do*. Eds. J. R. Paratore and R. L. McCormack. New York: The Guilford Press, 2007, pp. 195–209.

Weekly Tests

What are they?

- Tests designed to measure students' understanding of the skills and vocabulary words of the week
- Tests consisting of multiple-choice questions

Why would I choose them?

- To assess students' understanding of the vocabulary words, decoding skills, and comprehension skills of the week
- To monitor student mastery of skills

What do they test?

- Understanding of vocabulary words taught in a reading selection
- Phonics/word analysis skills
- Comprehension—target skills

When do I use them?

- At the end of Day 5 in each week

How do I use them?

- The tests are designed to be group-administered.

How do I use the results?

- To identify students who can successfully construct meaning from a reading selection and to identify which students need intervention
- To identify the specific vocabulary words, decoding skills, and comprehension skills a student has and has not mastered

A Students are tested on the week's introduced vocabulary words.

B The decoding skill of the week is tested.

C Students read a new passage for comprehension. Comprehension items cover passage content as well as the target and review skills.

D Students respond to the "Look Back and Write" assignment in the Student Edition.

Samples are from Grade 2 Weekly Tests.

Name _____

Bremen Town Musician

VOCABULARY

Directions
Read each sentence. Fill in the circle next to the word that fills the _____. **A**

1 There were many _____ at the park.
○ people
○ floors
○ pleasant

2 It will _____ rain today.
○ step
○ fine
○ probably

3 What _____ we eat for dinner?
○ sure
○ shall
○ jump

4 The street name is on the _____.
○ tire
○ cold
○ sign

5 Carla _____ a new book.
○ scared
○ bought
○ walked

49

PHONICS

Directions
Choose the correct plural form of the underlined word. Fill in the circle next to the answer. **B**

6 My box has green and white stripes.
○ boxs
○ box's
○ boxes

7 I packed a lunch for the picnic.
○ lunches
○ lunchs
○ lunchies

8 The baby giggled and smiled.
○ babys
○ babies
○ babyes

9 I read a book about pirates.
○ bookes
○ book's
○ books

10 My favorite flower is the daisy.
○ daisys
○ daisies
○ daisyes

50   Weekly Test 9   Unit 2 Week 4

Name _____

Bremen Town Musicians

COMPREHENSION

From Seed to Flower

C

Most plants begin as seeds. But how does a seed grow into a plant?

It starts when a seed falls to the ground. The seed has a hard shell to protect it. If it is too hot or cold, the seed will not grow. If it is too dry, the seed will not grow. The seed must get wet before it will grow.

When it gets enough water, the seed will start to grow. First, one part of the seed grows into the ground. This part will become the roots. The roots help make the plant strong. The roots also get food and water from the soil.

Another part of the seed grows out of the ground. It grows toward the sun. This part will become the stem and leaves of the plant. The leaves use the light from the sun to help the plant make food.

If the plant gets enough water and s_____ enough, it will stop growing.

Soon flowers will begin to grow on of leaves. Bugs, such as bees, like flow plants make new seeds. Later, the new seeds will start to make a new plant all

Weekly Test 9   Unit 2 Week 4

Name _____

Bremen Town Musicians

WRITTEN RESPONSE TO THE SELECTION

D

Look Back and Write Look back at the play. How do you know who is speaking? Using the elements of dialogue, write a scene about a fifth Bremen Town Musician.

Use the list in the box below to help you as you write.

REMEMBER—YOU SHOULD

☐ write a scene about a fifth Bremen Town Musician.

☐ use the elements of dialogue to write what each character will say in the scene.

☐ be sure your scene has a beginning, middle, and end.

☐ try to use correct spelling, capitalization, punctuation, grammar, and sentences.

Weekly Test 9   Unit 2 Week 4   53

Fresh Reads for Fluency and Comprehension

What are they?
- Tests that give students an opportunity to practice oral fluency and the comprehension skills of the week with a new selection, a "fresh read," matched to each student's instructional reading level
- Tests consisting of multiple-choice and constructed-response questions

Why would I choose them?
- To assess students' abilities to derive meaning from new selections at their instructional reading levels
- To retest a student's reading after administering a Weekly Test
- To check a student's reading rate
- To monitor student mastery of the Scott Foresman *Reading Street* Skills

What do they test?
- The target and review comprehension skills of the week
- Comprehension of the reading selection through literal, inferential, and critical-analysis questions
- Reading fluency

When do I use them?
- Throughout the year, each week after students have been taught the comprehension skill lesson

How do I use them?
- One option is for the student to read the passage aloud to you as a fluency check.
- Another option is for the student to do the pages as extra skill practice.
- Teachers choose which of the three types of reading passages for the week to give to each student: Strategic Intervention (SI), On-Level (OL), or Advanced (A).

How do I use the results?
- To gather additional information about a student's ability to comprehend a passage written at his or her instructional reading level
- To gather additional information about the specific comprehension skills a student has and has not mastered
- To monitor a student's progress in fluent reading

Name _____

Read the selection. Then answer the questions that follow.

First Place

Gene woke up nervous. The music contest was on Monday. Gene was scared.

"I can't do it," Gene said to his parents.

"First you need to practice. I will help you," Gene's dad said. They practiced the piano together every day.

Then Gene and his dad went to the contest. Gene heard the other students play. They played very well. *I don't have a chance*, Gene thought to himself.

Later it was Gene's turn. He looked at his dad and felt better. Gene played without any mistakes. He could not believe it when he heard his name called as the first-place winner.

Finally, Gene wasn't nervous anymore.

Turn the page.

Fresh Reads   Unit 1 Week 2 SI   7

(A)

Name _____

Read the selection. Then answer the questions that follow.

Henry's New Bed

My cat Henry could sleep almost anywhere and anytime. Sometimes I found him curled up in an armchair, or sleeping on a pile of clothes, or napping in my bed. One day my mom told me that it was time for Henry to have a bed of his own.

"Carl, you should make a bed for Henry," Mom said. "I'll help you."

First, we looked for a basket in the basement and found an old laundry basket that we didn't use anymore. Next, we needed something soft for Henry to sleep on. I suggested my pillow, but Mom didn't think that was a good idea. She found some old towels and put them in the basket. I wanted to show the bed to Henry right away, but Mom said that we should put one of his favorite toys in the basket first. I found Henry's toy mouse and put it in the basket.

"Now we need to find a place to put Henry's bed," Mom said.

We decided to put Henry's bed on the floor near my bed. When I showed Henry his new bed, he jumped right in, turned around a few times, and then quickly fell asleep. From then on, we found him in his own bed more often than in mine.

Turn the page.

Fresh Reads   Unit 1 Week 2 A   11

Name _____

Read the selection. Then answer the questions that follow.

The Backyard Party

Angie and Gina wanted to have a party because school was almost over for the	15
summer. They wanted to invite all their friends, but their houses were too small for	30
so many people. Gina thought that her big backyard would be perfect for the party,	45
so she asked her mom if she could have the party there. Gina's mom agreed, so the	62
girls began to make plans for the best party ever.	72
First, Angie and Gina made a list of their friends. Then they made fancy	86
invitations that told the time and place of the party. Next, Angie began writing names	101
on the cards, while Gina made a list of food to buy. Because the weather was warm,	118
Gina wanted to have ice cream for dessert.	126
"What games should we play?" Angie asked.	133
"Let's play the ring-toss game that we played last summer," Gina said.	145
Just then Gina's mom came into the room. "What's the date of the party?"	159
she asked.	161
Gina and Angie looked at each other and laughed. They had been so busy	175
making plans for the party that they'd forgotten to pick a day for it!	189

(C)

Turn the page.

Fresh Reads   Unit 1 Week 2 OL

Answer the questions below.

1 **What do you think Gina and Angie will do next?**
○ plan a beginning of the school year party
○ pick a day for the party
○ give Gina's mom a list of food to buy
○ practice the ring-toss game

2 **What clue words tell you the sequence of events in the second paragraph?**
○ made, began
○ first, then, next
○ told, because
○ time, place

3 **What did you learn about people from this story?**
○ When people work together, they sometimes disagree.
○ People who are busy enjoy life much more.
○ When people are excited, they can forget things.
○ People around the world celebrate differently.

4 **Which of the following happened first?**
○ Gina got permission to have the party.
○ Angie and Gina made invitations.
○ Gina's mom asked about the date of the party.
○ Gina and Angie made a list of friends to invite.

5 **If you were planning a party, what would you do first, second, and third?**

_____
_____
_____
_____
_____
_____
_____

(B)

10   Fresh Reads   Unit 1 Week 2 OL

(A) Passages of different instructional levels

(B) Questions on the target skill and review skill of the week

(C) Opportunity for fluency check

Samples are from Grade 3 Fresh Reads.

Unit Benchmark Tests

What are they?

- Tests designed to measure the students' ability to apply the target comprehension skills and other literacy skills taught during the unit

Why would I choose them?

- To assess students' understanding and use of specific skills
- To identify skill areas in which students need intervention and continued practice
- To know that there are sufficient items per individual skill to track a student's proficiency with that skill

What do they test?

- Unit reading comprehension skills through literal, inferential, and critical-analysis questions
- Vocabulary
- Phonics
- Writing conventions (grammar, usage, mechanics, and spelling)
- Writing—response to prompt
- Oral reading fluency

When do I use them?

- Throughout the year, at the end of each of the six-week units

How do I use them?

- All portions of the tests are designed to be group-administered except for the fluency passages.
- The fluency passages are to be individually administered.

How do I use the results?

- To identify students who can successfully construct meaning from a reading selection and to identify students who need intervention
- To identify specific skills students have and have not mastered
- As feedback about the effectiveness of your instruction and to help plan instruction for the next unit

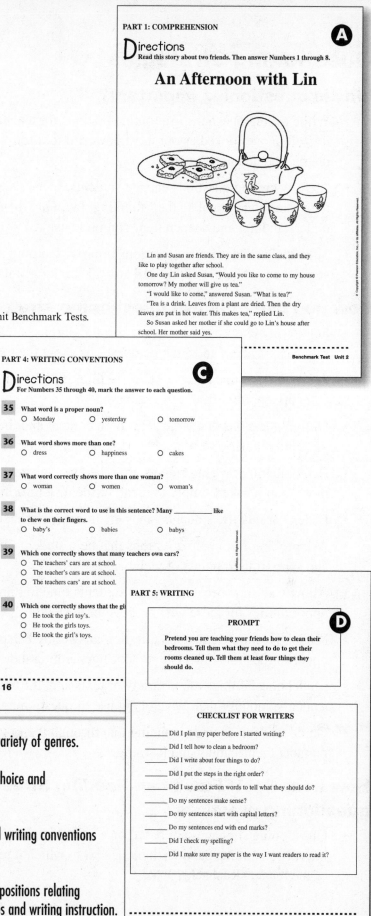

PART 1: COMPREHENSION

Directions
Read this story about two friends. Then answer Numbers 1 through 8.

An Afternoon with Lin

Lin and Susan are friends. They are in the same class, and they like to play together after school.

One day Lin asked Susan, "Would you like to come to my house tomorrow? My mother will give us tea."

"I would like to come," answered Susan. "What is tea?"

"Tea is a drink. Leaves from a plant are dried. Then the dry leaves are put in hot water. This makes tea," replied Lin.

So Susan asked her mother if she could go to Lin's house after school. Her mother said yes.

Benchmark Test Unit 2

Samples are from Grade 2 Unit Benchmark Tests.

1 Where was Lin's mother during the story?
- ○ at her own home
- ○ in China
- ○ at Lin's school

2 What happened first?
- ○ Susan's mother called Lin's mother on the telephone.
- ○ Lin asked Susan to come to her house for tea.
- ○ Lin's mother asked Susan if she liked tea.

3 How were Lin and Susan alike?
- ○ They played with the same friends.
- ○ They were both from China.
- ○ They liked to have tea together.

4 What happened when hot water was added to the dried leaves?
- ○ It became tea.
- ○ Susan dropped her cup.
- ○ Lin invited her friend over.

5 What would be another good title for the story?
- ○ Making New Friends at School
- ○ Learning All About China
- ○ Sharing Tea with a Friend

4   Benchmark Test Unit 2

PART 4: WRITING CONVENTIONS

Directions
For Numbers 35 through 40, mark the answer to each question.

35 What word is a proper noun?
- ○ Monday   ○ yesterday   ○ tomorrow

36 What word shows more than one?
- ○ dress   ○ happiness   ○ cakes

37 What word correctly shows more than one woman?
- ○ woman   ○ women   ○ woman's

38 What is the correct word to use in this sentence? Many _____ like to chew on their fingers.
- ○ baby's   ○ babies   ○ babys

39 Which one correctly shows that many teachers own cars?
- ○ The teachers' cars are at school.
- ○ The teacher's cars are at school.
- ○ The teachers cars' are at school.

40 Which one correctly shows that the gi
- ○ He took the girl toy's.
- ○ He took the girls toys.
- ○ He took the girl's toys.

16

PART 5: WRITING

PROMPT

Pretend you are teaching your friends how to clean their bedrooms. Tell them what they need to do to get their rooms cleaned up. Tell them at least four things they should do.

CHECKLIST FOR WRITERS

_____ Did I plan my paper before I started writing?

_____ Did I tell how to clean a bedroom?

_____ Did I write about four things to do?

_____ Did I put the steps in the right order?

_____ Did I use good action words to tell what they should do?

_____ Do my sentences make sense?

_____ Do my sentences start with capital letters?

_____ Do my sentences end with end marks?

_____ Did I check my spelling?

_____ Did I make sure my paper is the way I want readers to read it?

Benchmark Test Unit 2   17

A Students read selections in a variety of genres.

B Students respond to multiple-choice and writing questions.

C Vocabulary skills, phonics, and writing conventions skills are tested.

D Students produce original compositions relating selections in test to unit themes and writing instruction.

Questioning Strategies

Why is questioning important?

- While asking questions is a routine practice for teachers, it is often overlooked as our most powerful tool for instruction and assessment.

- Artfully crafted questions engage students, focus their attention, stimulate their thinking, facilitate their understanding, and deepen their comprehension.

- Students' self-generated questions improve learning and strengthen problem-solving and critical-thinking skills.

> "Our questions help us formulate our beliefs about teaching and learning, and those beliefs underlie our instructional decisions."
>
> (Keene & Zimmerman, 1997)

How do I use effective questioning strategies?

- Selectively choose questions for specific purposes (e.g., recall-level questions about sequence of ideas and analytic questions about the theme of a story).

- Ask questions that represent diverse thinking activities—recall, analysis, comparison, inference, and evaluation.

- Design questions that emphasize both content and the thinking needed to process the content, using verbs such as *list, define, compare, conclude*, and *defend*.

- Remember that when students are asked to analyze information, they will learn more than if asked simply to recall or identify information.

- Listen carefully to students' answers in order to shape skillful follow-up questions.

- Ask probing follow-up questions that help students extend their thinking and clarify and support their points of view.

- Allow wait time because it gives students time to think and provides answering opportunities for those who process more slowly.

- Model question-asking and question-answering behavior and provide repeated opportunities for students to practice generating their own questions.

- Model questioning with a variety of texts and, through reading conferences with the students, monitor their developing use of questioning.

- Guide students in understanding that through their own questions they can actively regulate their reading and learning.

How does Scott Foresman *Reading Street* support effective questioning practices?

- Questioning strategies are based on a question-answer framework suggesting an interaction among the question, the text to which it refers, and the prior knowledge of the reader (Raphael, 1986).

- Students are taught that answering comprehension questions in class and on tests demands thinking: they have to analyze the questions in order to provide the right answers.

- Students learn that answers to questions can be found **In the Book** and **In My Head.**

- **In the Book** questions can be:

  - **Right There** questions, which are *literal* and focus on ideas explicitly stated in the text. The words in the question may match the words in the passage.

  - **Think and Search** questions, which are also *literal* and require students to locate and integrate information from within different sections of the text.

- **In My Head** questions can be:

  - **Author and Me** questions, which are *inferential* in nature, requiring students to interpret information and connect themes and major ideas with their own background knowledge. The most demanding **Author and Me** questions necessitate use of critical analysis as readers evaluate and justify the purpose, content, and quality of text.

  - **On My Own** questions are not based on the text and can be answered from the students' general background knowledge and experience. These questions are often posed by teachers in order to activate prior knowledge before reading and/or to extend the learning beyond the lesson.

- The Scott Foresman *Reading Street* formal assessments offer students a variety of engaging narrative and expository texts, and students respond to test items designed to assess how they use their comprehension skills in constructing meaning.

- Literal, inferential, and critical-analysis questions on the formal assessments are based on the question-answer framework used in instruction and are similar to question types on high-stakes assessments.

- Daily practice in answering, analyzing, and asking **Right There, Think and Search,** and **Author and Me** questions will improve student achievement on high-stakes standardized tests.

Ongoing Teacher Observation

What is it?

- Observation that occurs in the context of teaching or classroom activities
- A way to check students' progress on a daily or weekly basis
- The basis for developing a concrete plan for dealing with individual students' classroom strengths or needs

How do I make observations?

- Choose one or more students to focus on each day.
- Select the literacy behavior, strategy, or skill that you wish to observe.
- Observe your focus students as they are participating in classroom activities.
- Using a clipboard, sticky note, customized form, or checklist, note a student's behavior or performance in the targeted skills.
- Include any comments, insights, or other information you regard as significant.
- Develop a record-keeping system that is convenient and informative for you.

Why should I record my observations?

- To remember information when you need to reflect on a student at the end of the day, week, grading period, or year
- As a helpful tool for presenting information to students, parents, and administrators
- For documentation when you need to explain why you've placed a student in a particular group or given a certain grade
- To plan intervention strategies for students needing special attention

Fluency Check

What is it?

- An individually-administered procedure of recording and analyzing a student's specific reading behaviors

- A method of deciding whether a text is at the appropriate instructional level for a student

- A means of determining the level of support a student will need while reading the material

What does it show?

- Teachers who administer regular fluency checks gather evidence about the following:

    - oral reading skills and fluency calculated as words correct per minute

    - decoding and word recognition strategies

    - reading strategies a student uses and how he or she uses them to derive meaning

When do I use it?

- As often as necessary to get a clear and ongoing picture of a student's precise reading behaviors (for example, at the beginning or end of a unit or grading period, or when you need to report progress to interested parties)

How do I use it?

- Use an excerpt from Scott Foresman *Reading Street*, from a trade book, or any other text that is at an appropriate reading level for the student.

- Make one photocopy of the passage for yourself and one for the student.

- Use a watch with a second hand to time the student's reading for exactly one minute.

- Observe the student closely as he or she reads aloud and note the miscues or errors that are made.

3 • Progress Monitoring

How do I use it?
(continued)

- Use the following notations and symbols for errors:
  - **Last Word Read ( ])** – Put a bracket after the last word the student reads in one minute.
  - **Mispronunciation/misreading (/)** – Write the student's pronunciation of the word.
  - **Substitutions** – Write the substituted word above the text word. Cross out the text word. If it is a nonsense word, write it phonetically.
  - **Self-correction (sc)** – Write *sc* in a circle next to the corrected word/text; this is not considered an error.
  - **Insertions (∧)** – Write the text word/phrase and the inserted word/phrase. Mark each insertion with a caret. Include any repetitions of words.
  - **Omissions** – Circle the word(s) or word part(s) omitted.

The formula is:

Total number of words read in one minute – Number of errors = Words correct per minute

Teacher Form
Retelling

What is retelling?

- A post-reading recall of what students can remember from reading or listening to a particular text
- An oral or written recounting of narrative or expository text in a student's own words
- A reminder for students that the purpose of reading is to make sense of text

What does it show?

- A holistic view of a student's understanding of text
- Students' ability to understand narrative text elements and author's purpose and to connect stories to personal experiences and other texts
- Students' ability to understand expository text—the relationship of main ideas and details, organizational structure, author's purpose, and inferences—and to connect texts to personal experiences and prior knowledge (Moss, 2004)
- Oral and written language development

What does the research say?

- Several researchers (Gambrell, Koskinen, and Kapinus, 1991; Gambrell, Pfeiffer, and Wilson, 1985; Morrow, 1986) have found that using retellings improves students' understanding of text.

How do I do it?

- In preparation:
  - Have students attempt to retell narrative or expository texts only after you have taught and modeled the procedure and students understand the task.
  - Have students practice in groups before retelling for assessment purposes.
  - Teach text structures (narrative and expository) separately to avoid confusing students.
- Oral retellings should be administered individually. Written retellings can be administered individually or in a group.
- For oral retellings, read the passage aloud to the student or have the student read the selected text. Remind the student to remember everything he or she has heard or read. Then ask the student to tell you everything about what was read. Use prompts such as "Can you tell me more about that?"; "What happened next?"; and "What else do you remember?" At the end of the retelling, use follow-up questions (e.g., main idea, author's purpose, personal response, etc.) to gain a deeper understanding of the student's comprehension.

How do I do it? (continued)

- For written retellings, read the text aloud to students or ask them to read it silently. Remind the students to remember everything they can. Immediately after reading, have students write out what they remember about the text.

How do I use the Retelling Forms?

- Record your scores and observations on either the narrative or the expository checklist. Try to record at least one narrative retelling and one expository retelling from each student per unit.

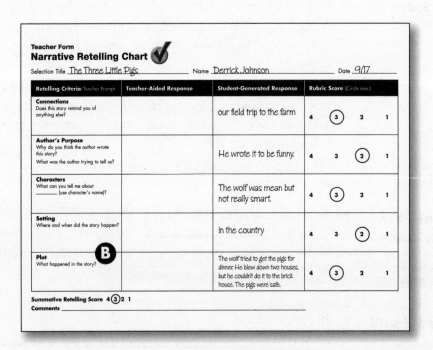

Teacher Form
Narrative Retelling Chart ✓

Selection Title _The Three Little Pigs_   Name _Derrick Johnson_   Date _9/17_

Retelling Criteria/Teacher Prompt	Teacher-Aided Response	Student-Generated Response	Rubric Score (Circle one.)			
Connections Does this story remind you of anything else?		our field trip to the farm	4	③	2	1
Author's Purpose Why do you think the author wrote this story? What was the author trying to tell us?		He wrote it to be funny.	4	3	②	1
Characters What can you tell me about _____ (use character's name)?		The wolf was mean but not really smart.	4	③	2	1
Setting Where and when did the story happen?		in the country	4	3	②	1
Plot What happened in the story?	**B**	The wolf tried to get the pigs for dinner. He blew down two houses, but he couldn't do it to the brick house. The pigs were safe.	4	③	2	1

Summative Retelling Score 4 ③ 2 1
Comments _____

A Criteria reflect comprehension skills.

B Criteria help students pinpoint key information.

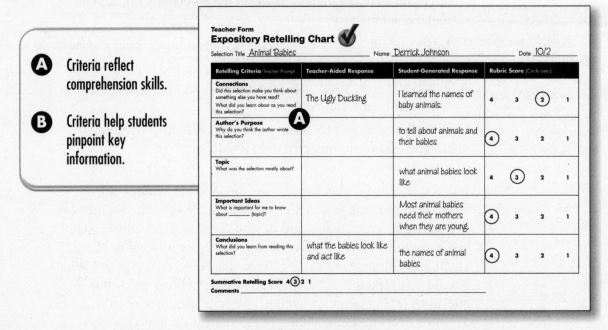

Teacher Form
Expository Retelling Chart ✓

Selection Title _Animal Babies_   Name _Derrick Johnson_   Date _10/2_

Retelling Criteria/Teacher Prompt	Teacher-Aided Response	Student-Generated Response	Rubric Score (Circle one.)			
Connections Did this selection make you think about something else you have read? What did you learn about as you read this selection?	The Ugly Duckling	I learned the names of baby animals.	4	3	②	1
Author's Purpose Why do you think the author wrote this selection?	**A**	to tell about animals and their babies	④	3	2	1
Topic What was the selection mostly about?		what animal babies look like	4	③	2	1
Important Ideas What is important for me to know about _____ (topic)?		Most animal babies need their mothers when they are young.	④	3	2	1
Conclusions What did you learn from reading this selection?	what the babies look like and act like	the names of animal babies	④	3	2	1

Summative Retelling Score 4 ③ 2 1
Comments _____

Forms for reproduction are on pages 143–144.

Teacher Form
Work Habits Conference Record

What is it?
- A means of assessing a student's understanding of tasks and time management behaviors

What does it show?
- A student's ability to set priorities and manage time
- A student's behavior toward problem-solving tasks

How do I use it?
- Plan to confer with each student at least once per grading period.
- Use the form for frequent, ongoing, informal conversations about the student's ability to manage time, set priorities, identify resources, follow directions, and articulate task completion processes.
- Tailor each conference to the student's needs, interests, and abilities; encourage him or her to take an active role.

3 • Progress Monitoring

A Did the student understand the assignment's purpose and procedures? Did he or she follow directions?

B Was the student able to decide which parts of the assignment had to be done first?

C Did the student allot time appropriately and use the time productively?

D Did the student know when it was time to seek help? Did he or she seek out the right resources (books, peers, teacher, and so on)?

E Was the student able to clearly articulate how he or she carried out the assignment, as well as the goals set in the process?

Teacher Form
Work Habits Conference Record

Student Eriko Sato

Use the key at the bottom of the page to assess student's performance.

Date	Understands tasks	Sets priorities	Uses time appropriately	Solves problems effectively	Seeks help when needed	Completes tasks on time	Can explain process/ project effectively	Comments
9/20	2	2	3	2	1	2	1	Needs to bring more of herself to discussion group.
10/24	2	2	3	2	2	2	2	Doing more independent thinking.
	A	B	C	D			E	

4 Does more than expected　　**3** Does what was expected　　**2** Does less than expected　　**1** Does not fulfill the assignment or does not complete the assignment

Form for reproduction is on page 145.

Teacher Form
Skills Conference Record

What is it?
- A means of focusing and recording results of conversations with a student about his or her reading, writing, speaking, and listening

What does it show?
- A student's behaviors, strategies, and proficiencies in the areas of reading, writing, speaking, and listening

How do I use it?
- Plan to confer with each student at least once per grading period.
- Use the form for frequent, ongoing, informal conversations about the student's progress, strengths, and areas for improvement.
- Tailor each conference to the student's needs, interests, and abilities; encourage him or her to take an active role.

A Specific criteria in each area show particular strengths and needs.

B Comments can be made to record a student's behavior or a specific concern.

C Checklist covers the continuum of student's skill growth.

Form for reproduction is on page 146.

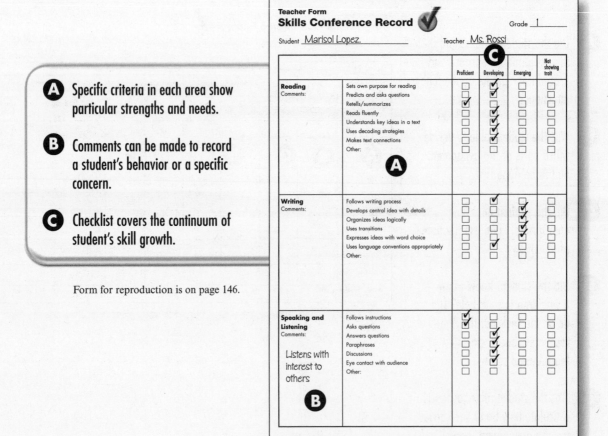

Teacher Form
Observing English Language Learners

What is it?	• A form to record your ongoing observations about how English language learners process what they read
What does it show?	• How English language learners use strategies to make sense of materials they read • Students' growth and development in processing what they read
How do I use it?	• Work with students individually as they read a new selection. • Record your observations about how students deal with new words and concepts. • Continue to review and record students' behaviors periodically as needed. • Consider using the information on the form in parent conferences.

A Behaviors identify common strategies for success in reading a new language.

B Space is provided to record students' development over time.

Teacher Form
Observing English Language Learners

Student: Tomás Alvarez

B

Behaviors Observed	Date: 10/27			Date: 11/18			Date:			Date:		
The student **A**	Yes	No	Sometimes	Yes	No	Sometimes	Yes	No	Sometimes	Yes	No	Sometimes
• uses context clues to figure out new words		✓				✓						
• uses prior knowledge to figure out new words			✓	✓								
• uses visuals to decipher meaning	✓			✓								
• uses strategies to decipher meaning		✓				✓						
• can identify the strategies he or she is using		✓				✓						
• understands why he or she is using a particular strategy		✓		✓								
• assesses his or her own progress			✓	✓								
• generally understands what the class is reading			✓			✓						

General Comments

10/27: need to work harder on strategies with Tomás

11/18: Tomás doing much better at drawing on prior knowledge. Is beginning to see the logic of strategies.

Form for reproduction is on page 147.

Parent Form
Observing My Child's Reading

What is it?

- A form to allow parents to monitor, evaluate, and comment on their child's reading
- A way to keep parents knowledgeable about and involved in their child's reading progress

What does it show?

- Reading behaviors that parents notice as their child reads aloud to them

How do parents use it?

- Give multiple copies of the form to parents during a conference or other meeting early in the school year.
- Ask parents to use the forms every few weeks to note their responses as their child reads aloud to them.
- Encourage parents to include comments on any other noteworthy aspects of their child's reading progress.

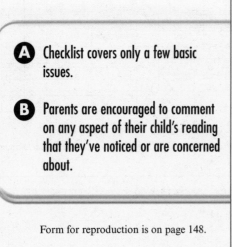

A Checklist covers only a few basic issues.

B Parents are encouraged to comment on any aspect of their child's reading that they've noticed or are concerned about.

Form for reproduction is on page 148.

Student Form
Student Self-Assessment

What is it?
- A form that allows students to assess their own growth as readers, writers, and learners
- An opportunity for students to make some of their own decisions and become more independent learners

What is the purpose?
- To help students recognize their own strengths and weaknesses
- To help students set their own goals for improvement

How is it used?
- Students assess themselves or a piece of work at least once per grading period.
- Confer with students about their self-evaluations, goals, and progress
- Place the forms in students' portfolios and share them at parent conferences.

A Students select the work, project, or time frame to be assessed.

B Students assess their own growth as learners by positively reflecting on some of their successes.

C Students reflect on things they still want to learn or improve.

D Students think about how they would like to work on or improve their learning.

E Students set future learning goals related to this or other projects.

Form for reproduction is on page 154.

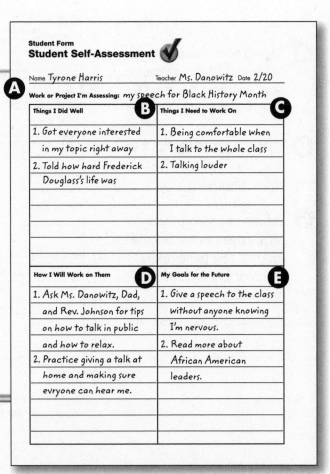

Student Form
Student Self-Assessment

Name *Tyrone Harris* Teacher *Ms. Danowitz* Date *2/20*

Work or Project I'm Assessing: *my speech for Black History Month*

Things I Did Well	Things I Need to Work On
1. Got everyone interested in my topic right away	1. Being comfortable when I talk to the whole class
2. Told how hard Frederick Douglass's life was	2. Talking louder

How I Will Work on Them	My Goals for the Future
1. Ask Ms. Danowitz, Dad, and Rev. Johnson for tips on how to talk in public and how to relax.	1. Give a speech to the class without anyone knowing I'm nervous.
2. Practice giving a talk at home and making sure evryone can hear me.	2. Read more about African American leaders.

Student Form
Peer Assessment

What is it?

- A form that allows students to evaluate and comment on each other's work
- A way to help students become aware of and value different points of view

What does it show?

- Constructive feedback that students provide to their peers
- Different perspectives students have on their peers' work and/or performance

How do students use it?

- Students should assess a piece of a peer's work at least once per grading period.
- Students might keep this form in their portfolios and use it during peer conferences.

A Students assess their peers' work and/or performance in a positive way by reflecting on some of the things they like best.

B Students suggest things that their peers might want to work on and/or improve.

C Students have the opportunity to make suggestions that their peers might not have considered for improving their work and/or performance.

Form for reproduction is on page 153.

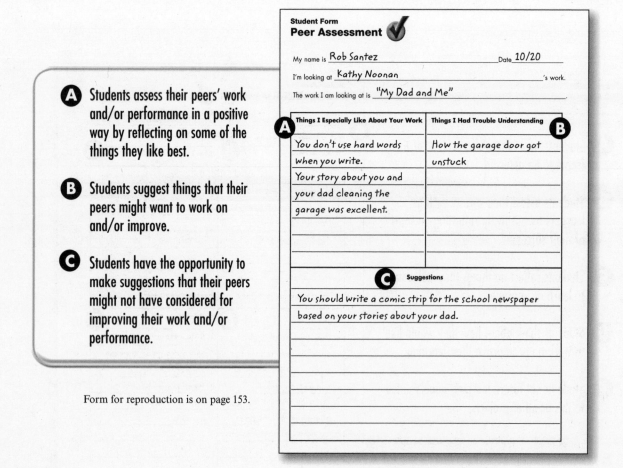

Student Form
Group Assessment

What is it?

- A form that allows students to assess their work in groups
- A way for students to evaluate both their own contributions to group work and those of other group members

What does it show?

- Group members' evaluation of their own work on a project
- How members view the work of the group as a whole
- Areas of the project that succeeded and failed, as well as goals for the future

How do students use it?

- Students may use the form to evaluate any assignment or project in which several students participate.
- Students should evaluate their own roles and contribute to an assessment of the whole group's work.

3 • Progress Monitoring

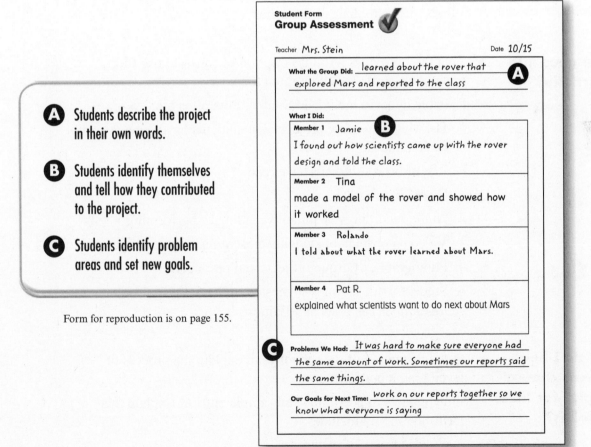

A Students describe the project in their own words.

B Students identify themselves and tell how they contributed to the project.

C Students identify problem areas and set new goals.

Form for reproduction is on page 155.

Student Form
Group Assessment

Teacher _Mrs. Stein_   Date _10/15_

What the Group Did: _learned about the rover that explored Mars and reported to the class_ **A**

What I Did:

Member 1 Jamie **B**
I found out how scientists came up with the rover design and told the class.

Member 2 Tina
made a model of the rover and showed how it worked

Member 3 Rolando
I told about what the rover learned about Mars.

Member 4 Pat R.
explained what scientists want to do next about Mars

C **Problems We Had:** _It was hard to make sure everyone had the same amount of work. Sometimes our reports said the same things._

Our Goals for Next Time: _work on our reports together so we know what everyone is saying_

Student Portfolios

What is a portfolio?

- A teacher-guided process in which students collect representative samples of their own reading, writing, speaking, and listening as a means of demonstrating growth over time

- A method of documenting growth by using the actual products students create during normal day-to-day learning

- A way to encourage students to feel ownership of their learning

What is the purpose of a portfolio?

Portfolios may accomplish any or all of the following:

- – Demonstrate students' growth and progress

- – Show students' strengths and needs

- – Help you make instructional decisions about students

- – Encourage students to assess their own growth and progress and to set new goals

- – Make it possible to share evidence of students' growth during parent conferences

- – Compile representative samples of students' work that you can pass along to their next teachers

What goes into a portfolio?

- Chapter 7 provides a full description of forms to use for organizing portfolios throughout the year.

- Possible items to include in Student Portfolios are:

  - – Drawing or writing projects that students have done at school or at home

  - – List of books students have read

  - – Works in progress

  - – Audio recordings of students reading or performing

  - – Video recordings of students presenting projects or performing

  - – Photographs of group projects and products

  - – Student work samples suggested in the Scott Foresman *Reading Street* Teacher's Editions

How do I help students choose samples for their portfolios?

- At the beginning of the school year, explain the process of developing a portfolio.

- Show models of portfolios and sample entries. Explain that portfolios should include:

  - – a wide variety of materials

  - – samples that demonstrate learning experiences

How do I help students choose samples for their portfolios? (continued)

- – pieces that show growth or improvement over time
- – materials that indicate that students have challenged themselves to try something different
- – self-assessments and future learning goals

- Periodically set aside time for students to examine their work and think about which pieces they would like to include in their portfolios.
  - – Ask students to complete a Portfolio Selection Slip that can be attached to each piece of work selected for inclusion in the portfolio.
  - – Ask students to briefly describe the work sample, the rationale for including it, and a reflection on the quality of the work (for example, *What I Chose, Why I Chose It,* and *What I Like About It*).
- Encourage students to include other documentation of literacy growth and progress, such as journal entries, inventories, writing drafts and revised copies, reading and writing logs, and peer assessments of portfolio work.

How do I involve the family in the portfolio process?

- At the beginning of the year, send home a letter to parents informing them about portfolios.
- Share students' portfolios during parent conferences as students explain the contents, how projects were developed, and how portfolio pieces were selected.
- While viewing portfolios with parents, point out students' strengths and progress over time.

What can I do at the end of each grading period?

- Hold portfolio conferences toward the end of each grading period to help students reflect on the contents of their portfolios.
- Have students decide which pieces to take home, which pieces to keep in their portfolios, and which pieces to lend to you to update their Portfolio Guides.

What can I do at the end of the school year?

- Hold final conferences with students to help them reflect on their portfolios and decide what to save and what to eliminate.
- Have students decide what to take home and what to pass along to their next teachers (for example, the pieces they are most proud of or the ones that show the most growth).

3 • Progress Monitoring

Student Form
Reading Log

What is it?

- A form to help students keep track of the literature they have read

What does it show?

- Literature students have read and how they evaluate what they read

- A student's reading growth over time

How do students use it?

- Students can list *Reading Street* text selections or trade books, as well as pieces of literature they have selected on their own.

- Students may put this form in their portfolios as a way of documenting what they have read.

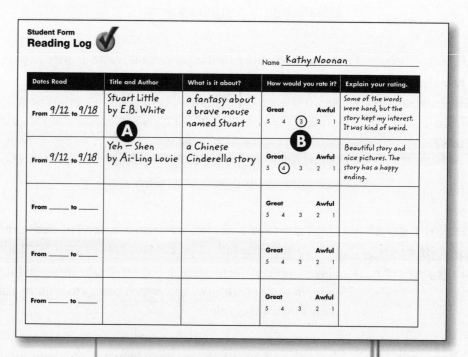

Student Form
Reading Log

Name _Kathy Noonan_

Dates Read	Title and Author	What is it about?	How would you rate it?	Explain your rating.
From _9/12_ to _9/18_	Stuart Little by E.B. White Ⓐ	a fantasy about a brave mouse named Stuart	Great Awful 5 4 ③ 2 1 Ⓑ	Some of the words were hard, but the story kept my interest. It was kind of weird.
From _9/12_ to _9/18_	Yeh – Shen by Ai-Ling Louie	a Chinese Cinderella story	Great Awful 5 ④ 3 2 1	Beautiful story and nice pictures. The story has a happy ending.
From ___ to ___			Great Awful 5 4 3 2 1	
From ___ to ___			Great Awful 5 4 3 2 1	
From ___ to ___			Great Awful 5 4 3 2 1	

Form for reproduction is on page 149.

Ⓐ Students list titles and authors of selections they have read.

Ⓑ Have students circle the rating they would give each selection. Students should give a reason or two to explain or support their ratings.

Student Form
About My Reading

What is it?	• A way for students to describe and evaluate their own reading progress
What does it show?	• Students' assessments of their own reading abilities and attitudes • Students' evaluations of reading selections that they particularly liked
How do students use it?	• Students complete the form at various points during the year, but at least once each grading period. • Students should keep completed forms in their portfolios and periodically review them to assess progress over time.

A Students evaluate their reading strengths and weaknesses.

B Students describe a specific reading selection that they enjoyed.

Form for reproduction is on page 150.

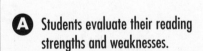

Student Form
About My Reading

Name Kathy Noonan   Date 1/31

1. Compared with earlier in the year, I am enjoying reading
   ☐ more   ☐ less   ☑ about the same

   A

2. When I read now, I understand
   ☑ more than I used to   ☐ about the same as I used to

3. One thing that has helped me with my reading is
   stopping while I'm reading a story and trying to figure
   out what will happen next

4. One thing that could make me a better reader is   **A**
   being able to figure out the meanings of more words
   while I read

5. Here is one selection or book that I really enjoyed reading:
   Stuart Little by E.B. White

   B

6. Here are some reasons why I liked it:
   Stuart wasn't afraid to try things. I liked his bird. I
   like the way the author told about things.

Student Form
Writing Log

What is it?	• A form to help students keep track of and reflect on the pieces they have written
What does it show?	• Titles and genres of compositions students have written
	• Students' feelings toward their writing and what they liked or disliked about each piece
How do students use it?	• Students can make notes on their Writing Logs during any stage of the writing process for any pieces they choose.
	• Students may put this form in their portfolios as a way of keeping track of what they have written.

A Students list pieces of writing by genre—for example, personal narrative, sports story, folk tale, biography, and so on.

B Have students circle the rating they would give each piece.

C Encourage students to assess their own writing and to point out the strengths of the piece.

Form for reproduction is on page 151.

Student Form
Writing Log

Name _Sami Smith_   Date _10/20_
Teacher _Ms. Brewer_   Grade _4_

Date	Title	Type of Writing **(A)**	How I felt about this this piece	What I liked or disliked	Put in Portfolio
10/20	My Camping Trip	Narrative	④ 3 2 1	I described everything on the trip.	✓
11/15	Chimpanzees	Expository	4 3 ② 1	I couldn't find information. **C**	
			4 3 2 **B**		
			4 3 2 1		
			4 3 2 1		
			4 3 2 1		

Key
4 = Excellent
3 = Good
2 = Fair
1 = Poor

Student Form
About My Writing

What is it?	• A way for students to describe and evaluate their own writing progress
What does it show?	• Students' assessments of their own writing abilities and attitudes • Students' evaluations of original pieces of writing that they thought turned out well
How do students use it?	• Students may complete the form at various points during the year, but at least once each grading period. • Students should keep completed forms in their portfolios and periodically review them to assess progress over time.

A Students evaluate their writing strengths and weaknesses.

B Students assess an original piece of writing.

Form for reproduction is on page 152.

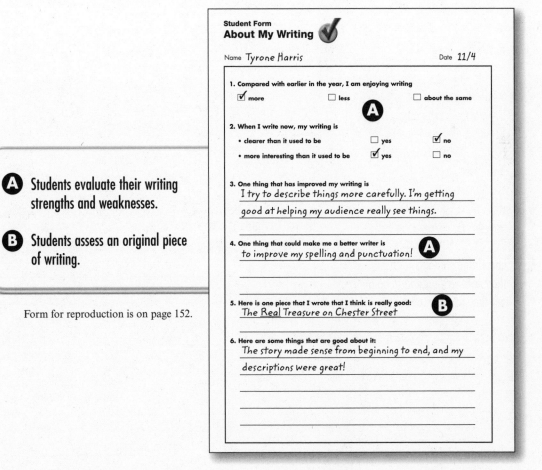

Student Form
About My Writing

Name _Tyrone Harris_   Date _11/4_

1. **Compared with earlier in the year, I am enjoying writing**
   ☑ more   ☐ less   ☐ about the same   **A**

2. **When I write now, my writing is**
   • clearer than it used to be   ☐ yes   ☑ no
   • more interesting than it used to be   ☑ yes   ☐ no

3. **One thing that has improved my writing is**
   I try to describe things more carefully. I'm getting good at helping my audience really see things.

4. **One thing that could make me a better writer is**   **A**
   to improve my spelling and punctuation!

5. **Here is one piece that I wrote that I think is really good:**   **B**
   The Real Treasure on Chester Street

6. **Here are some things that are good about it:**
   The story made sense from beginning to end, and my descriptions were great!

Chapter 4 | Summative Assessment: What to Do After Instruction Has Taken Place

Overview

Summative assessments are formal assessments used to determine how well students have met or exceeded state reading and language arts curriculum standards. They are designed to document long-term growth in the development of literacy skills and include state-required assessments as well as Scott Foresman *Reading Street* assessments and tests developed by school districts. They focus on yearly and end-of-year standards and outcomes.

What are the benefits of summative assessments?

Summative assessments help you determine if all students are making expected academic growth and provide you with information to:

- determine your students' progress in meeting or exceeding state reading and language arts curriculum standards;

- gather information in a systematic way to validate judgments and decisions about learning;

- standardize opportunities for each student taking the test;

    - Each student receives the same directions.

    - Each test is scored by the same criteria.

- give feedback to your students that enables them to learn about their own literacy development; and

- continually refine and modify instruction in your classroom to meet the needs of your students.

What is the purpose of using summative assessments?

Summative assessments are used for measuring long-term growth. The results of summative assessment tests can be used to:

- determine the degree to which your students have achieved the goals defined by a given standard or group of standards; and

- gather specific information about students with particular needs, such as English language learners and students with disabilities.

What do I want to learn from summative assessments?

Summative assessments provide you with information about how well your students have mastered the content of previously taught lessons. They include feedback on student achievement of standards in the following grade level strands of national and state reading and language arts standards.

- Phonics, word analysis, and vocabulary development
- Reading comprehension
- Written language conventions (e.g., sentence structure, grammar, punctuation, capitalization, spelling)
- Writing ability
- Reading fluency

What type of assessments should be used as summative assessment?

- Use formal assessments that provide a detailed analysis of how well your students have mastered the knowledge and skills described in the national and state reading and language arts standards.

When do I gather the information?

- Summative assessments should be given at the end of the year.

What techniques and tools are available?

FORMAL ASSESSMENT TOOL AND TECHNIQUES FOR SUMMATIVE ASSESSMENT

- **Scott Foresman *Reading Street* End-of-Year Benchmark Test**
  (See pages 88–89.)
  A group-administered, summative assessment is used to determine your students' growth in mastering the content in the national and state reading and language arts standards and to document achievement of skills taught throughout the school year.

INFORMAL ASSESSMENT TOOLS AND TECHNIQUES FOR SUMMATIVE ASSESSMENT

- Additional classroom-based assessment forms can be found in Chapter 7. These include:
  – Reading Strategy Assessment
  – Writing Strategy Assessment
  – Cumulative Folder Form

Want to learn more about summative assessment?

If you are interested in learning more about research that supports the use of summative assessment tools and practices, you will find the following resources interesting.

References

Afflerbach, P. "Teaching Reading Self-Assessment Strategies." In *Comprehension Instruction: Research-Based Best Practices*. Eds. C. Block and M. Pressley. New York: Guilford Press, 2001, pp. 96–111.

Guthrie, J. T. "Preparing Students for High-Stakes Test Taking in Reading." In *What Research Has to Say About Reading Instruction*. Eds. A. E. Farstrup and S. J. Samuels. Newark, DE: International Reading Association, 2002, pp. 370–391.

Howell, K. W., and V. Nolet. *Curriculum-Based Evaluation: Teaching and Decision Making*, 3rd Ed. Belmont, CA: Wadsworth and Thompson Learning Company, 2000.

Johnston, P., and P. Costello. "Principles for Literacy Assessment." *Reading Research Quarterly*, vol. 40, no. 2 (2005), pp. 256–267.

Marzano, R., et al. *Classroom Instruction That Works: Research-Based Strategies for Increasing Student Achievement*. Alexandria, VA: ASCD, 2001.

Pearson, P. D.; S. Vyas; L. M. Sensale; and Y. Kim. "Making Our Way Through the Assessment and Accountability Maze: Where Do We Go Now?" *The Clearing House*, vol. 74, no. 4 (2001), pp. 175–182.

Shepard, L. "The Role of Classroom Assessment in Teaching and Learning." In *Handbook of Research on Teaching*, 4th Ed. Ed. V. K. Richardson. Washington, DC: American Educational Research Association, 2001, pp. 1066–1101.

Valencia, S. W. "Inquiry-Oriented Assessment." In *Classroom Literacy Assessment: Making Sense of What Students Know and Do*. Eds. J. R. Paratore and R. L. McCormack. New York: The Guilford Press, 2007, pp. 3–20.

Wixson, K. K., S. W. Valencia, and M. Y. Lipson. "Issues in Literacy Assessment: Facing the Realities of Internal and External Assessment." *Journal of Reading Behavior*, vol. 26, no. 3 (1994), pp. 315–337.

4 • Summative

Scott Foresman *Reading Street* End-of-Year Benchmark Test

What is it?

- A multiple-choice and constructed-response test designed to measure your students' mastery of state reading and language arts curriculum standards
- A means to document your students' long-term growth
- A test coded to the state reading and language arts curriculum standards

Why would I choose it?

- To evaluate your students' end-of-year mastery in specific language arts skills coded to the state reading and language arts curriculum standards
- To identify skill areas in which students need intervention and continued practice
- To document academic growth

What does it test?

The grades 2 and 3 End-of-Year Benchmark Tests include subtests for the following grade-level strands:

- Reading comprehension
- Vocabulary
- Phonics and word analysis
- Writing conventions—usage, mechanics, grammar, and spelling
- Writing application—response to a prompt
- Oral reading fluency

When do I use it?

- At the end of the year

How do I use it?

- The test is designed to be group-administered.
- The fluency check is to be administered individually.

How do I use the results?

- To document and record individual students' growth in cumulative skills taught during the school year
- To diagnose and record individual students' needs for the next year
- To inform and improve the delivery of curriculum and instruction
- To provide guidance for teacher teams in the next school year who plan interventions for students who need additional support
- To provide helpful feedback to students and parents
- To help determine students' overall grades
- To guide parents in working with their students during vacation, so learning continues throughout the summer months

Samples are from Grade 3 End-of-Year Benchmark Test.

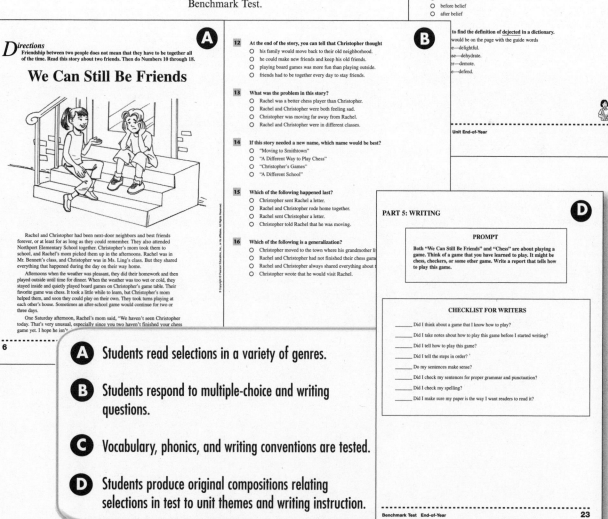

PART 2: VOCABULARY

Directions
Fill in the circle beside your answer choice for Numbers 28 through 36.

28 Which of these is a compound word?
   ○ enough
   ○ attended
   ○ everything
   ○ demonstrate

29 In chess, the queen is a player's most **powerful** weapon.
   Which of these means the same as **powerful**?
   ○ without power
   ○ more power
   ○ full of power
   ○ less power

30 "Baseball?" Jackie answered in **disbelief.**
   What does the word **disbelief** mean?
   ○ toward belief
   ○ without belief
   ○ before belief
   ○ after belief

Directions
Friendship between two people does not mean that they have to be together all of the time. Read this story about two friends. Then do Numbers 10 through 18.

We Can Still Be Friends

Rachel and Christopher had been next-door neighbors and best friends forever, or at least for as long as they could remember. They also attended Northport Elementary School together. Christopher's mom took them to school, and Rachel's mom picked them up in the afternoons. Rachel was in Mr. Bennett's class, and Christopher was in Ms. Ling's class. But they shared everything that happened during the day on their way home.

Afternoons when the weather was pleasant, they did their homework and then played outside until time for dinner. When the weather was too wet or cold, they stayed inside and quietly played board games on Christopher's game table. Their favorite game was chess. It took a little while to learn, but Christopher's mom helped them, and soon they could play on their own. They took turns playing at each other's house. Sometimes an after-school game would continue for two or three days.

One Saturday afternoon, Rachel's mom said, "We haven't seen Christopher today. That's very unusual, especially since you two haven't finished your chess game yet. I hope he isn't...

12 At the end of the story, you can tell that Christopher thought
   ○ his family would move back to their old neighborhood.
   ○ he could make new friends and keep his old friends.
   ○ playing board games was more fun than playing outside.
   ○ friends had to be together every day to stay friends.

13 What was the problem in this story?
   ○ Rachel was a better chess player than Christopher.
   ○ Rachel and Christopher were both feeling sad.
   ○ Christopher was moving far away from Rachel.
   ○ Rachel and Christopher were in different classes.

14 If this story needed a new name, which name would be best?
   ○ "Moving to Smithtown"
   ○ "A Different Way to Play Chess"
   ○ "Christopher's Games"
   ○ "A Different School"

15 Which of the following happened last?
   ○ Christopher sent Rachel a letter.
   ○ Rachel and Christopher rode home together.
   ○ Rachel sent Christopher a letter.
   ○ Christopher told Rachel that he was moving.

16 Which of the following is a generalization?
   ○ Christopher moved to the town where his grandmother li...
   ○ Rachel and Christopher had not finished their chess gam...
   ○ Rachel and Christopher always shared everything about t...
   ○ Christopher wrote that he would visit Rachel.

...to find the definition of **dejected** in a dictionary.
...would be on the page with the guide words

4 • Summative

PART 5: WRITING

PROMPT

Both "We Can Still Be Friends" and "Chess" are about playing a game. Think of a game that you have learned to play. It might be chess, checkers, or some other game. Write a report that tells how to play this game.

CHECKLIST FOR WRITERS

_____ Did I think about a game that I know how to play?
_____ Did I take notes about how to play this game before I started writing?
_____ Did I tell how to play this game?
_____ Did I tell the steps in order?
_____ Do my sentences make sense?
_____ Did I check my sentences for proper grammar and punctuation?
_____ Did I check my spelling?
_____ Did I make sure my paper is the way I want readers to read it?

A Students read selections in a variety of genres.

B Students respond to multiple-choice and writing questions.

C Vocabulary, phonics, and writing conventions are tested.

D Students produce original compositions relating selections in test to unit themes and writing instruction.

Unit End-of-Year   15

Benchmark Test End-of-Year   23

| Chapter 5 | # Writing as Learning and Assessment |

Overview

Writing is an important component of the state reading and language arts curriculum standards. Writing facilitates learning by providing a means through which students can develop complex thinking and express depth of understanding. As you design writing instruction, you will not only want to consider how to assess the development of writing, but also how your students use writing as a tool for demonstrating knowledge and skills.

Writing as Learning

The process and products of writing are in themselves educative. The act of writing helps your students organize and clarify their thoughts. It helps them discover meaning and express what they understand about a topic or concept. Writing gives your students an opportunity to explore thoughts and deepen their understanding. When your students write down their ideas and then have an opportunity to rethink and revise them, they also have an opportunity to expand their thinking. During this process, their ideas are extended and refined, especially if you are able to give students opportunities to participate in writing conferences in which they share their drafts with you and their peers. Some activities that give your students opportunities to learn as they write are:

- Making lists of ideas as they brainstorm information on a specific topic
- Creating concept maps
- Completing graphic organizers
- Describing what they have learned in logs or journals
- Taking notes as they use media, listen to lectures, or research topics
- Writing responses to literature and analyzing literary texts
- Writing reports
- Reflecting on what they have learned while completing projects
- Writing observations and lab reports during science investigations

Writing as a Demonstration of Knowledge and Skill

Because writing illustrates thinking, it provides you with an opportunity to assess what your students have learned during or following instruction. Constructed responses, whether short (e.g., two or three sentences describing how they solved a mathematics problem, a short paragraph describing the causes of a historical event) or extended (e.g., multiple paragraphs identifying and supporting themes found in a piece of literature), are very effective forms of assessment. The checklists and rubrics used to evaluate constructed-response items allow you to provide clear feedback to your students so that they can improve their performance.

Assessment and Evaluation of Writing

Writing assessment is an essential part of a comprehensive writing program. In order to ensure growth in writing, a balanced approach to assessment is needed—one that includes entry-level, progress-monitoring, and summative assessments. Through the combination of these assessments, you will gain an in-depth view of your students' knowledge and skill in using the stages of writing (e.g., pre-writing, drafting, revising, editing, postwriting). The assessments labeled progress-monitoring tools in this handbook provide ongoing feedback on the progress your students make toward achievement of skills and knowledge.

What are the benefits of a balanced approach to writing assessment?

- Using a balanced approach to writing assessment allows you to collect data throughout the year and respond specifically to the learning trajectory of your students.

  - Entry-level writing assessments, given at the beginning of the year, help you diagnose where to begin writing instruction for individual students and help you plan specific instructional activities designed to meet the learning needs of each of the writers in your class.

  - Progress-monitoring assessments, given throughout the year, help you determine if all students are making expected progress toward the goal of writing a well-constructed paragraph with a main idea and supporting details.

  - Summative assessment at the end of the year determines how well your students have learned the writing skills you have taught and how well how your students have met or exceeded statewide and district-wide curriculum standards.

- You can guide your students' writing development better if you have an up-to-date understanding of their current performance levels—wasting no time on skills they have already mastered and focusing instead on the areas that represent the next step in their growing writing proficiency or areas that need additional attention.

- Because high standards in writing achievement are most reliably achieved in small, consistent increases that occur over time, a balanced approach to writing assessment affords you the opportunity to monitor and adjust curriculum and instruction as needed to maximize the writing improvement for all students.

- Providing feedback to students about their performances on writing assessments will help them develop skills required to successfully complete writing tasks (e.g., constructed-response questions in mathematics, science, social studies, and language arts) included in high-stakes assessments.

What are the purposes of writing assessment?

- To promote continuous improvement in your students' successful use of the writing process and language conventions

- To identify mastery of state curriculum standards both at the individual student level and the class level, which address:

  - Organization and focus

  - Penmanship

  - Research

  - Evaluation and revision

  - Written language conventions (sentence structure, grammar, punctuation, capitalization, spelling)

- To determine when differentiation of instruction is required for individuals or groups of students who have not demonstrated mastery in writing

- To provide a basis for focused instructional decision-making, mini-lessons on the writing process and skills, and feedback to be shared during writing conferences with your students

- To encourage student self-assessment and evaluation by helping students learn how to make judgments about the quality of their writing

- To determine report card grades and/or communicate progress to parents

- To evaluate instructional approaches and modify curriculum to reflect results from writing assessments

When do I use writing assessments?

- Use entry-level writing assessments at the beginning of the year to gather baseline data regarding students' writing proficiency levels.

- Use progress-monitoring writing assessments throughout the school year to measure students' growth in developing writing proficiency.

- Use summative writing assessments to determine students' proficiency levels in the area of writing at the close of each grading period and at the end of the year.

How do I help students assess their own writing?

Self-assessment is very important to your students' writing development. Although you are the primary evaluator of your students' writing, you should give your students opportunities to engage in ongoing self-assessment and peer assessment. The benefits are many—such assessments will help them analyze their writing and the writing of their peers, set goals for improvement, and evaluate their performances in achieving the goals.

- **How can I help students become better self-assessors?**

  - Model self-monitoring by sharing your thoughts with students as you evaluate and reflect on a writing project you are doing.

  - Make the criteria on which students are assessed (e.g., checklists, rubrics) public so that they can use this information to self-assess.

  - Schedule regular times for self-assessment.

  - Give students opportunities to draft criteria for assessing their own work.

  - Provide opportunities for students to engage in activities that encourage thinking, writing, and talking about their writing.

- **What kind of activities support self-assessment?**

  - Writing conferences with you

  - Writing conferences with classmates

  - Reflections about writing goals and progress in achieving the goals

  - Reviews of student portfolios

  - Use of self-assessment checklists and rubrics

  - Student-led parent-teacher conferences

The Role of Rubrics in Assessing Writing

Rubrics play an important role in assessing writing. They identify criteria upon which writing is evaluated, and they identify levels of performance. Using rubrics helps you and your students in many ways.

- Rubrics help you focus your students' attention on elements of quality writing, especially if you share the rubrics with them before they begin writing.

- Rubrics help you achieve consistency when evaluating your students' work.

- Rubrics allow you to provide focused feedback to students so that they can improve their writing.

- Rubrics help you identify objectives for individuals and groups of students.

- Your students will become better writers by using rubrics to guide their self-assessment.

- Peer assessment will be more effective when students have rubrics to guide their analysis of writing samples.

There are several types of rubrics:

- Some rubrics are general and describe the features of good writing that can be applied to a variety of genres.

- Some rubrics describe the features of a specific type or genre of writing.

- Some rubrics are holistic, assessing writing on how well the parts (e.g., ideas, organization, voice, conventions) interact to create a quality piece of writing.

- Some rubrics are analytic, assessing the individual characteristics of writing that serve as criteria for assessing the quality of a piece of writing.

A general four-point writing rubric is included in this chapter.

For guidance in creating your own rubric see page 127.

What techniques and tools are available?

ENTRY-LEVEL ASSESSMENT TOOL AND TECHNIQUES

- **Myself as a Reader and Writer** (See page 41.)

  An informal questionnaire that gives students an opportunity to share information about their writing interests.

PROGRESS-MONITORING ASSESSMENT TOOLS AND TECHNIQUES

- **Unit Benchmark Tests** (See pages 62–63.)
  These tests are designed to measure your students' ability to apply target comprehension skills and other literacy skills. Included in each assessment is a writing prompt that elicits a narrative, expository, persuasive, or friendly letter response.

- **Ongoing Teacher Observation** (See page 66.)
  Observation of your students allows you to monitor their performance in the context of classroom writing activities and provide helpful feedback while students are in the process of learning, rather than after the fact.

- **Skills Conference Record** (See page 72.)
  This checklist allows you to capture information about your students' writing.

- **Student Self-Assessment** (See page 75.)
  This form provides your students with an opportunity to assess themselves as writers.

- **Peer Assessment** (See page 76.)
  This form affords your students an opportunity to assess a peer's work and apply what they are learning about the quality of effective writing.

5 • Writing

- **Student Portfolios** (See pages 78–79.)
  Maintaining a writing portfolio is a process that allows your students to use work samples to document and reflect on their growth in writing.

- **Writing Log** (See page 82.)
  This form helps students keep track of the pieces they have written, as well as rate the quality of their own writing.

- **About My Writing** (See page 83.)
  This form encourages your students to describe and evaluate their own writing progress.

SUMMATIVE ASSESSMENT TOOL

- **End-of-Year Benchmark Test** (See pages 88–89.)
  A group-administered, summative assessment used to determine your students' growth in mastering the Scott Foresman *Reading Street* content. Additionally, this test documents achievement of skills taught throughout the school year. The Writing subtest requires students to write to a prompt based on one of the reading passages on the test.

Want to learn more about writing assessment?

If you would like to learn more about how to use writing assessment practices in your classroom, you will find the following resources interesting.

References

Bromley, K. "Assessing Student Writing." In *Classroom Literacy Assessment: Making Sense of What Students Know and Do.* Eds. J. R. Paratore and R. L. McCormack. New York: The Guilford Press, 2007, pp. 227–245.

Calfee, R. C. "Writing Portfolios: Activity, Assessment, Authenticity." In *Perspectives on Writing: Research, Theory, and Practice.* Eds. R. Indrisano and J. R. Squire. Newark, DE: International Reading Association, 2000, pp. 278–304.

Fisher, D., and N. Frey. *Checking for Understanding: Formative Assessment Techniques for Your Classroom.* Alexandria, VA: Association for Supervision and Curriculum Development, 2007.

Glazer, S. M. "A Classroom Portfolio System: Assessment Instruction." In *Classroom Literacy Assessment: Making Sense of What Students Know and Do.* Eds. J. R. Paratore and R. L. McCormack. New York: The Guilford Press, 2007, pp. 227–245.

Spandel, V. *Seeing with New Eyes: A Guidebook on Teaching and Assessing Beginning Writers.* Portland, OR: Northwest Regional Educational Laboratory, 1998.

Spandel, V. *Creating Writers Through 6-Trait Writing Assessment and Instruction.* Boston: Allyn and Bacon, 2000.

Vacca, R. T., and J. L. Vacca. "Writing Across the Curriculum." In *Perspectives on Writing: Research, Theory, and Practice.* Eds. R. Indrisano and J. R. Squire. Newark, DE: International Reading Association, 2000, pp. 214–232.

Zamel, V. "Writing: The Process of Discovering Meaning." *TESOL Quarterly*, vol. 16, no. 2 (1982), pp. 195–209.

Four-Point Scoring Rubric—Grades 2–3

4 **The writing—**

- *Clearly* addresses the writing task.

- Demonstrates a *clear* understanding of purpose.

- Maintains a *consistent* point of view, focus, and organizational structure, including paragraphing when appropriate.

- Includes a *clearly presented* central idea with relevant facts, details, and/or explanations.

- Includes sentence variety.

- Contains *few or no* errors in the conventions of the English language (e.g., grammar, punctuation, capitalization, spelling). These errors do **not** interfere with the reader's understanding of the writing.

3 **The writing—**

- Addresses *most* of the writing task.

- Demonstrates a *general* understanding of purpose.

- Maintains a *mostly consistent* point of view, focus, and organizational structure, including paragraphing when appropriate.

- Presents a central idea with *mostly* relevant facts, details, and/or explanations.

- Includes *some* sentence variety.

- Contains *some* errors in the conventions of the English language (e.g., grammar, punctuation, capitalization, spelling). These errors do **not** interfere with the reader's understanding of the writing.

2 **The writing—**

- Addresses *some* of the writing task.

- Demonstrates *little* understanding of the purpose.

- Maintains an *inconsistent* point of view, focus, and/or organizational structure; may lack appropriate paragraphing.

- *Suggests* a central idea with *limited* facts, details, and/or explanations.

- Includes little sentence variety.

- Contains *many errors* in the conventions of the English language (e.g., grammar, punctuation, capitalization, spelling). These errors **may** interfere with the reader's understanding of the writing.

1 **The writing—**

- Addresses *only one part or none* of the writing task.

- Demonstrates *no* understanding of purpose.

- *Lacks* a clear point of view, focus, and/or organizational structure; may contain inappropriate paragraphing.

- *Lacks* a central idea but may contain *marginally related* facts, details, and/or explanations.

- Includes *no* sentence variety.

- Contains *serious errors* in the conventions of the English language (e.g., grammar, punctuation, capitalization, spelling). These errors interfere with the reader's understanding of the writing.

5 • Writing

Student Portfolios

What is a portfolio as it relates to writing?

- A teacher-guided process in which students collect representative samples of their own writing as a means of demonstrating growth over time

- A way to encourage students to feel ownership of their writing

What is the purpose of a portfolio as it relates to writing?

Portfolios may accomplish any or all of the following:

- Demonstrate students' writing progress

- Show students' writing strengths and needs

- Help you make instructional decisions for each student's writing

- Encourage students to assess their own growth and progress and to set new writing goals

- Make it possible to share evidence of students' writing growth during parent conferences

- Compile representative samples of students' writing that you can pass along to their next teachers

Which writing pieces go into a portfolio?

- Chapters 3 and 7 provide full descriptions of techniques and forms to use for compiling and organizing portfolios.

- Possible writing pieces to include in Student Portfolios are:
  - Drawing or writing projects that students have done at school or at home
  - Works in progress
  - Examples of pre-writing activities
  - Examples of first drafts
  - Examples of revision at the paragraph, multi-paragraph, and self-composition levels
  - Documentation of peer assessment
  - Documentation of self-assessment
  - Examples of a variety of genres, including:
    - Expository descriptions of objects, people, places, or events
    - Narratives (fictional or autobiographical)
    - Written responses to literature
    - Summaries

How do I help students choose writing samples for their portfolios?

- At the beginning of the school year, explain the process of developing a portfolio.

- Show models of portfolios and sample writing entries. Explain that portfolios should include:

  - a wide variety of written works

  - samples that demonstrate learning experiences in writing

  - pieces that show growth or improvement in writing over time

  - materials that indicate that students have challenged themselves to try something different with their writing

  - self-assessments and future learning goals in the area of writing

- Periodically set aside time for students to examine their writing samples and think about which pieces they would like to include in their portfolios.

What can I do at the end of each grading period?

- Hold writing conferences toward the end of each grading period to help students reflect on the written pieces they have placed in their portfolios.

- Have students decide which pieces to take home, which ones to keep in their portfolios, and which ones to lend to you to update their Portfolio Guides.

What can I do at the end of the school year?

- Hold final conferences with students to help them reflect on their writing and decide which pieces to save and which to eliminate.

- Have students decide which writing samples to take home and which to pass along to their next teachers (for example, the pieces they are most proud of or the ones that show the most growth).

| Chapter 6 | # Chapter 6: Assessing the Progress of English Language Learners |

Overview

Classrooms throughout the United States are populated with students representing diverse cultures, ethnicities, and languages. This diversity offers rich benefits to learners, but also places enormous demands upon teachers, who are expected to guide *all* students with vastly different literacy and learning abilities toward achievement of state reading and language arts standards.

English language learners pose unique challenges to educators. Teachers must monitor the language acquisition of these students in an ongoing, systematic way, in addition to assessing their understanding of concepts, skills, and strategies. This chapter is designed to assist teachers of English language learners in recognizing the assessment challenges, utilizing appropriate assessment accommodations, preparing students for high-stakes tests, and implementing classroom-based strategies for assessing the strengths and needs of English language learners.

What are the unique challenges in assessing achievement of English language learners?

- Many English language learners may quickly master *social* English, the conversational language skills and conventions used in everyday interactions with classmates. These same learners frequently encounter difficulty with the *academic* English found on formal assessments.

- The structure of academic English is complex, e.g., fiction and nonfiction text structures; paragraph organization; and syntax, including prepositional phrases, introductory clauses, and pronoun references. There are structural analysis constraints at the word, sentence, paragraph, and text levels.

- The vocabulary of academic English consists of specialized meanings of common words, abstract concepts, multiple-meaning words, and words based on Latin and Greek roots. (Bielenberg, 2004/2005)

- The topics and concepts of comprehension passages are frequently unfamiliar, and the purposes of assessment tasks divorced from real-life contexts can be difficult to perceive.

- Formal assessments often fail to reflect the diverse cultural and linguistic experiences of English language learners and then have limited value for helping teachers select appropriate instructional strategies. (Garcia, 1994)

How are Scott Foresman *Reading Street* assessments sensitive to the needs of English language learners?

- Both formal and informal classroom-based *Reading Street* assessments help teachers monitor growth in the basic reading and expression skills of alphabetic understanding, decoding, sight vocabulary, and grammar, along with measurement of the more complex skills of fluency, comprehension, and vocabulary.

- Reading comprehension test passages reflect diverse ethnic content and cultural experiences.

- Texts are matched to the age, interest, and background knowledge of students.

- Most assessment tasks are embedded in contexts with which students are familiar. The comprehension assessments are generally based on themes and topics explored in instruction; vocabulary is assessed within the context of the passage; and writing tasks relate to central ideas of the texts.

- The language of the test directions and assessment items is straightforward and unambiguous.

What instructional strategies will help prepare my English language learners for formal assessments?

- Preteach the "language of tests" encountered in directions and test items, including:
  - Question words, such as *who, what, which, where, when, why,* and *how*
  - Emphasis words, such as *not, except, most likely, probably, major, both, neither, either, most,* and *least*
  - Action words, such as *explain, describe, discuss, persuade,* and *support with experience*

- Teach use of context clues to interpret meaning of unfamiliar terms.

- Highlight and discuss routinely the *academic* language, vocabulary, syntax, and narrative and expository text structures encountered in textbooks and trade books.

- Coach students in oral and written retelling and summarization, so they develop a "sense" of text types, features, conventions, and organization. English language learners relate to the concrete nature of expository text, and expository summarization helps to familiarize them with common text structures, such as sequence, description, classification, compare/contrast, cause/effect, and problem/solution.

- Provide regular opportunities for meaningful oral language experiences in which English language learners participate in discussion of important topics and perform the activities required on tests, such as explaining, describing, and stating and supporting opinions. Encourage them to use vocabulary that will support academic language development.

- Read aloud, think aloud, and model purposeful and strategic behaviors of effective readers, speakers, and writers of English.

- Provide repeated opportunities for practicing all the techniques above.

What accommodations are appropriate to use with the Scott Foresman *Reading Street* assessments?

- Accommodating the needs of English language learners ensures fairness and full participation in formal assessments. A general rule of thumb is to use the same accommodations in testing situations as used in instruction. For instance, if students receive part of their instruction in their first languages, then it is appropriate to translate test directions and comprehension questions into the students' first languages.

- Other acceptable accommodations might include the following:

  - providing additional testing time and allowing frequent or extended breaks

  - administering the tests at times most beneficial to students

  - administering the tests in small groups or in one-on-one settings

  - reading test directions to students in English (or in the students' first languages, if this is possible), and repeating as often as needed

  - simplifying the language and sentence structure of test directions

  - requesting that students restate and clarify test directions in their own words

  - discussing the pictures and any graphics, such as maps, to ensure that students can interpret them

  - reading test passages to students in English, and repeating as often as necessary, when listening comprehension is being assessed

  - reading comprehension questions orally in English or in the students' first languages

  - allowing students to respond orally to questions or dictate answers for transcription

  - encouraging students to draw pictures to demonstrate their thinking and learning

- In providing accommodations to students, it is important not to compromise the intent of the assessment. It is never appropriate to read aloud the *reading* comprehension passages or the vocabulary and grammar questions to students in English or their first languages. These practices alter the constructs of the assessments. For example, the reading comprehension assessments are designed to measure both word recognition and understanding, so reading the selections to students actually changes the intent of the test.

- While the language-specific modifications above may be most appropriate for English language learners, many of the listed accommodations are also beneficial for students with learning and reading disabilities and other special needs. The use of appropriate accommodations in assessment ensures that all students have fair and equal opportunities to demonstrate evidence of learning and achievement.

- Following the administration of the formal assessments, note which accommodations were used, and interpret scores with that information in mind.

6 • English Learners

What are the *best* ways to assess the strengths and needs of English language learners?

- Through informal and on-going classroom-based assessment, teachers can observe, monitor, and judge the quality of student work.

- Using multiple assessments mirrors the learning process, while single assessments capture one moment at a time, much like the difference between an album of photographs and a single snapshot.

- Ask students frequently to communicate orally or in writing their understanding of concepts and processes. In this way, teachers are provided with instant insight about students' thinking and depth of learning.

- Observing small, consistent increases in learning over time is most reliable. The goal is continuous improvement.

- Frequent monitoring addresses learning in progress, allows for correction of misconceptions as they occur, and provides helpful feedback to English language learners.

- Teaching students to self-assess their reading progress helps to build independence in language and learning. For example, encourage them to monitor their progress by comparing work samples and voice recordings over time.

- Authentic assessment activities enhance, rather than diminish, instructional time because they are inseparable from instruction. Activities include classroom observation, language-experience stories, storytelling or writing, voice recordings of oral reading, reading-response logs, and journals. (Garcia, 1994)

- Scott Foresman *Reading Street* provides many resources to help you tailor instruction and assessment for all your students; administer and score entry-level, progress-monitoring, and summative assessments; interpret scores; and make decisions based on test results.

What are examples of classroom-based assessment techniques and tools?

- **Profile of English Language Learners** (See pages 109–110.)

  a checklist that identifies the strengths and needs of English language learners

- **Observing English Language Learners** (See page 111.)

  a form that allows you to record ongoing observations about your English language learners' progress in developing reading skills

6 • English Learners

References

Afflerbach, P. *Understanding and Using Reading Assessment K–12.* Newark, DE: International Reading Association, 2007.

Bielenberg, B., and L. W. Fillmore. "The English They Need for the Test." *Educational Leadership*, 2004, pp. 45–49.

Garcia, G. E. "Assessing the Literacy Development of Second-Language Students: A Focus on Authentic Assessment." In *Kids Come in All Languages: Reading Instruction for ESL Students*. Eds. K. Spangenberg-Urbshat and R. Pritchard. Newark, DE: International Reading Association, 1994, pp. 180–205.

Lenters, K. "No Half Measures: Reading Instruction for Young Second-Language Learners." *The Reading Teacher*, vol. 58 (2004), pp. 328–336.

Moss, B. "Teaching Expository Text Structures through Information Trade Book Retellings." *The Reading Teacher*, vol. 57 (2004), pp. 710–718.

Zwiers, J. "The Third Language of Academic English." *Educational Leadership*, vol. 62, no. 4 (2004), pp. 60–63.

Survey
Profile of English Language Learners

What is it?

- This checklist helps to identify the strengths and needs of students whose first language is not English. Complete this profile at the time the student enters your classroom and update it periodically throughout the school year.

What does it show?

- An English language learner's proficiency with speaking, reading, and writing English

How do I use it?

- Identify students whose English proficiency you are uncertain about.

- Use the criteria on the form to assess students' abilities in the various language areas, noting specific examples.

- Use the form as a rough guideline of where students are and where they may need help.

What do I do next?

Scott Foresman *Reading Street* offers many instructional resources to advance the achievement of your English language learners.

- Standards-based instruction addresses all levels of language acquisition—Beginning, Early Intermediate, Intermediate, Early Advanced, and Advanced levels of English-language proficiency.

- The English Language Learners Handbook and the English language learner student materials together provide before-, during-, and after-reading support for English language learners to allow them to successfully participate in and progress through the daily lessons of the basic program with their peers.

6 • English Learners

What do I do next? (continued)

- The English Language Learners Handbook offers instructional material and comprehensive guidance for teachers and effective, efficient, and explicit instruction for English language learners, with scaffolded comprehension and vocabulary development. It builds on the *Reading Street* Student Editions and on literacy instruction in each Teacher's Edition. The guide uses program components including ELL Posters, ELL Readers, and English Language Support (blackline masters) for activities that engage students with the English language, literature, and comprehension skills.

A Checklist format is easy to interpret.

B Space is provided for you to note your own responses.

Form for reproduction is on page 140.

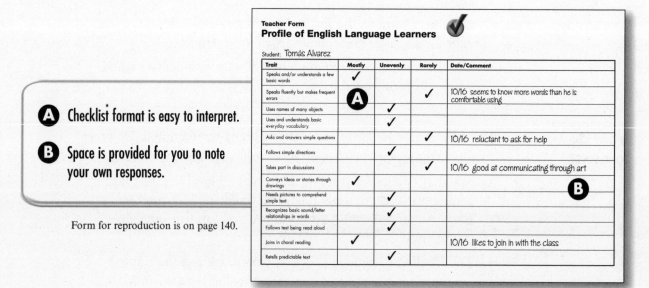

Teacher Form
Profile of English Language Learners

Student: Tomás Alvarez

Trait	Mostly	Unevenly	Rarely	Date/Comment
Speaks and/or understands a few basic words	✓			
Speaks fluently but makes frequent errors			✓	10/16 seems to know more words than he is comfortable using
Uses names of many objects		✓		
Uses and understands basic everyday vocabulary		✓		
Asks and answers simple questions			✓	10/16 reluctant to ask for help
Follows simple directions		✓		
Takes part in discussions			✓	10/16 good at communicating through art
Conveys ideas or stories through drawings	✓			
Needs pictures to comprehend simple text		✓		
Recognizes basic sound/letter relationships in words		✓		
Follows text being read aloud		✓		
Joins in choral reading	✓			10/16 likes to join in with the class
Retells predictable text		✓		

Observing English Language Learners

What is it?	• A form to record your ongoing observations about how English language learners process what they read
What does it show?	• How English language learners use strategies to make sense of materials they read • Students' growth and development in processing what they read
How do I use it?	• Work with students individually as they read a new selection. • Record your observations about how students deal with new words and concepts. • Continue to review and record students' behaviors periodically as needed. • Consider using the information on the form in parent conferences.

Ⓐ Behaviors identify common strategies for success in reading a new language.

Ⓑ Space is provided to record students' development over time.

Teacher Form
Observing English Language Learners

Student: Tomás Alvarez

Behaviors Observed	Date: 10/27			Date: 11/18			Date:			Date:		
The student	Yes	No	Sometimes	Yes	No	Sometimes	Yes	No	Sometimes	Yes	No	Sometimes
• uses context clues to figure out new words		✓				✓						
• uses prior knowledge to figure out new words			✓	✓								
• uses visuals to decipher meaning	✓			✓								
• uses strategies to decipher meaning		✓				✓						
• can identify the strategies he or she is using		✓				✓						
• understands why he or she is using a particular strategy		✓		✓								
• assesses his or her own progress			✓	✓								
• generally understands what the class is reading			✓			✓						

General Comments

10/27: need to work harder on strategies with Tomás

11/18: Tomás doing much better at drawing on prior knowledge. Is beginning to see the logic of strategies.

Form for reproduction is on page 147.

6 • English Learners

111

| Chapter 7 | # Collecting, Evaluating, and Reporting Evidence of Learning |

Overview

Information about the three levels of assessment, entry-level (diagnostic and screening), progress-monitoring, and summative assessment, explained in Chapters 2–4, suggests that teachers will be compiling large amounts of information about students. Access to this data informs sound decision-making related to the focus of curriculum instruction, effectiveness of instruction, meaningful feedback to students and parents, and improved achievement.

Teacher Record Keeping

Learning goals are met by shaping effective instruction and assessment to meet the needs of each student. Checking for understanding contributes to improved instruction and learning. The evidence of this learning can be collected on a variety of record forms.

Why collect evidence of learning?

- A roadmap of each student's learning is created by keeping records of learning from classroom assessment, including:
  - the Scott Foresman *Reading Street* Baseline Group Test, entry-level (diagnostic) inventories, surveys (Chapter 2)
  - progress-monitoring discussions, logs, journal entries, essays, portfolios, projects, and Scott Foresman *Reading Street* tests (Chapter 3)
  - summative measurements, such as state-required tests, the Scott Foresman *Reading Street* End-of-Year Benchmark Test, and district tests (Chapter 4)
- Pace, content, and type of instruction may be adjusted after evaluating the student's collected evidence of learning to see that learning goals are met.

How do I collect evidence of learning?

- Collect records of students' learning throughout the year—at the beginning of the school year, daily, weekly, after clusters of instructional time such as units, and at the end of the year.
- Collect a variety of records of students' learning (e.g., notes from observations, responses to questions, checklists, portfolios, self-assessment, rubric and test scores, and grading).
- Collect key indicators about skills and concepts (e.g., words correct per minute, recognition of multiple meanings, summaries of readings).

Tools and Techniques for Teacher Record Keeping

- **Teacher Summary Reports** (See page 121.)
  compilations of assessment data that help describe your students' growth in reading, writing, speaking, and listening

- **Reading Strategy Assessment** (See page 122.)
  a checklist that allows you to synthesize the information you have gathered about each student's knowledge and use of reading strategies

- **Writing Strategy Assessment** (See page 123.)
  a checklist that allows you to synthesize the information you have gathered about each student's knowledge and use of writing strategies

- **Cumulative Folder Form** (See page 124.)
  a cumulative record of students' reading progress that can be placed in their permanent files and follow them from year to year

How do I share assessment information?

- Assessment information is shared in two ways, communication and grading. Communication of assessment information may occur as written remarks or as conversation in which the quality or level of learning is discussed.

- Conferences provide excellent opportunities to convey assessment information and to maintain ongoing communication between teacher and student, teacher and parent, and student and student.

  - Teacher-student conferences can be part of your classroom routine and allow you time to learn about the unique learning needs and successes of individual students in your class.

  - Teacher-parent conferences are held formally during regularly scheduled school conference days, but they can also be held informally when you want to share concerns and accomplishments with your students' parents.

  - Student-led conferences with a teacher and parent allow students to talk about personal strengths and weaknesses and set goals for their next steps in learning, as well as help students become more aware of what to say and do about their learning.

- Conferencing about reading, writing, speaking, or listening or collections of work may include:

  - examining and discussing a reading response with comments about why its attributes meet a learning standard

  - analyzing and discussing how the traits on written work match the descriptions on a rubric

  - providing feedback about an inference skill or questioning strategy

  - explaining the reasons for a score on a vocabulary progress test

- discussing a student's self-assessment reflection

- evaluating a collection of work in a portfolio together with the student

• Evaluative communication provides feedback with a judgment about the quality of the work. This type of formal communication is typically shared by mark or symbol—check, score, or grade to designate the quality or level of learning. Symbols are often used on

- checklists

- continuums

- assessment reports

- report cards

• Narrative statements are often found on students' work, in portfolios, or as an addition to a report marked with symbols.

Student Portfolios

A portfolio is a collection of representative student work in reading, writing, speaking, and listening, serving as documentation of change and growth over a period of time. It centers discussion about learning among teachers, students, and parents on actual samples of work. The collection may be evaluated in process or as a completed product with narrative comments or symbols, such as rubric scores, and it is a credible form of progress-monitoring. A rubric is a valuable way to score entries in the portfolio because criteria in a rubric serve as a clear vision for students during the writing process, in drafting as well as the final product. The final rubric scores awarded in the portfolio contribute to an overall evaluation of learning along with other requirements for a grade.

What is the teacher's role?

- To make decisions with students about the purpose, process, content, and time line of the portfolio

- To consider options for the format of the portfolio (e.g., folder, binder, or electronic versions)

- To decide the method for evaluating the process and contents of the portfolio (e.g., conferencing with the student and parents, narrative feedback, scoring, grading, or perhaps review by other teachers or students)

- To share examples of portfolios, showing students how portfolios might be organized and what might be kept in a portfolio

- To model metacognition (the awareness of the internal thinking that influences the choices for selection and revision of portfolio contents) by keeping a personal portfolio and sharing how you select and reflect on the pieces you include in it

What is the student's role?

- To add, change, or remove portfolio items demonstrating evidence of reading, writing, speaking, and listening to their portfolios with decreasing assistance from the teacher

- To explain and reflect about their collections of work

- To set and monitor goals for learning, as well as discuss strengths and weaknesses with teachers and family

- To participate in self-assessment and peer-assessment activities to improve their skills in collecting and learning from evidence in their portfolios

Tools and Techniques for Maintaining Portfolios

- **Student Portfolios** (See pages 78–79.)
  Maintaining a portfolio is a process that allows your students to use work samples to document and reflect on their growth in reading, writing, speaking, and listening.

- **Portfolio Guide** (See page 125.)
  This form helps you manage the contents of students' portfolios.

- **Portfolio Selection Slips** (See page 126.)
  These forms help your students select items to include in their portfolios and reflect on how the items demonstrate their growing skills in reading, writing, speaking, and listening.

- **Peer Assessment** (See page 76.)
  This form affords your students an opportunity to assess a peer's work and apply what they are learning about the quality of effective reading, writing, speaking, and listening.

- **Reading Log** (See page 80.)
  This form allows students to keep track of the literature they have read, as well as rate the quality of the selections.

- **About My Reading** (See page 81.)
  This form encourages your students to describe and evaluate their own reading progress.

- **Writing Log** (See page 82.)
  This form helps students keep track of and reflect on the pieces they have written.

- **About My Writing** (See page 83.)
  This form encourages your students to describe and evaluate their own writing progress.

Grading

As mentioned earlier in this chapter, grading is a formal, summative form of communication about learning. Grading provides information for students, parents, teacher record-keeping, and sometimes district reporting, and it often leads to decisions about future learning goals for the student. Guidelines about grading attempt to ensure fairness to the student and sound grading practices.

What is a grade?

A grade is the evaluative symbol reported at the end of an instructional unit of time. It is a summary of performance or achievement, showing whether the student met learning goals or standards. The symbol is usually a number or letter and answers, "How well is the student achieving at this point in time?" The primary purposes of grading are

- to inform students, parents, teachers, and others about the student's current level of achievement

- to support learning goals and inform progress of learning

- to improve students' achievement by providing feedback that explains the criteria upon which the grade is based

- to answer the question, "Has the student met the intended learning goals for this period?"

What are some general guidelines for grading?

- Base grades on academic achievement. Feedback on effort, behavior, ability, and attendance should be documented and reported separately.

- Communicate achievement of clear learning goals and standards with grades.

- Discuss expectations for grading with students and parents at the beginning of the instruction. Explain the criteria for grades in the classroom and school. Display models of graded work to students and parents at the beginning of the year to clarify and demonstrate expectations for students.

- Develop criteria for grades which may include test scores, rubric scores, completed work, and narrative records.

- Use rubrics as a lead-in to fair grading with clear descriptive criteria for scoring and alignment to learning standards.

- Add narrative and descriptive feedback with grades whenever possible.

- Do not grade all work—some work is in draft form or for practice only.

- Use *recent* summative classroom assessments to measure achievement of learning goals.
- Determine marking period grades from multiple types of scores. Summarize overall achievement for a marking period into one score or grade.
- Check with the district's grading policy to ensure that your procedures are fair and consistent with the guidelines established by your school and district.

What are some opportunities for grading in Scott Foresman *Reading Street*?

The program offers many opportunities to grade students' work, including:

- activities and projects
- writing assignments
- pages from the Reader's and Writer's Notebook
- pages from the Fresh Reads for Fluency and Comprehension
- oral presentations
- Weekly Tests
- Unit Benchmark Tests
- End-of-Year Benchmark Test

Tools and Techniques for Grading

- **Rubrics in the Teacher's Editions**

  Your Scott Foresman *Reading Street* Teacher's Editions contain a variety of rubrics to help you assess your students' performances.

- **Creating a Rubric** (See page 127.)

  This form is used to identify criteria for assessing reading, writing, speaking, and listening and to evaluate how well students meet those criteria on various assignments.

- **Grading Writing** (See page 128.)

  Teachers can use the Creating a Rubric form to develop grading criteria for students' responses to writing prompts.

- **Grading Products and Activities** (See page 129–132.)

  Teachers can use the Creating a Rubric form to develop grading criteria for a wide variety of students' products and activities.

7 • Evidence of Learning

Want to learn more about record keeping and grading?

If you are interested in learning more about record keeping and sharing assessment information, you will find the following resources interesting.

References

Afflerbach, P. *Understanding and Using Reading Assessment, K–12.* Newark, DE: International Reading Association, 2007.

Fisher, D., and N. Frey. *Checking for Understanding: Formative Assessment Techniques for Your Classroom.* Alexandria, VA: Association for Supervision and Curriculum Development, 2007.

Guskey, T. R. *How's My Kid Doing? A Parent's Guide to Grades, Marks, and Report Cards.* San Francisco, CA: Jossey-Bass, 2002.

Marzano, R. J. *Transforming Classroom Grading.* Alexandria, VA: Association for Supervision and Curriculum Development, 2000.

O'Connor, K. *How to Grade for Learning.* Arlington Heights, IL: Skylight Professional Development, 2002.

Stiggins, R.; J. Arter; J. Chappuis; and S. Chappuis. *Classroom Assessment for Student Learning: Doing it Right—Using it Well.* Portland, OR: Assessment Training Institute, 2004.

Teacher Forms
Teacher Summary Reports

What are they?	• Various forms that teachers can compile as a way of summarizing and assessing a student's literacy growth over time
What do they show?	• A student's reading, writing, speaking, and listening behaviors and strategies
How do I use them?	• In order to document a student's progress, compile and synthesize information from any or all of these sources:

- – Ongoing teacher observations
- – Behavior checklists
- – Profiles and inventories
- – Self, peer, and group assessments
- – Conference records
- – Reading and writing logs
- – Strategy assessments
- – Rubrics
- – Student portfolios
- – Cumulative folder form
- – Test scores

• Use what you have gathered when you prepare grades and as you get ready for conferences with students, parents, administrators, or resource teachers.

Teacher Form
Reading Strategy Assessment

What is it?	• A form to use at the end of each grading period to help synthesize the information gathered about a student's reading progress
What does it show?	• A student's knowledge and use of reading strategies, including self-assessment • A student's reading proficiency levels at the end of a grading period
How do I use it?	• Use the checklist to summarize a student's progress in applying reading strategies or to help you transfer information to a more traditional reporting form.

Ⓐ Criteria help you synthesize the information you've compiled from any of the forms and checklists you used throughout the grading period.

Form for reproduction is on page 158.

Teacher Form
Reading Strategy Assessment ✔

Student _Kathy Noonan_   Date _11/3_
Teacher _Mrs. Hill_   Grade _4_

		Proficient	Developing	Emerging	Not showing yet
Building Background Comments: Is usually very interested in what she is reading.	Previews	☑	☐	☐	☐
	Ask questions	☑	☐	☐	☐
	Predicts	☑	☐	☐	☐
	Activates prior knowledge	☑	☐	☐	☐
Ⓐ	Sets own purposes for reading	☑	☐	☐	☐
	Other:	☐	☐	☐	☐
Comprehension Comments: Needs to work on decoding skills. Kathy comprehends well unless vocabulary is problematic. Is sometimes reluctant to try new approaches (e.g. reading ahead).	Retells/summarizes	☑	☐	☐	☐
	Questions, evaluates ideas	☐	☑	☐	☐
	Paraphrases	☑	☐	☐	☐
	Rereads/reads ahead for meaning	☑	☐	☑	☐
	Visualizes	☑	☐	☐	☐
	Uses text structure to locate information	☐	☑	☐	☐
	Uses decoding strategies	☐	☑	☐	☐
	Uses vocabulary strategies	☐	☑	☐	☐
	Understands key ideas of a text	☐	☑	☐	☐
	Relates text to other texts, experiences, or understanding	☑	☐	☐	☐
	Other:	☐	☐	☐	☐
Fluency Comments: Reads dialogue with expression.	Reads fluently and accurately	☑	☐	☐	☐
	Paces appropriately	☐	☑	☐	☐
	Uses appropriate intonation and expression	☑	☐	☐	☐
	Other:	☐	☐	☐	☐
Self-Assessment Comments: Thinks that she reads more than she does. Kathy shies away from collaborative learning activities.	Is aware of: Strengths	☐	☑	☐	☐
	Needs	☐	☑	☐	☐
	Improvement/Achievement	☐	☑	☐	☐
	Sets and implements learning goals	☑	☐	☐	☐
	Maintains logs, records, portfolio	☑	☐	☐	☐
	Works with others	☐	☐	☑	☐
	Shares ideas and materials	☑	☐	☐	☐
	Other: accepts suggestions for improvement	☐	☑	☐	☐

Teacher Form
Writing Strategy Assessment

What is it?	• A form to use at the end of each grading period to help synthesize the information gathered about a student's writing progress
What does it show?	• A student's knowledge and use of writing strategies • A student's writing proficiency levels at the end of a grading period
How do I use it?	• Use the checklist to summarize a student's progress in applying writing strategies or to help you transfer information to a more traditional reporting form.

A Criteria help you synthesize the information you've compiled from any of the forms and checklists you used throughout the grading period.

Form for reproduction is on page 159.

Teacher Form
Writing Strategy Assessment ✓ **A**

Student _Kari Snow_   Date _10/15_
Teacher _Ms. Brewer_   Grade _4_

		Competent	Developing	Emerging	Not showing yet
Focus/Ideas Comments: needs to expand details	Addresses the writing task	✓			
	Demonstrates understanding of purpose	✓			
	States central idea	✓			
	Details support central idea		✓		
	Conclusion reinforces central idea		✓		
	Other:				
Organization Comments: difficulty with conclusions	Product of writing process	✓			
	Clearly presents central idea with details	✓	✓		
	Begins with a topic sentence	✓			
	Uses transitions between sentences and paragraphs		✓		
	Uses order words (first, then, after, finally)		✓		
	Other:				
Voice Comments: doesn't have a grasp on voice	Speaks directly to audience		✓		
	Voice matches writer's purpose		✓		
	Shows rather than tells		✓		
	Shows writer's feelings and personality		✓		
	Keeps reader's attention		✓		
	Other:				
Word Choice Comments:	Uses vivid words to elaborate ideas	✓	✓		
	Avoids slang and jargon	✓	✓		
	Uses strong images or figurative language		✓		
	Uses action verbs versus linking verbs	✓	✓		
	Uses new words to express ideas		✓		
	Other:				
Sentences Comments:	Expresses thoughts in lively, varied sentences		✓		
	Mixes short and long sentences		✓		
	Includes questions, commands, and exclamations	✓			
	Sentences flow logically from one to another		✓		
	Avoids choppy and wordy sentences		✓		
	Other:				
Conventions Comments: great spelling and grammar	Uses subjects and verbs in agreement	✓			
	Uses correct punctuation for grade level	✓			
	Capitalizes proper nouns and sentence beginnings	✓			
	Forms noun plurals correctly	✓			
	Spells words correctly	✓			
	Other:				

Teacher Form
Cumulative Folder Form

What is it?

- A cumulative record of a student's reading progress, to be placed in the student's permanent record that follows him or her from year to year

What does it show?

- The most basic and permanent information on how the student performed during each school year—namely, his or her score on the Baseline Group Test, scores for each Unit Benchmark Test, group placement, and any additional comments from the teacher.

How do I use it?

- Record scores and comments from unit to unit.
- Place the form into the student's cumulative folder at the end of the school year.

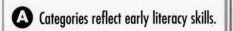

A Categories reflect early literacy skills.

B Scores serve as guide for flexible group placement.

Form for reproduction is on page 160.

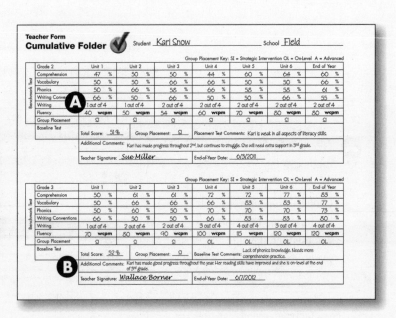

Teacher Form
Portfolio Guide

What is it?

- A form for managing the contents of a student's portfolio, whether teacher- or student-selected
- A cover sheet showing the portfolio contents at-a-glance

What does it show?

- An overall composite of a student's strengths, needs, interests, and attitudes throughout the year
- A student's selected work throughout the year

How do I use it?

- Track forms and work samples submitted at various times during the year.
- Fill in dates as a reminder of when items were submitted and when to collect additional submissions.

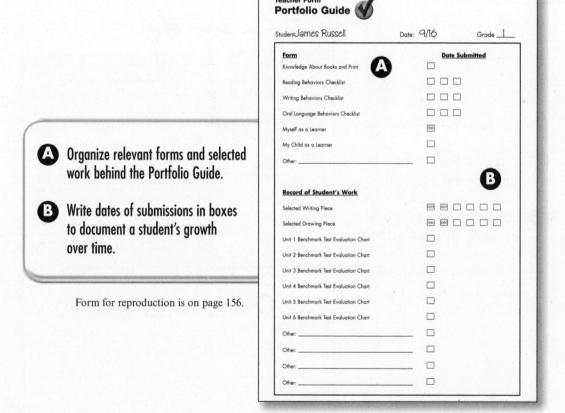

A Organize relevant forms and selected work behind the Portfolio Guide.

B Write dates of submissions in boxes to document a student's growth over time.

Form for reproduction is on page 156.

Student Form
Portfolio Selection Slips

What are they?
- Forms to help students select work samples to include in their portfolios
- Opportunities for students to think about what they have included in their portfolios and why they have chosen those items

What do they show?
- A student's rationale for including each piece in the portfolio
- What students think of their own work

How do students use them?
- Give students time to look over their work, decide which items to submit to their portfolios, and complete the forms.
- Attach one slip to each work sample and place it in the portfolio for future review of contents.

A Form gives students a chance to assess their work.

B Form gives students a chance to assess their own growth as learners.

Form for reproduction is on page 157.

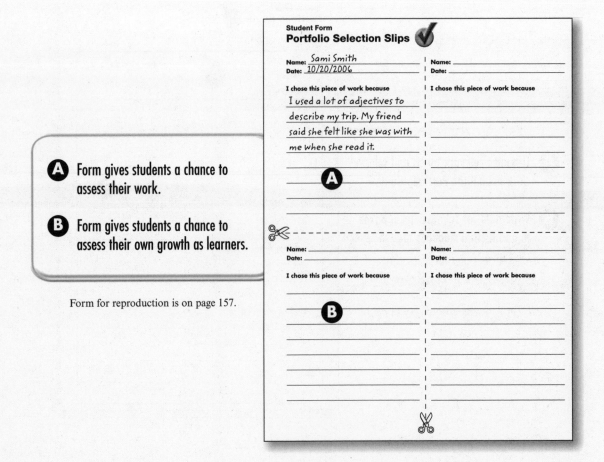

126

Teacher Form
Creating a Rubric

What is it?
- A form that may be used for evaluation of reading, writing, speaking, or listening assignments
- A tool that allows you to focus assessment on the key concepts emphasized during instruction

What does it show?
- How well a student exhibits his or her understanding of the key features of the assignment
- Areas in which a student may require additional instruction

How do I use it?
- Decide which assessment criteria are most relevant to a particular assignment. List them in the Features column.
- Rate and comment on those features as you assess the assignment.
- If desired, teacher may choose to convert the ratings into letter grades.

A The open-endedness of this form allows you to customize assessment features to meet the needs of every assignment.

B Your comments help you remember why you arrived at a rating and give you a starting point for discussing the assignment with the student or family.

C When desired, the rating may be turned into a letter grade.

Form for reproduction is on page 161.

Teacher Form
Creating a Rubric

Student Eriko Sato   Teacher Mr. Everett   Date 10/27

Assignment Make-believe story — The Beautiful Princess

Features	Rating	Comments
Entertaining	4 ③ 2 1	Story shows a sense of humor. Needs to get to the point quicker.
	4 3 2 1	
Beginning, middle, end	④ 3 2 1	Understands sequence and story progression.
	4 3 2 1	
Interesting characters	4 ③ 2 1	Doing better at descriptions of characters.
	4 3 2 1	
Setting and plot	④ 3 2 1	Main character strives for goal and reaches it.
	4 3 2 1	
Use of dialogue	4 3 ② 1	Dialogue would bring story to life.
	4 3 2 1	
	4 3 2 1	
	4 3 2 1	
Total	③	

Key: **4** - Has more than expected
  3 - Has what was expected
  2 - Has less than expected
  1 - Did not fulfill assignment or did not complete the assignment

Read by:

7 • Evidence of Learning

Teacher Form
Grading Writing

Grading Responses to Writing Prompts

- Writing prompts occur in several places in Scott Foresman *Reading Street*:

  – Following each selection and in the end-of-unit writing-process activity in the Teacher's Edition

  – In the Unit Benchmark Tests and the End-of-Year Benchmark Test

- To grade students's writing, you can use the Creating a Rubric form. For your convenience, an example scale for a how-to response has been completed for you below. Actual determinations about what score equals which grade will, however, vary with different teachers and districts.

A List the features of a how-to article and add your own criteria if you wish.

B Comments help you remember why you arrived at a rating and give you a starting point for discussing the writing with the student.

C To determine the possible score, multiply the number of features by 4 (5 features x 4 = 20). Then add the ratings you've given the features to find the student's actual score. In this example 17 out of 20 = B.

Score	Grade
18–20	A
15–17	B
12–14	C
10–11	D
9 and below	F

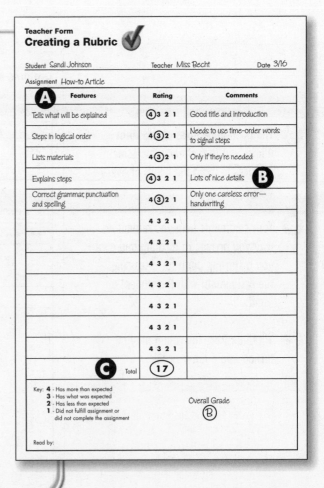

Teacher Form
Creating a Rubric

Student Sandi Johnson   Teacher Miss Becht   Date 3/16

Assignment How-to Article

A Features	Rating	Comments
Tells what will be explained	④ 3 2 1	Good title and introduction
Steps in logical order	4 ③ 2 1	Needs to use time-order words to signal steps
Lists materials	4 ③ 2 1	Only if they're needed
Explains steps	④ 3 2 1	Lots of nice details **B**
Correct grammar, punctuation and spelling	4 ③ 2 1	Only one careless error— handwriting
	4 3 2 1	
	4 3 2 1	
	4 3 2 1	
	4 3 2 1	
	4 3 2 1	
	4 3 2 1	
	4 3 2 1	
C Total	⑰	

Key: **4** - Has more than expected
3 - Has what was expected
2 - Has less than expected
1 - Did not fulfill assignment or did not complete the assignment

Overall Grade Ⓑ

Read by:

Form for reproduction is on page 161.

Teacher Form
Grading Products and Activities

Grading Products and Activities

- The Creating a Rubric form lends itself to grading a variety of students' products and activities, including:
  - Class discussions
  - Speeches
  - Retellings
  - Oral readings and dramatizations
  - Drawings, sculptures, and other artwork
  - Graphic organizers such as Venn diagrams, story maps, concept maps, and KWL charts
- Two examples and grading scales—for a class discussion and for a graphic organizer—are provided here. Actual determinations about what score equals which grade will, however, vary with different teachers and districts.
- In determining the criteria on which to evaluate students' work, you may find it helpful to refer to the various teacher summary reports described earlier or to the other checklists in this handbook.

7 • Evidence of Learning

A Example for a CLASS DISCUSSION

B To get a grade:
5 features x 4 = 20;
18 out of 20 = A.

Score	Grade
18–20	A
15–17	B
12–14	C
10–11	D
9 and below	F

A

Teacher Form
Creating a Rubric

Student Dawn Kolak   Teacher Miss Bolt   Date 5/10

Assignment Class Discussion

Features	Rating	Comments
Gave detailed, thoughtful answers	④ 3 2 1	Came prepared to discuss
Backed up opinions with fact	④ 3 2 1	Great!
Asked questions to clarify	4 ③ 2 1	A little quiet but improving
Was supportive of others' ideas and opinions	4 ③ 2 1	Needs to show more outward reactions
Connected text to self	4 ③ 2 1	Good—related to a family experience
	4 3 2 1	
	4 3 2 1	
	4 3 2 1	
	4 3 2 1	
	4 3 2 1	
	4 3 2 1	
	4 3 2 1	
B Total	⑱	

Key: **4** - Has more than expected
3 - Has what was expected
2 - Has less than expected
1 - Did not fulfill assignment or did not complete the assignment

Overall Grade
Ⓐ

Read by:

C Example for a GRAPHIC ORGANIZER

D To determine a grade:
4 features x 4 = 16;
14 out of 16 = B.

Score	Grade
15–16	A
13–14	B
11–12	C
10	D
9 and below	F

Form for reproduction is on page 161.

C

Teacher Form
Creating a Rubric

Student Laura Damon   Teacher Ms. Dolan   Date 11/3

Assignment Graphic Organizer

Features	Rating	Comments
Set up clear categories	4 3 ② 1	Categories were mixed between general & specific
Showed relationships between parts	4 ③ 2 1	Some relationships shown nicely
Included all important information	④ 3 2 1	Synthesized information very well
Was neat and well drawn	4 3 ② 1	Needs to work on presentation
	4 3 2 1	
	4 3 2 1	
	4 3 2 1	
	4 3 2 1	
	4 3 2 1	
	4 3 2 1	
	4 3 2 1	
	4 3 2 1	
D Total	⑪	

Key: **4** - Has more than expected
3 - Has what was expected
2 - Has less than expected
1 - Did not fulfill assignment or did not complete the assignment

Overall Grade
Ⓒ

Read by:

Grading Group Activities

Grading Group Activities

- You can use the Creating a Rubric form to assign grades for group work. Students can be graded in one of two ways:

  – As group members working together

  – As individuals contributing to the group effort

- When evaluating the group as a unit, use criteria that emphasize students' ability to work together in an efficient and cooperative manner. Be mindful that cooperative or group grading can unfairly reward or penalize individual students.

- When assigning grades to individual students in a group, use criteria that emphasize the specific tasks the student must do. You might use students' reviews of their work on the Group Assessment form described in chapter 3.

- The examples provided here show ways to evaluate and grade groups as well as individual students within groups. Actual determinations about what score equals which grade will vary with different teachers and districts.

A Example for a COOPERATIVE GROUP ACTIVITY

B These criteria assess students' ability to work together cooperatively and effectively.

C These criteria assess the actual product that students created.

D To get a grade:
6 features x 4 = 24;
22 out of 24 = A.

Score	Grade
22–24	A
18–21	B
15–17	C
14–16	D
13 and below	F

Teacher Form
Creating a Rubric ✓

Student Ian, Lisa, James   Teacher Mr. King   Date 2/14

A Assignment Writing and Illustrating a Book

Features	Rating	Comments
B Collaborated cooperatively and effectively	4 ③ 2 1	Worked independently but did consult often
Topic interesting to all in group	④ 3 2 1	Yes. All three love dogs.
Divided tasks equally	④ 3 2 1	Definitely!
Story has a strong, consistent plot	④ 3 2 1	Plot tracked well; especially strong ending
C Close match between text and illustration	4 ③ 2 1	One mismatch; pictured wrong dog
Writing and illustration styles match	④ 3 2 1	Perfect! Very whimsical
	4 3 2 1	
	4 3 2 1	
	4 3 2 1	
	4 3 2 1	
	4 3 2 1	
	4 3 2 1	
D Total	㉒	

Key: **4** - Has more than expected
3 - Has what was expected
2 - Has less than expected
1 - Did not fulfill assignment or did not complete the assignment

Overall Grade Ⓐ

Read by:

E Example for an INDIVIDUAL IN A GROUP

F These criteria assess individual students according to the specific tasks they have performed.

G To get a grade:
3 features x 4 = 12;
10 out of 12 = B.

Score	Grade
11–12	A
10	B
9	C
8	D
7 and below	F

Teacher Form
Creating a Rubric ✓

Student Ian Murphy   Teacher Mr. King   Date 2/14

Assignment Writing/Illustrating a Book **E**

Features	Rating	Comments
Created half of book illustrations **F**	④ 3 2 1	Worked conscientiously; finished ahead of schedule
Created illustrations that hit highlights of text	④ 3 2 1	Ian's illustrations were right on target.
Participated in development of story line	4 3 ② 1	Less attention to this than to doing the art
	4 3 2 1	
	4 3 2 1	
	4 3 2 1	
	4 3 2 1	
	4 3 2 1	
	4 3 2 1	
	4 3 2 1	
	4 3 2 1	
	4 3 2 1	
G Total	⑩	

Key: **4** - Has more than expected
3 - Has what was expected
2 - Has less than expected
1 - Did not fulfill assignment or did not complete the assignment

Overall Grade Ⓑ

Read by:

Form for reproduction is on page 161.

Classroom-based Assessment Tools

Myself as a Reader and Writer

Name _____ Date _____

	A Lot	Sometimes	Not at All
1. I like to read			
realistic fiction	☐	☐	☐
fantasy stories (for example, tall tales, myths, mysteries)	☐	☐	☐
historical fiction	☐	☐	☐
plays	☐	☐	☐
biographies and autobiographies	☐	☐	☐
nonfiction articles	☐	☐	☐
other:	☐	☐	☐
2. The subjects I like to read about most are			
students my age	☐	☐	☐
sports	☐	☐	☐
famous people	☐	☐	☐
exploration and adventure	☐	☐	☐
how things work	☐	☐	☐
things that are funny	☐	☐	☐
other:	☐	☐	☐
3. I like to write			
made-up stories	☐	☐	☐
true stories	☐	☐	☐
letters	☐	☐	☐
poems	☐	☐	☐
reports	☐	☐	☐
plays	☐	☐	☐
other:	☐	☐	☐

4. The best book or story I have read in the last year is

_____

_____

5. The best thing I have written in the last year is a piece about

_____

_____

Student Form
Reading and Me

Name   Date

Mark the box next to the answer that tells how you feel.

1. How often do you like to read?

- ☐ All of the time
- ☐ Sometimes
- ☐ Not too often
- ☐ Never

2. When I read I

- ☐ always try my best.
- ☐ try my best most of the time.
- ☐ don't try very hard.
- ☐ often give up.

3. In general, when I read I

- ☐ really enjoy it.
- ☐ think it's OK.
- ☐ don't like it very much.
- ☐ dislike it a lot.

4. I think reading is

- ☐ my favorite thing to do.
- ☐ one of my favorite things to do.
- ☐ not one of my favorite things to do.
- ☐ my least favorite thing to do.

5. I read

- ☐ a lot better than my classmates.
- ☐ a little better than my classmates.
- ☐ about the same as my classmates.
- ☐ worse than my classmates.

6. When I am reading by myself, I understand

- ☐ most of what I read.
- ☐ some of what I read.
- ☐ not much of what I read.
- ☐ very little of what I read.

7. I am

- ☐ a great reader.
- ☐ a good reader.
- ☐ an OK reader.
- ☐ a poor reader.

8. I care what other kids think about my reading.

- ☐ Never
- ☐ Not too often
- ☐ Sometimes
- ☐ Always

9. I think that reading is

- ☐ very easy.
- ☐ kind of easy.
- ☐ kind of hard.
- ☐ very hard.

10. When I read in school I usually

- ☐ feel good about it.
- ☐ feel OK about it.
- ☐ feel not too good about it.
- ☐ feel terrible about it.

Name _____   Date _____

Mark the box next to the answer that tells how you feel.

11. I talk with my friends about the things that I read

- ☐ all of the time.
- ☐ sometimes.
- ☐ not too often.
- ☐ never.

12. People who read a lot are

- ☐ very interesting.
- ☐ kind of interesting.
- ☐ not very interesting.
- ☐ pretty boring.

13. I think that reading in school is

- ☐ very important.
- ☐ important.
- ☐ somewhat important.
- ☐ not too important.

14. I think that reading at home is

- ☐ very important.
- ☐ important.
- ☐ somewhat important.
- ☐ not too important.

15. I like getting a book for a present.

- ☐ All the time
- ☐ Sometimes
- ☐ Not very often
- ☐ Never

16. I read newspapers

- ☐ very well.
- ☐ pretty well.
- ☐ not too well.
- ☐ not well at all.

17. I read schoolbooks

- ☐ very well.
- ☐ pretty well.
- ☐ not too well.
- ☐ not well at all.

18. I read comics

- ☐ very well.
- ☐ pretty well.
- ☐ not too well.
- ☐ not well at all.

19. I read magazines

- ☐ very well.
- ☐ pretty well.
- ☐ not too well.
- ☐ not well at all.

20. I read storybooks or novels

- ☐ very well.
- ☐ pretty well.
- ☐ not too well.
- ☐ not well at all.

Teacher Form
Reading Behaviors Checklist

Student   Date

Behavior	Yes	No	Not Applicable
Recognizes letters of the alphabet			
Recognizes name in print			
Recognizes some environmental print, such as signs and logos			
Knows the difference between letters and words			
Knows the difference between capital and lowercase letters			
Understands function of capitalization and punctuation			
Recognizes that book parts such as cover, title page, and table of contents offer information			
Recognizes that words are represented in writing by specific sequences of letters			
Recognizes words that rhyme			
Distinguishes rhyming and nonrhyming words			
Knows sound-letter correspondences			
Identifies and isolates initial sounds in words			
Identifies and isolates final sounds in words			
Blends sounds to make spoken words			
Segments one-syllable/two-syllable spoken words into individual phonemes			
Reads consonant blends and digraphs			
Reads and understands endings such as -es, -ed, -ing			
Reads vowels and vowel diphthongs			
Reads and understands possessives			
Reads and understands compound words			
Reads simple sentences			
Reads simple stories			
Understands simple story structure			
Other:			

Writing Behaviors Checklist

Student   Date

Behavior	Yes	No	Not Applicable
Produces detailed and relevant drawings			
Dictates messages for others to write			
Writes using scribble, drawing, or letterlike forms			
Distinguishes between writing and drawing			
Writes own name and other important words			
Writes all letters of the alphabet, capital and lowercase			
Writes labels or captions for illustrations and possessions			
Writes messages that move from left to right and top to bottom			
Uses phonological knowledge to map sounds to letters when writing			
Holds pencil and positions paper correctly			
Uses basic capitalization and punctuation			
Writes messages that can be understood by others			
Shows understanding of sequence in writing			
Stays on topic when writing			
Expresses original ideas			
Elaborates with details			
Has an identifiable voice			
Chooses precise and vivid words			
Takes risks with vocabulary			
Uses descriptive words			
Writes in different forms			
Writes for different audiences and purposes			
Writes to record ideas and reflections			
Other:			

Teacher Form
Oral Language Behaviors Checklist

Student   Date

Behavior	Yes	No	Example
Follows simple oral directions			
Follows directions of several steps			
Listens to stories read aloud			
Participates actively when predictable rhymes and songs are read aloud			
Understands and retells spoken messages			
Gives precise directions			
Expresses ideas clearly			
Responds appropriately to questions			
Knows and uses many words			
Participates in conversations and discussions			
Listens in small-group situations			
Listens in whole-group situations			
Stays on topic in discussions			
Uses language conventions appropriately			
Listens to others courteously, without interrupting			
Can retell simple stories in sequence			
Recalls details from stories			
Reads orally with appropriate fluency			
Listens and speaks for various purposes			
Adapts speaking to audience			
Listens critically to oral readings, discussions, and messages			
Connects cultural experiences and prior knowledge through speaking and listening			
Other:			

Teacher Form

Profile of English Language Learners

Student: _____

Trait	Mostly	Unevenly	Rarely	Date/Comment
Speaks and/or understands a few basic words				
Speaks fluently but makes frequent errors				
Uses names of many objects				
Uses and understands basic everyday vocabulary				
Asks and answers simple questions				
Follows simple directions				
Takes part in discussions				
Conveys ideas or stories through drawings				
Needs pictures to comprehend simple text				
Recognizes basic sound/letter relationships in words				
Follows text being read aloud				
Joins in choral reading				
Retells predictable text				

Student Form

How Do I Learn?

Name _____   Date _____

1. Which statement is most true about you?

a. ☐ I nearly always understand things better if I see a picture or diagram.

b. ☐ When someone explains something, I usually understand it just by listening.

c. ☐ Sometimes I need pictures to help me understand; other times I don't.

2. If you have a choice, you would rather work

a. ☐ in a group with three or four others.

b. ☐ with one partner.

c. ☐ by yourself.

3. You want to remember a story you read. The best way for you to do this would be to

a. ☐ draw a picture of it.

b. ☐ act out a scene from it.

c. ☐ discuss it with a partner or group.

d. ☐ do this instead:

_____

_____

4. You go to a museum. The kind of exhibit you like best has

a. ☐ a film to go with it.

b. ☐ levers and buttons you can play with.

c. ☐ a book where you can write what you liked and didn't like.

d. ☐ something else:

_____

_____

5. Your group is planning a presentation about castles for younger students. The part you would like to do best is

a. ☐ design the invitations.

b. ☐ build a model of the castle.

c. ☐ talk to the students after the presentation to see how they liked it.

d. ☐ something else:

_____

_____

Parent Form
My Child as a Learner

Name   Date

Please comment and provide examples of your child's learning in the following areas.			
My child	**Yes**	**No**	**Comments/Examples**
1. usually • reads daily • writes daily • watches TV daily	☐ ☐ ☐	☐ ☐ ☐	
2. often • is curious • keeps on with what he or she is doing • does things in new ways • becomes easily frustrated • likes trying new things • likes to express opinions	☐ ☐ ☐ ☐ ☐ ☐	☐ ☐ ☐ ☐ ☐ ☐	
3. understands what he or she is • reading • writing • watching	☐ ☐ ☐	☐ ☐ ☐	
4. explores ideas by • reading • writing • drawing • watching • talking	☐ ☐ ☐ ☐ ☐	☐ ☐ ☐ ☐ ☐	
5. enjoys working • with others • alone	☐ ☐	☐ ☐	
6. is someone who • is proud of achievement • recognizes his or her growth • considers new possibilities • sets goals for himself or herself	☐ ☐ ☐ ☐	☐ ☐ ☐ ☐	
7. likes to read about			
8. likes to write about			
9. likes to watch			
10. Additional comments and reactions:			
My name		Relationship to child	
I can be reached at			

Teacher Form

Narrative Retelling Chart

Selection Title _____

Name _____ Date _____

Retelling Criteria/Teacher Prompt	Teacher-Aided Response	Student-Generated Response	Rubric Score (Circle one.)
Connections Does this story remind you of anything else?			4 3 2 1
Author's Purpose Why do you think the author wrote this story? What was the author trying to tell us?			4 3 2 1
Characters What can you tell me about _____ (use character's name)?			4 3 2 1
Setting Where and when did the story happen?			4 3 2 1
Plot What happened in the story?			4 3 2 1

Summative Retelling Score 4 3 2 1

Comments _____

143

Teacher Form

Expository Retelling Chart

Selection Title _____ Name _____ Date _____

Retelling Criteria/Teacher Prompt	Teacher-Aided Response	Student-Generated Response	Rubric Score (Circle one.)			
Connections Did this selection make you think about something else you have read? What did you learn about as you read this selection?			4	3	2	1
Author's Purpose Why do you think the author wrote this selection?			4	3	2	1
Topic What was the selection mostly about?			4	3	2	1
Important Ideas What is important for me to know about _____ (topic)?			4	3	2	1
Conclusions What did you learn from reading this selection?			4	3	2	1

Summative Retelling Score 4 3 2 1

Comments _____

144

Teacher Form

Work Habits Conference Record

Student

Use the key at the bottom of the page to assess student's performance.

Date	Understands tasks	Sets priorities	Uses time appropriately	Solves problems effectively	Seeks help when needed	Completes tasks on time	Can explain process/ project effectively	Comments

4 Does more than expected   **3** Does what was expected   **2** Does less than expected   **1** Does not fulfill the assignment or does not complete the assignment

Skills Conference Record

Grade _____

Student _____   Teacher _____

	Proficient	Developing	Emerging	Not showing trait
Reading Comments: Sets own purpose for reading Predicts and asks questions Retells/summarizes Reads fluently Understands key ideas in a text Uses decoding strategies Makes text connections Other:	☐ ☐ ☐ ☐ ☐ ☐ ☐ ☐	☐ ☐ ☐ ☐ ☐ ☐ ☐ ☐	☐ ☐ ☐ ☐ ☐ ☐ ☐ ☐	☐ ☐ ☐ ☐ ☐ ☐ ☐ ☐
Writing Comments: Follows writing process Develops central idea and with details Organizes ideas logically Uses transitions Expresses ideas with word choice Uses language conventions appropriately Other:	☐ ☐ ☐ ☐ ☐ ☐ ☐	☐ ☐ ☐ ☐ ☐ ☐ ☐	☐ ☐ ☐ ☐ ☐ ☐ ☐	☐ ☐ ☐ ☐ ☐ ☐ ☐
Speaking and Listening Comments: Follows instructions Asks questions Answers questions Paraphrases Discussions Eye contact with audience Other:	☐ ☐ ☐ ☐ ☐ ☐ ☐	☐ ☐ ☐ ☐ ☐ ☐ ☐	☐ ☐ ☐ ☐ ☐ ☐ ☐	☐ ☐ ☐ ☐ ☐ ☐ ☐

Teacher Form

Observing English Language Learners

Student:

Behaviors Observed	Date:			Date:			Date:		
	Yes	No	Sometimes	Yes	No	Sometimes	Yes	No	Sometimes
The student									
• uses context clues to figure out new words									
• uses prior knowledge to figure out new words									
• uses visuals to decipher meaning									
• uses strategies to decipher meaning									
• can identify the strategies he or she is using									
• understands why he or she is using a particular strategy									
• assesses his or her own progress									
• generally understands what the class is reading									

General Comments

147

Parent Form
Observing My Child's Reading

Child   Parent/
                         Guardian   Date

---

1. Story or article my child read to me:

---

2. Here are some things I noticed about my child's

Vocabulary

- understands most words that he or she reads   ☐ yes   ☐ no   ☐ not sure

- can figure out word meanings from other words
  in story or article   ☐ yes   ☐ no   ☐ not sure

- is not afraid to attempt reading new words   ☐ yes   ☐ no   ☐ not sure

Comprehension

- understands what he or she is reading   ☐ yes   ☐ no   ☐ not sure

- remembers the important ideas from a reading   ☐ yes   ☐ no   ☐ not sure

- can tell back what he or she has read   ☐ yes   ☐ no   ☐ not sure

- remembers the order things happened in   ☐ yes   ☐ no   ☐ not sure

Read-Aloud Ability

- reads most sentences without pausing   ☐ yes   ☐ no   ☐ not sure

- reads in a manner that shows he or she
  makes sense of what is being read   ☐ yes   ☐ no   ☐ not sure

- reads with expression   ☐ yes   ☐ no   ☐ not sure

- pronounces most words correctly   ☐ yes   ☐ no   ☐ not sure

---

3. Here are some general comments about what I noticed as my child read:

Student Form
Reading Log

Name _____

Dates Read	Title and Author	What is it about?	How would you rate it?	Explain your rating.
From ____ to ____			**Great** 5 4 3 2 1 **Awful**	
From ____ to ____			**Great** 5 4 3 2 1 **Awful**	
From ____ to ____			**Great** 5 4 3 2 1 **Awful**	
From ____ to ____			**Great** 5 4 3 2 1 **Awful**	
From ____ to ____			**Great** 5 4 3 2 1 **Awful**	

About My Reading

Name   Date

---

1. Compared with earlier in the year, I am enjoying reading

☐ more   ☐ less   ☐ about the same

2. When I read now, I understand

☐ more than I used to   ☐ about the same as I used to

3. One thing that has helped me with my reading is

_____

_____

_____

4. One thing that could make me a better reader is

_____

_____

_____

5. Here is one selection or book that I really enjoyed reading:

_____

_____

6. Here are some reasons why I liked it:

_____

_____

_____

_____

_____

_____

Student Form

Writing Log

Student _____ Date _____

Teacher _____ Grade _____

Date	Title	Type of Writing	How I felt about this piece	What I liked or disliked	Put in Portfolio
			4 3 2 1		
			4 3 2 1		
			4 3 2 1		
			4 3 2 1		
			4 3 2 1		
			4 3 2 1		

Key
4 = Excellent
3 = Good
2 = Fair
1 = Poor

About My Writing ✓

Name   Date

---

1. Compared with earlier in the year, I am enjoying writing

☐ more   ☐ less   ☐ about the same

2. When I write now, my writing is

• clearer than it used to be   ☐ yes   ☐ no

• more interesting than it used to be   ☐ yes   ☐ no

3. One thing that has improved my writing is

_____

_____

_____

4. One thing that could make me a better writer is

_____

_____

5. Here is one piece that I wrote that I think is really good:

_____

_____

6. Here are some things that are good about it:

_____

_____

_____

_____

_____

Peer Assessment ✓

My name is _____ Date_____

I'm looking at _____'s work.

The work I am looking at is _____

Things I Especially Like About Your Work	Things I Had Trouble Understanding
_____	_____
_____	_____
_____	_____
_____	_____
_____	_____
_____	_____
_____	_____

Suggestions

_____

_____

_____

_____

_____

_____

_____

_____

Student Self-Assessment

Name _____ Teacher _____ Date _____

Work or Project I'm Assessing: _____

Things I Did Well	Things I Need to Work On

How I Will Work on Them	My Goals for the Future

Student Form
Group Assessment

Teacher _____ Date _____

What the Group Did: _____

_____

_____

What I Did:

Member 1
Member 2
Member 3
Member 4

Problems We Had: _____

_____

_____

Our Goals for Next Time: _____

_____

Teacher Form
Portfolio Guide ✓

Student: _____ Date: _____ Grade _____

Form   ### Date Submitted

Knowledge About Books and Print   ☐

Reading Behaviors Checklist   ☐ ☐ ☐

Writing Behaviors Checklist   ☐ ☐ ☐

Oral Language Behaviors Checklist   ☐ ☐ ☐

Myself as a Learner   ☐

My Child as a Learner   ☐

Other: _____   ☐

Record of Student's Work

Selected Writing Piece   ☐ ☐ ☐ ☐ ☐ ☐

Selected Drawing Piece   ☐ ☐ ☐ ☐ ☐ ☐

Unit 1 Benchmark Test Evaluation Chart   ☐

Unit 2 Benchmark Test Evaluation Chart   ☐

Unit 3 Benchmark Test Evaluation Chart   ☐

Unit 4 Benchmark Test Evaluation Chart   ☐

Unit 5 Benchmark Test Evaluation Chart   ☐

Unit 6 Benchmark Test Evaluation Chart   ☐

Other: _____   ☐

Other: _____   ☐

Other: _____   ☐

Other: _____   ☐

Student Form
Portfolio Selection Slips

Name: _____

Date: _____

I chose this piece of work because

_____

_____

_____

_____

_____

_____

_____

_____

Name: _____

Date: _____

I chose this piece of work because

_____

_____

_____

_____

_____

_____

_____

_____

Name: _____

Date: _____

I chose this piece of work because

_____

_____

_____

_____

_____

_____

Name: _____

Date: _____

I chose this piece of work because

_____

_____

_____

_____

_____

_____

157

Teacher Form
Reading Strategy Assessment

Student _____ Date _____

Teacher _____ Grade _____

		Proficient	Developing	Emerging	Not showing trait
Building Background Comments:	Previews	☐	☐	☐	☐
	Asks questions	☐	☐	☐	☐
	Predicts	☐	☐	☐	☐
	Activates prior knowledge	☐	☐	☐	☐
	Sets own purposes for reading	☐	☐	☐	☐
	Other:	☐	☐	☐	☐
Comprehension Comments:	Retells/summarizes	☐	☐	☐	☐
	Questions, evaluates ideas	☐	☐	☐	☐
	Paraphrases	☐	☐	☐	☐
	Rereads/reads ahead for meaning	☐	☐	☐	☐
	Visualizes	☐	☐	☐	☐
	Uses text structure to locate information	☐	☐	☐	☐
	Uses decoding strategies	☐	☐	☐	☐
	Uses vocabulary strategies	☐	☐	☐	☐
	Understands key ideas of a text	☐	☐	☐	☐
	Relates text to other texts, experiences, or understanding	☐	☐	☐	☐
	Other:	☐	☐	☐	☐
Fluency Comments:	Reads fluently and accurately	☐	☐	☐	☐
	Paces appropriately	☐	☐	☐	☐
	Uses appropriate intonation and expression	☐	☐	☐	☐
	Other:	☐	☐	☐	☐
Self-Assessment Comments:	Is aware of: Strengths	☐	☐	☐	☐
	Needs	☐	☐	☐	☐
	Improvement/Achievement	☐	☐	☐	☐
	Sets and implements learning goals	☐	☐	☐	☐
	Maintains logs, records, portfolio	☐	☐	☐	☐
	Works with others	☐	☐	☐	☐
	Shares ideas and materials	☐	☐	☐	☐
	Other:	☐	☐	☐	☐

Teacher Form
Writing Strategy Assessment

Student _____ Date _____

Teacher _____ Grade _____

		Proficient	Developing	Emerging	Not showing trait
Focus/Ideas Comments:	Addresses the writing task	☐	☐	☐	☐
	Demonstrates understanding of purpose	☐	☐	☐	☐
	States central idea	☐	☐	☐	☐
	Details support central idea	☐	☐	☐	☐
	Conclusion reinforces central idea	☐	☐	☐	☐
	Other:	☐	☐	☐	☐
Organization Comments:	Product of writing process	☐	☐	☐	☐
	Clearly presents central idea with details	☐	☐	☐	☐
	Begins with a topic sentence	☐	☐	☐	☐
	Uses transitions between sentences and paragraphs	☐	☐	☐	☐
	Uses order words (first, then, after, finally)	☐	☐	☐	☐
	Other:	☐	☐	☐	☐
Voice Comments:	Speaks directly to audience	☐	☐	☐	☐
	Voice matches writer's purpose	☐	☐	☐	☐
	Shows rather than tells	☐	☐	☐	☐
	Shows writer's feelings and personality	☐	☐	☐	☐
	Keeps reader's attention	☐	☐	☐	☐
	Other:	☐	☐	☐	☐
Word Choice Comments:	Uses vivid words to elaborate ideas	☐	☐	☐	☐
	Avoids slang and jargon	☐	☐	☐	☐
	Uses strong images or figurative language	☐	☐	☐	☐
	Uses action verbs versus linking verbs	☐	☐	☐	☐
	Uses new words to express ideas	☐	☐	☐	☐
	Other:	☐	☐	☐	☐
Sentences Comments:	Expresses thoughts in lively, varied sentences	☐	☐	☐	☐
	Mixes short and long sentences	☐	☐	☐	☐
	Includes questions, commands, and exclamations	☐	☐	☐	☐
	Sentences flow logically from one to another	☐	☐	☐	☐
	Avoids choppy and wordy sentences	☐	☐	☐	☐
	Other:	☐	☐	☐	☐
Conventions Comments:	Uses subjects and verbs in agreement	☐	☐	☐	☐
	Uses correct punctuation for grade level	☐	☐	☐	☐
	Capitalizes proper nouns and sentence beginnings	☐	☐	☐	☐
	Forms noun plurals correctly	☐	☐	☐	☐
	Spells words correctly	☐	☐	☐	☐
	Other:	☐	☐	☐	☐

Teacher Form
Cumulative Folder

Student _____   School _____

Group Placement Key: SI = Strategic Intervention OL = On-level A = Advanced

Benchmark Test

Grade 2	Unit 1	Unit 2	Unit 3	Unit 4	Unit 5	Unit 6	End of Year
Comprehension	%	%	%	%	%	%	%
Vocabulary	%	%	%	%	%	%	%
Phonics	%	%	%	%	%	%	%
Writing Conventions	%	%	%	%	%	%	%
Writing							
Fluency	wcpm	wcpm	wcpm	wcpm	wcpm	wcpm	wcpm
Group Placement							

Baseline Test

Total Score: _____   Group Placement: _____   Placement Test Comments:

Additional Comments:

Teacher Signature: _____   End-of-Year Date: _____

Group Placement Key: SI = Strategic Intervention OL = On-level A = Advanced

Benchmark Test

Grade 3	Unit 1	Unit 2	Unit 3	Unit 4	Unit 5	Unit 6	End of Year
Comprehension	%	%	%	%	%	%	%
Vocabulary	%	%	%	%	%	%	%
Phonics	%	%	%	%	%	%	%
Writing Conventions	%	%	%	%	%	%	%
Writing							
Fluency	wcpm	wcpm	wcpm	wcpm	wcpm	wcpm	wcpm
Group Placement							

Baseline Test

Total Score: _____   Group Placement: _____   Baseline Test Comments:

Additional Comments:

Teacher Signature: _____   End-of-Year Date: _____

Teacher Form
Creating a Rubric

Student _____ Teacher _____ Date _____

Assignment _____

Features	Rating	Comments
	4 3 2 1	
	4 3 2 1	
	4 3 2 1	
	4 3 2 1	
	4 3 2 1	
	4 3 2 1	
	4 3 2 1	
	4 3 2 1	
	4 3 2 1	
	4 3 2 1	
	4 3 2 1	
	4 3 2 1	
Total		

Key: **4** - Has more than expected
    3 - Has what was expected
    2 - Has less than expected
    1 - Did not fulfill assignment or
       did not complete the assignment

Read by: _____

Second Grade Formal Assessment Tools

Forms from Second Grade Baseline Group Test Teacher's Manual

Phonemic Awareness Scoring Sheet

Student's Name _____ Date _____

Directions: Follow the instructions for scoring as given for each section below. Record notes and observations in the box at the bottom. Count up the total number correct, and record the results of this assessment on the Evaluation Chart for Grade 2.

Element	Points
Segmentation/Blending of Phonemes:	Underline each correct sound/blend that the student says. All sounds in a word must be identified to score 1 point for each word. (Maximum: 4 points)
1. /d/ /r/ /o/ /p/	
2. /k/ /l/ /ē/ /n/	
3. /k/ /r/ /u/ /n/ /ch/	
4. /b/ /ē/ /g/ /a/ /n/	
	Underline and score 1 point for each word that the student says correctly. (Maximum: 4 points)
5. left	
6. gold	
7. stand	
8. wagon	
Segmentation/Blending of Syllables:	Underline the number of syllables if the student answers correctly. Score 1 point for each word. (Maximum: 4 points)
9. 3	
10. 3	
11. 4	
12. 4	
	Underline the word if the student answers correctly. Each word is worth 1 point. (Maximum: 4 points)
13. wonderful	
14. remember	
15. elevator	

16. impossible	
Rhyming Words:	Underline the word if the student answers correctly. Each word is worth 1 point. (Maximum: 4 points)
17. hard	
18. sign	
19. clown	
20. feather	
PHONEMIC AWARENESS TOTAL:	_____ (Maximum: 20 points)

Notes and Observations:

Grade 2 Baseline Test Evaluation Chart

Student's Name _____ Date _____

Teacher's Name _____ Class _____

SUBTEST Skills/ Item Numbers		Subtest Percentages	SUBTEST Skills/ Item Numbers		Subtest Percentages
Phonics _____ /12 Correct			**Reading Comprehension**		
1.	0 1	1=8%	_____/18 Correct		
2.	0 1	2=16%	1.	0 1	1=6%
3.	0 1	3=25%	2.	0 1	2=12%
4.	0 1	4=34%	3.	0 1	3=18%
5.	0 1	5=42%	4.	0 1	4=22%
6.	0 1	6=50%	5.	0 1	5=28%
7.	0 1	7=58%	6.	0 1	6=33%
8.	0 1	8=66%	7.	0 1	7=39%
9.	0 1	9=75%	8.	0 1	8=44%
10.	0 1	10=83%	9.	0 1	9=50%
11.	0 1	11=91%	10.	0 1	10=56%
12.	0 1	12=100%	11.	0 1	11=61%
Word Knowledge _____/10 Correct			12.	0 1	12=67%
			13.	0 1	13=72%
1.	0 1	1=10%	14.	0 1	14=78%
2.	0 1	2=20%	15.	0 1	15=83%
3.	0 1	3=30%	16.	0 1	16=89%
4.	0 1	4=40%	17.	0 1	17=94%
5.	0 1	5=50%	18.	0 1	18=100%
6.	0 1	6=60%	**Phonemic Awareness**		
7.	0 1	7=70%			
8.	0 1	8=80%	_____/20 Correct		
9.	0 1	9=90%			
10.	0 1	10=100%	Total Test _____/70 Correct		
Vocabulary _____ /10 Correct			**Fluency** _____		
1.	0 1	1=10%	**Alternate Baseline Test**		
2.	0 1	2=20%			
3.	0 1	3=30%	_____/61 Correct		
4.	0 1	4=40%			
5.	0 1	5=50%			
6.	0 1	6=60%			
7.	0 1	7=70%			
8.	0 1	8=80%			
9.	0 1	9=90%			
10.	0 1	10=100%			

Total # Correct	Total Percentage	Total # Correct	Total Percentage	Total # Correct	Total Percentage	Total # Correct	Total Percentage
1	1%	19	27%	37	53%	55	79%
2	2%	20	29%	38	54%	56	80%
3	4%	21	30%	39	56%	57	81%
4	6%	22	31%	40	57%	58	82%
5	7%	23	33%	41	59%	59	84%
6	9%	24	34%	42	60%	60	86%
7	10%	25	36%	43	61%	61	87%
8	11%	26	37%	44	63%	62	89%
9	13%	27	39%	45	64%	63	90%
10	14%	28	40%	46	66%	64	91%
11	16%	29	41%	47	67%	65	92%
12	17%	30	43%	48	69%	66	94%
13	19%	31	44%	49	70%	67	96%
14	20%	32	46%	50	71%	68	97%
15	21%	33	47%	51	72%	69	99%
16	23%	34	49%	52	74%	70	100%
17	24%	35	50%	53	76%		
18	26%	36	51%	54	77%		

Initial Placement: **Strategic Intervention**   **On-Level**   **Advanced**

Fluency Forms

Class Fluency Progress Chart

Child's Name	Initial		Unit 1		Unit 2		Unit 3		Unit 4		Unit 5		Unit 6	
	Date	WCPM	Date	WCPM	Date	WCPM	Date	WCPM	Date	WCPM	Date	WCPM	Date	WCPM
1.														
2.														
3.														
4.														
5.														
6.														
7.														
8.														
9.														
10.														
11.														
12.														
13.														
14.														
15.														
16.														
17.														
18.														
19.														
20.														
21.														
22.														
23.														
24.														
25.														
26.														
27.														
28.														
29.														
30.														
31.														
32.														
33.														
34.														
35.														

Individual Fluency Progress Chart, Grade 2

Name _____

WCPM

	1	2	3	4	5	6	7	8	9	10	11	12	13	14	15	16	17	18	19	20	21	22	23	24	25	26	27	28	29	30	31	32	33	34	35	36
125																																				
120																																				
115																																				
110																																				
105																																				
100																																				
95																																				
90																																				
85																																				
80																																				
75																																				
70																																				
65																																				
60																																				
55																																				
50																																				
45																																				
40																																				
35																																				
30																																				

Timed Reading/Week

171

Forms from Second Grade Weekly Tests Teacher's Manual

Scott Foresman *Reading Street*
Class Weekly Test Progress Chart—Grade 2

Teacher's Name: _____

Child's Name	1	2	3	4	5	6	7	8	9	10	11	12	13	14	15	16	17	18	19	20	21	22	23	24	25	26	27	28	29	30

(Weekly Test Total Score across columns; Child's Name rows 1–30)

1																															
2																															
3																															
4																															
5																															
6																															
7																															
8																															
9																															
10																															
11																															
12																															
13																															
14																															
15																															
16																															
17																															
18																															
19																															
20																															
21																															
22																															
23																															
24																															
25																															
26																															
27																															
28																															
29																															
30																															

Scott Foresman *Reading Street*
Student Weekly Test Progress Chart—Grade 2

Name: _____

Test	Vocabulary	Phonic/Word Analysis	Comprehension	TOTAL
Weekly Test 1	/5	/5	/5	/15
Weekly Test 2	/5	/5	/5	/15
Weekly Test 3	/5	/5	/5	/15
Weekly Test 4	/5	/5	/5	/15
Weekly Test 5	/5	/5	/5	/15
Weekly Test 6	/5	/5	/5	/15
Weekly Test 7	/5	/5	/5	/15
Weekly Test 8	/5	/5	/5	/15
Weekly Test 9	/5	/5	/5	/15
Weekly Test 10	/5	/5	/5	/15
Weekly Test 11	/5	/5	/5	/15
Weekly Test 12	/5	/5	/5	/15
Weekly Test 13	/5	/5	/5	/15
Weekly Test 14	/5	/5	/5	/15
Weekly Test 15	/5	/5	/5	/15
Weekly Test 16	/5	/5	/5	/15
Weekly Test 17	/5	/5	/5	/15
Weekly Test 18	/5	/5	/5	/15
Weekly Test 19	/5	/5	/5	/15
Weekly Test 20	/5	/5	/5	/15
Weekly Test 21	/5	/5	/5	/15
Weekly Test 22	/5	/5	/5	/15
Weekly Test 23	/5	/5	/5	/15
Weekly Test 24	/5	/5	/5	/15
Weekly Test 25	/5	/5	/5	/15
Weekly Test 26	/5	/5	/5	/15
Weekly Test 27	/5	/5	/5	/15
Weekly Test 28	/5	/5	/5	/15
Weekly Test 29	/5	/5	/5	/15
Weekly Test 30	/5	/5	/5	/15

Comprehension Target Skill Coverage

How can the Weekly Tests predict student success on Unit Benchmark Tests?

Each Unit Benchmark Test, as well as assessing overall student reading ability, concentrates on two skills taught and/or reviewed during the unit by including several questions on those skills. In order to ensure that comprehension target skill can be accurately learned and then tested, students learn each target skill through a combination of being taught and reviewing the skill multiple times before testing occurs. The charts below show the units/weeks where the target comprehension skills are taught and where they are tested on Weekly Tests. Based on the student's number of correct answers for each tested target skill, the teacher will know whether a student has gained the necessary skill knowledge before the Unit Test is given. A low score on the Weekly Tests probably indicates a need for closer review of the student's performance and perhaps additional instruction. It is important to understand that these tests provide only one look at the student's progress and should be interpreted in conjunction with other assessments and the teacher's observation.

Using the Comprehension Target Skill Coverage Chart

To score target skill knowledge, use the Comprehension Target Skill Coverage Chart.

1. Make a copy of the appropriate Comprehension Target Skill Coverage chart for each student.

2. To score, circle the number of correct answers the student had for that skill on the appropriate Weekly Test.

3. Using the total number of correct answers for a skill, check the appropriate box under *Student Trend* to indicate whether or not the student has acquired the target skill knowledge. We recommend 90% correct as the criterion for skill acquisition at this level. Add any notes or observations that may be helpful to you and the student in later instruction.

Grade 2 — Comprehension Target Skill Coverage Chart

Student Name _____

Unit 1 Tested Skills	Weekly Test Locations	Number Correct	Student Trend
Literary Elements: Character/Setting	Weekly Test 1	0 1 2 3 4 5	_____ Skill knowledge acquired
	Weekly Test 3	0 1 2 3 4 5	_____ Skill needs further review
Main Idea and Supporting Details	Weekly Test 2	0 1 2 3 4 5	_____ Skill knowledge acquired
	Weekly Test 4	0 1 2 3 4 5	_____ Skill needs further review

Unit 2 Tested Skills	Weekly Test Locations	Number Correct	Student Trend
Compare and Contrast	Weekly Test 10	0 1 2 3 4 5	_____ Skill knowledge acquired _____ Skill needs further review
Cause and Effect	Weekly Test 6	0 1 2 3 4 5	_____ Skill knowledge acquired
	Weekly Test 9	0 1 2 3 4 5	_____ Skill needs further review

Grade 2 — Comprehension Target Skill Coverage Chart

Student Name _____

Unit 3 Tested Skills	Weekly Test Locations	Number Correct	Student Trend
Sequence	Weekly Test 14	0 1 2 3 4 5	____ Skill knowledge acquired ____ Skill needs further review
Author's Purpose	Weekly Test 7	0 1 2 3 4 5	____ Skill knowledge acquired ____ Skill needs further review
	Weekly Test 11	0 1 2 3 4 5	

Unit 4 Tested Skills	Weekly Test Locations	Number Correct	Student Trend
Fact and Opinion	Weekly Test 15	0 1 2 3 4 5	____ Skill knowledge acquired ____ Skill needs further review
	Weekly Test 18	0 1 2 3 4 5	
Draw Conclusions	Weekly Test 12	0 1 2 3 4 5	____ Skill knowledge acquired ____ Skill needs further review
	Weekly Test 16	0 1 2 3 4 5	

Grade 2 — Comprehension Target Skill Coverage Chart

Student Name _____

Unit 5 Tested Skills	Weekly Test Locations	Number Correct	Student Trend
Main Idea and Supporting Details	Weekly Test 2	0 1 2 3 4 5	
	Weekly Test 4	0 1 2 3 4 5	_____ Skill knowledge acquired
	Weekly Test 25	0 1 2 3 4 5	_____ Skill needs further review
Cause and Effect	Weekly Test 6	0 1 2 3 4 5	
	Weekly Test 9	0 1 2 3 4 5	_____ Skill knowledge acquired
	Weekly Test 22	0 1 2 3 4 5	_____ Skill needs further review

Unit 6 Tested Skills	Weekly Test Locations	Number Correct	Student Trend
Draw Conclusions	Weekly Test 12	0 1 2 3 4 5	
	Weekly Test 16	0 1 2 3 4 5	_____ Skill knowledge acquired
	Weekly Test 28	0 1 2 3 4 5	_____ Skill needs further review
Facts and Details	Weekly Test 5	0 1 2 3 4 5	
	Weekly Test 8	0 1 2 3 4 5	_____ Skill knowledge acquired
	Weekly Test 30	0 1 2 3 4 5	_____ Skill needs further review

Weekly Test Item Analysis—Grade 2

TEST	SECTION	ITEMS	SKILL
Weekly Test 1	**Vocabulary**	1–5	Understand and use new vocabulary
	Phonics	6–10	Short vowels and consonants
	Comprehension	11–15	◉ Character and setting
	Written Response	Look Back and Write	Respond to literature
Weekly Test 2	**Vocabulary**	1–5	Understand and use new vocabulary
	Phonics	6–10	Long vowels VCe
	Comprehension	11–15	◉ Main idea
	Written Response	Look Back and Write	Respond to literature
Weekly Test 3	**Vocabulary**	1–5	Understand and use new vocabulary
	Phonics	6–10	Consonant blends
	Comprehension	11–15	◉ Character and setting
	Written Response	Look Back and Write	Respond to literature
Weekly Test 4	**Vocabulary**	1–5	Understand and use new vocabulary
	Phonics	6–10	Inflected endings
	Comprehension	11–15	◉ Main idea
	Written Response	Look Back and Write	Respond to literature
Weekly Test 5	**Vocabulary**	1–5	Understand and use new vocabulary
	Phonics	6–10	Consonant digraphs
	Comprehension	11–15	◉ Facts and details
	Written Response	Look Back and Write	Respond to literature

Weekly Test Item Analysis—Grade 2

TEST	SECTION	ITEMS	SKILL
Weekly Test 6	**Vocabulary**	1–5	Understand and use new vocabulary
	Phonics	6–10	*r*-controlled vowels *ar, or, ore, oar*
	Comprehension	11–15	◉ Cause and effect
	Written Response	Look Back and Write	Respond to literature
Weekly Test 7	**Vocabulary**	1–5	Understand and use new vocabulary
	Phonics	6–10	Contractions
	Comprehension	11–15	◉ Author's purpose
	Written Response	Look Back and Write	Respond to literature
Weekly Test 8	**Vocabulary**	1–5	Understand and use new vocabulary
	Phonics	6–10	*r*-controlled vowels *er, ir, ur*
	Comprehension	11–15	◉ Facts and details
	Written Response	Look Back and Write	Respond to literature
Weekly Test 9	**Vocabulary**	1–5	Understand and use new vocabulary
	Phonics	6–10	Plurals
	Comprehension	11–15	◉ Cause and effect
	Written Response	Look Back and Write	Respond to literature
Weekly Test 10	**Vocabulary**	1–5	Understand and use new vocabulary
	Phonics	6–10	Vowel patterns *a, ai, ay*
	Comprehension	11–15	◉ Compare and contrast
	Written Response	Look Back and Write	Respond to literature

Weekly Test Item Analysis—Grade 2

TEST	SECTION	ITEMS	SKILL
Weekly Test 11	**Vocabulary**	1–5	Understand and use new vocabulary
	Phonics	6–10	Vowels patterns *e, ee, ea, y*
	Comprehension	11–15	◉ Author's purpose
	Written Response	Look Back and Write	Respond to literature
Weekly Test 12	**Vocabulary**	1–5	Understand and use new vocabulary
	Phonics	6–10	Vowels patterns *o, oa, ow*
	Comprehension	11–15	◉ Draw conclusions/ make inferences
	Written Response	Look Back and Write	Respond to literature
Weekly Test 13	**Vocabulary**	1–5	Understand and use new vocabulary
	Word Analysis	6–10	Compound words
	Comprehension	11–15	◉ Compare and contrast
	Written Response	Look Back and Write	Respond to literature
Weekly Test 14	**Vocabulary**	1–5	Understand and use new vocabulary
	Phonics	6–10	Vowel patterns *i, e, igh, y*
	Comprehension	11–15	◉ Sequence
	Written Response	Look Back and Write	Respond to literature
Weekly Test 15	**Vocabulary**	1–5	Understand and use new vocabulary
	Word Analysis	6–10	Comparative endings *-er, -est*
	Comprehension	11–15	◉ Fact and opinion
	Written Response	Look Back and Write	Respond to literature

Weekly Test Item Analysis—Grade 2

TEST	SECTION	ITEMS	SKILL
Weekly Test 16	**Vocabulary**	1–5	Understand and use new vocabulary
	Phonics	6–10	Final syllable -*le*
	Comprehension	11–15	◉ Draw conclusions/ make inferences
	Written Response	Look Back and Write	Respond to literature
Weekly Test 17	**Vocabulary**	1–5	Understand and use new vocabulary
	Phonics	6–10	Vowels patterns *oo, u*
	Comprehension	11–15	◉ Sequence
	Written Response	Look Back and Write	Respond to literature
Weekly Test 18	**Vocabulary**	1–5	Understand and use new vocabulary
	Phonics	6–10	Diphthongs *ou, ow, oi, oy*
	Comprehension	11–15	◉ Fact and opinion
	Written Response	Look Back and Write	Respond to literature
Weekly Test 19	**Vocabulary**	1–5	Understand and use new vocabulary
	Phonics	6–10	Syllable patterns
	Comprehension	11–15	◉ Plot and theme
	Written Response	Look Back and Write	Respond to literature
Weekly Test 20	**Vocabulary**	1–5	Understand and use new vocabulary
	Phonics	6–10	Vowel digraphs *oo, ue, ew*
	Comprehension	11–15	◉ Plot and theme
	Written Response	Look Back and Write	Respond to literature

Weekly Test Item Analysis—Grade 2

TEST	SECTION	ITEMS	SKILL
Weekly Test 21	**Vocabulary**	1–5	Understand and use new vocabulary
	Phonics	6–10	Suffixes *-ly, -iful, -er, -or, -ish*
	Comprehension	11–15	◉ Fact and opinion
	Written Response	Look Back and Write	Respond to literature
Weekly Test 22	**Vocabulary**	1–5	Understand and use new vocabulary
	Phonics	6–10	Prefixes *un-, re-, pre-, dis-*
	Comprehension	11–15	◉ Cause and effect
	Written Response	Look Back and Write	Respond to literature
Weekly Test 23	**Vocabulary**	1–5	Understand and use new vocabulary
	Phonics	6–10	Consonant patterns *kn, wr, gn, mb*
	Comprehension	11–15	◉ Plot and theme
	Written Response	Look Back and Write	Respond to literature
Weekly Test 24	**Vocabulary**	1–5	Understand and use new vocabulary
	Phonics	6–10	Consonant patterns *ph, gh, ck, ng*
	Comprehension	11–15	◉ Character and setting
	Written Response	Look Back and Write	Respond to literature
Weekly Test 25	**Vocabulary**	1–5	Understand and use new vocabulary
	Phonics	6–10	Vowel patterns *aw, au, au(gh), al*
	Comprehension	11–15	◉ Main idea
	Written Response	Look Back and Write	Respond to literature

Weekly Test Item Analysis—Grade 2

TEST	SECTION	ITEMS	SKILL
Weekly Test 26	**Vocabulary**	1–5	Understand and use new vocabulary
	Phonics	6–10	Inflected endings
	Comprehension	11–15	◉ Compare and contrast
	Written Response	Look Back and Write	Respond to literature
Weekly Test 27	**Vocabulary**	1–5	Understand and use new vocabulary
	Word Analysis	6–10	Abbreviations
	Comprehension	11–15	◉ Author's purpose
	Written Response	Look Back and Write	Respond to literature
Weekly Test 28	**Vocabulary**	1–5	Understand and use new vocabulary
	Word Analysis	6–10	Final syllables -*tion, -ture, -ion*
	Comprehension	11–15	◉ Draw conclusions/ make inferences
	Written Response	Look Back and Write	Respond to literature
Weekly Test 29	**Vocabulary**	1–5	Understand and use new vocabulary
	Word Analysis	6–10	Suffixes -*ness, -less*
	Comprehension	11–15	◉ Sequence
	Written Response	Look Back and Write	Respond to literature
Weekly Test 30	**Vocabulary**	1–5	Understand and use new vocabulary
	Word Analysis	6–10	Prefixes *mis-, mid-*
	Comprehension	11–15	◉ Facts and details
	Written Response	Look Back and Write	Respond to literature

Forms from Grade 2 Unit and End-of-Year Benchmark Tests Teacher's Manual

CLASS RECORD CHART
Grade 2 Unit Benchmark Tests

Teacher Name _____ Class _____

Student Name	Unit 1		Unit 2		Unit 3		Unit 4		Unit 5		Unit 6	
	Pt 1–4	Pt 5	Pt 1–4	Pt 5	Pt 1–4	Pt 5	Pt 1–4	Pt 5	Pt 1–4	Pt 5	Pt 1–4	Pt 5
1.												
2.												
3.												
4.												
5.												
6.												
7.												
8.												
9.												
10.												
11.												
12.												
13.												
14.												
15.												
16.												
17.												
18.												
19.												
20.												
21.												
22.												
23.												
24.												
25.												
26.												
27.												
28.												
29.												
30.												

Evaluation Chart: Grade 2 — Unit 1 Benchmark Test

Student Name _____ **Date** _____

Item	Tested Skill	Item Type*	Score (circle one)
Reading – Parts 1–4			
Item	**Tested Skill**	**Item Type***	**Score** (circle one)
Reading – Part 1: Comprehension			
1.	Literary elements: setting	L	0 1
2.	Literary elements: plot	I	0 1
3.	Literary elements: character	C	0 1
4.	Literary elements: plot	I	0 1
5.	Main idea and details	C	0 1
6.	Literary elements: plot	I	0 1
7.	Literary elements: theme	C	0 1
8.	Main idea and details	C	0 1
A.	Constructed-response text-to-self connection		0 1 2
9.	Literary elements: plot	I	0 1
10.	Main idea and details	L	0 1
11.	Literary elements: character	I	0 1
12.	Literary elements: setting	C	0 1
13.	Literary elements: plot	I	0 1
14.	Literary elements: character	I	0 1
15.	Literary elements: plot	I	0 1
16.	Literary elements: theme	C	0 1
B.	Constructed-response text-to-text connection		0 1 2
Reading – Part 2: High-Frequency Words			
17.	High-frequency words		0 1
18.	High-frequency words		0 1
19.	High-frequency words		0 1
20.	High-frequency words		0 1
21.	High-frequency words		0 1
22.	High-frequency words		0 1
Reading – Part 3: Phonics			
23.	Consonant blends: 2-letter initial; digraph *th*		0 1
24.	Consonant digraph: *ng*; g /j/		0 1
25.	Consonant blends: 2-letter ending, *nk*		0 1
26.	Consonant digraphs: *th, tch*		0 1
27.	Short *e: ea*		0 1
28.	Base words and ending -*ing* with spelling change		0 1

Reading – Part 3: Phonics (continued)		
29.	Consonant sounds: *s/z/, c/s/*	0 1
30.	Long vowel: CVCe	0 1
31.	Consonant blends: 3-letter blends	0 1
32.	Short vowels: CVC, CVCC, CCVC	0 1
33.	Inflected ending *-ing* with spelling change	0 1
34.	Consonant digraphs: *sh, ch*	0 1
Reading – Part 4: Writing Conventions		
35.	Sentences	0 1
36.	Sentences	0 1
37.	Sentences	0 1
38.	Sentences	0 1
39.	Sentences	0 1
40.	Sentences	0 1
Student's Reading Total Score/Total Possible Score		**/44**

*L = literal   I = inferential   C = critical analysis

Reading – Parts 1–4 percentage score: _____ ÷ 44 = _____ × 100 = _____%

(student's total score)   (percentage score)

Writing – Part 5

Writing Score (Complete one.)   _____/6   _____/5   _____/4   _____/3

Notes/Observations:

Evaluation Chart: Grade 2 — Unit 2 Benchmark Test

Student Name _____ **Date** _____

Item	Tested Skill	Item Type*	Score (circle one)		
Reading – Parts 1–4					
Reading – Part 1: Comprehension					
1.	Literary elements: setting	I	0	1	
2.	Sequence	L	0	1	
3.	Compare and contrast	I	0	1	
4.	Cause and effect	I	0	1	
5.	Main idea and details	I	0	1	
6.	Literary elements: character	I	0	1	
7.	Cause and effect	I	0	1	
8.	Cause and effect	I	0	1	
A.	Constructed-response text-to-self connection		0	1	2
9.	Literary elements: plot	L	0	1	
10.	Literary elements: character	I	0	1	
11.	Cause and effect	I	0	1	
12.	Compare and contrast	I	0	1	
13.	Cause and effect	I	0	1	
14.	Compare and contrast	I	0	1	
15.	Literary elements: theme	C	0	1	
16.	Compare and contrast	I	0	1	
B.	Constructed-response text-to-text connection		0	1	2
Reading – Part 2: High-Frequency Words					
17.	High-frequency words		0	1	
18.	High-frequency words		0	1	
19.	High-frequency words		0	1	
20.	High-frequency words		0	1	
21.	High-frequency words		0	1	
22.	High-frequency words		0	1	
Reading – Part 3: Phonics					
23.	Long *a: ay*		0	1	
24.	Plural *-ies* (change y to i)		0	1	
25.	r-Controlled *ir*		0	1	
26.	Contractions: *'re*		0	1	
27.	r-Controlled *or*		0	1	
28.	Plural *-es*		0	1	

Reading – Part 3: Phonics (continued)

29.	Contraction *'m*	0	1
30.	Long *a: ai*	0	1
31.	Contraction *'ll*	0	1
32.	r-Controlled *ore*	0	1
33.	r-Controlled *ar:* syllables VCCV	0	1
34.	Contraction *'s*	0	1
Student's Regrouping Multiple-Choice Score/Total Possible Score		_____ /34	

Reading – Part 4: Writing Conventions

35.	Nouns	0	1
36.	Nouns	0	1
37.	Nouns	0	1
38.	Nouns	0	1
39.	Possessive nouns	0	1
40.	Possessive nouns	0	1
Student's Reading Total Score/Total Possible Score		_____ /44	

*L = literal   I = inferential   C = critical analysis

Regrouping (Reading – Parts 1–3) percentage: _____ ÷ 34 = _____ × 100 = _____%
(student's score)   (percentage score)

Reading – Parts 1–4 percentage score: _____ ÷ 44 = _____ × 100 = _____%
(student's total score)   (percentage score)

Writing – Part 5

Writing Score (Complete one.) _____/6 _____/5 _____/4 _____/3

Notes/Observations:

Evaluation Chart: Grade 2 — Unit 3 Benchmark Test

Student Name _____ Date _____

Item	Tested Skill	Item Type*	Score (circle one)		
Reading – Parts 1–4					
Reading – Part 1: Comprehension					
1.	Cause and effect	I	0	1	
2.	Sequence	L	0	1	
3.	Literary elements: character	I	0	1	
4.	Sequence	I	0	1	
5.	Sequence	I	0	1	
6.	Author's purpose	C	0	1	
7.	Draw conclusions	I	0	1	
8.	Literary elements: plot	C	0	1	
A.	Constructed-response text-to-self connection		0	1	2
9.	Main idea and details	C	0	1	
10.	Draw conclusions	C	0	1	
11.	Draw conclusions	I	0	1	
12.	Sequence	I	0	1	
13.	Sequence	I	0	1	
14.	Sequence	L	0	1	
15.	Main idea and details	I	0	1	
16.	Author's purpose	C	0	1	
B.	Constructed-response text-to-text connection		0	1	2
Reading – Part 2: High-Frequency Words					
17.	High-frequency words		0	1	
18.	High-frequency words		0	1	
19.	High-frequency words		0	1	
20.	High-frequency words		0	1	
21.	High-frequency words		0	1	
22.	High-frequency words		0	1	
Reading – Part 3: Phonics					
23.	Long *i: ie*		0	1	
24.	Comparative ending *er*		0	1	
25.	Compound words		0	1	
26.	Long *e: y*		0	1	
27.	Comparative ending *est*		0	1	
28.	Long *e: ee*		0	1	

Reading – Part 3: Phonics (continued)			
29.	Long *i: i* in iCC	0	1
30.	Long *o: o* in oCC; syllables VCV (open)	0	1
31.	Long *e: ea*	0	1
32.	Long *o: ow*	0	1
33.	Compound words	0	1
34.	Long *i: y*	0	1
Student's Regrouping Multiple-Choice Score/Total Possible Score _____/34			
Reading – Part 4: Writing Conventions			
35.	Verbs	0	1
36.	Verbs	0	1
37.	Verbs	0	1
38.	Verbs	0	1
39.	Verbs	0	1
40.	Verbs	0	1
Student's Reading Total Score/Total Possible Score _____/44			

*L = literal   I = inferential   C = critical analysis

Regrouping (Reading – Parts 1–3) percentage: _____ $\div$ 34 = _____ $\times$ 100 = _____%

(student's score)   (percentage score)

Reading – Parts 1–4 percentage score: _____ $\div$ 44 = _____ $\times$ 100 = _____%

(student's total score)   (percentage score)

Writing – Part 5

Writing Score (Complete one.) _____/6 _____/5 _____/4 _____/3

Notes/Observations:

Evaluation Chart: Grade 2 — Unit 4 Benchmark Test

Student Name _____ **Date** _____

Item	Tested Skill	Item Type*	Score (circle one)		
Reading – Parts 1–4					
Reading – Part 1: Comprehension					
1.	Compare and contrast	L	0	1	
2.	Compare and contrast	I	0	1	
3.	Fact and opinion	I	0	1	
4.	Fact and opinion	I	0	1	
5.	Main idea	I	0	1	
6.	Fact and opinion	I	0	1	
7.	Draw conclusions	C	0	1	
8.	Fact and opinion	I	0	1	
A.	Constructed-response text-to-self connection		0	1	2
9.	Draw conclusions	I	0	1	
10.	Literary element: theme	C	0	1	
11.	Draw conclusions	I	0	1	
12.	Literary element: plot	I	0	1	
13.	Literary element: character	I	0	1	
14.	Draw conclusions	I	0	1	
15.	Compare and contrast	I	0	1	
16.	Author's purpose	C	0	1	
B.	Constructed-response text-to-text connection		0	1	
Reading – Part 2: Vocabulary					
17.	Context clues: multiple-meaning words		0	1	
18.	Word structures: suffix *-ful*		0	1	
19.	Word structures: prefix *un-*		0	1	
20.	Antonyms		0	1	
21.	Context clues: multiple-meaning words		0	1	
22.	Context clues: multiple-meaning words		0	1	
Reading – Part 3: Phonics					
23.	Syllables: consonant + *le*		0	1	
24.	Vowel *oo* (short /oo/)		0	1	
25.	Vowel diphthong *ou, ow* /ou/		0	1	
26.	Vowel diphthong *oi, oy* /oi/		0	1	
27.	Syllables: two consonants together		0	1	
28.	Vowel pattern *ew, ue* (long /oo/)		0	1	

Reading – Part 3: Phonics (continued)			
29.	Vowel diphthong *ou, ow* /ou/	0	1
30.	Vowel pattern *ew, oo* (long /oo/)	0	1
31.	Vowel *u* as in *put*	0	1
32.	Syllables: consonant + *le*	0	1
33.	Vowel diphthong *ou* /ou/	0	1
34.	Syllables: digraph/diphthong combination	0	1
Student's Regrouping Multiple-Choice Score/Total Possible Score _____/34			
Reading – Part 4: Writing Conventions			
35.	Adverbs	0	1
36.	Adjectives	0	1
37.	Adverbs	0	1
38.	Adverbs	0	1
39.	Adjectives	0	1
40.	Adjectives	0	1
Student's Reading Total Score/Total Possible Score _____/44			

*L = literal   I = inferential   C = critical analysis

Regrouping (Reading – Parts 1–3) percentage: _____ ÷ 34 = _____ × 100 = _____%
                                         (student's score)   (percentage score)

Reading – Parts 1–4 percentage score: _____ ÷ 44 = _____ × 100 = _____%
                                      (student's total score)   (percentage score)

Writing – Part 5
Writing Score (Complete one.)   _____/6   _____/5   _____/4   _____/3
Notes/Observations:

Evaluation Chart: Grade 2 — Unit 5 Benchmark Test

Student Name _____ **Date** _____

Reading – Parts 1–4			
Item	**Tested Skill**	**Item Type***	**Score** (circle one)
Reading – Part 1: Comprehension			
1.	Literary element: plot	L	0　　1
2.	Cause and effect	I	0　　1
3.	Main idea	I	0　　1
4.	Facts and details	L	0　　1
5.	Cause and effect	L	0　　1
6.	Literary element: theme	C	0　　1
7.	Author's purpose	I	0　　1
8.	Main idea	I	0　　1
A.	Constructed-response text-to-self connection		0　　1　　2
9.	Sequence	L	0　　1
10.	Cause and effect	L	0　　1
11.	Cause and effect	L	0　　1
12.	Main idea	I	0　　1
13.	Literary element: plot	I	0　　1
14.	Main idea	I	0　　1
15.	Literary element: theme	C	0　　1
16.	Author's purpose	C	0　　1
B.	Constructed-response text-to-text connection		0　　1　　2
Reading – Part 2: Vocabulary			
17.	Word structure: compound words		0　　1
18.	Word structure: suffixes		0　　1
19.	Word structure: compound words		0　　1
20.	Word structure: suffixes		0　　1
21.	Word structure: compound words		0　　1
22.	Word structure: suffixes		0　　1
Reading – Part 3: Phonics			
23.	Silent consonant *kn*		0　　1
24.	Silent consonant *wr*		0　　1
25.	Vowel *al*		0　　1
26.	Suffix *-ly*		0　　1
27.	Prefix *un-*		0　　1

Reading – Part 3: Phonics (continued)			
28.	Silent consonant *gn*	0	1
29.	Suffix *-ful*	0	1
30.	Consonant pattern *ph* /f/	0	1
31.	Suffix *-er* (agent)	0	1
32.	Vowel *aw*	0	1
33.	Prefix *re-*	0	1
34.	Consonant pattern *gh* /f/	0	1
Student's Regrouping Multiple-Choice Score/Total Possible Score _____ /34			
Reading – Part 4: Writing Conventions			
35.	Pronouns	0	1
36.	Pronouns	0	1
37.	Contractions	0	1
38.	Contractions	0	1
39.	Pronouns	0	1
40.	Pronouns	0	1
Student's Reading Total Score/Total Possible Score _____ /44			

*L = literal   I = inferential   C = critical analysis

Regrouping (Reading – Parts 1–3) percentage: _____ ÷ 34 = _____ × 100 = _____%
                                                          (student's score)   (percentage score)

Reading – Parts 1–4 percentage score: _____ ÷ 44 = _____ × 100 = _____%
                                                  (student's total score)   (percentage score)

Writing – Part 5

Writing Score (Complete one.) _____ /6 _____ /5 _____ /4 _____ /3

Notes/Observations:

Evaluation Chart: Grade 2 — Unit 6 Benchmark Test

Student Name _____ **Date** _____

	Reading – Parts 1–4		
Item	**Tested Skill**	**Item Type***	**Score** (circle one)
Reading – Part 1: Comprehension			
1.	Compare and contrast	I	0 1
2.	Main idea	I	0 1
3.	Cause and effect	I	0 1
4.	Fact and opinion	I	0 1
5.	Draw conclusions	I	0 1
6.	Cause and effect	L	0 1
7.	Facts and details	L	0 1
8.	Draw conclusions	I	0 1
A.	Constructed-response text-to-self connection		0 1 2
9.	Cause and effect	I	0 1
10.	Draw conclusions	I	0 1
11.	Draw conclusions	I	0 1
12.	Main idea	I	0 1
13.	Fact and opinion	I	0 1
14.	Cause and effect	I	0 1
15.	Compare and contrast	I	0 1
16.	Author's purpose	I	0 1
B.	Constructed-response text-to-text connection		0 1 2
Reading – Part 2: Vocabulary			
17.	Context clues: multiple-meaning words		0 1
18.	Context clues: multiple-meaning words		0 1
19.	Context clues: multiple-meaning words		0 1
20.	Context clues: unfamiliar words		0 1
21.	Context clues: unfamiliar words		0 1
22.	Context clues: unfamiliar words		0 1
Reading – Part 3: Phonics			
23.	Base words and ending -est		0 1
24.	Base words and ending -ed		0 1
25.	Prefix mid-		0 1
26.	Common syllable -tion		0 1
27.	Abbreviations		0 1
28.	Suffix -ness		0 1

Reading – Part 3: Phonics (continued)

29.	Common syllable *-tion*	0	1
30.	Suffix *-less*	0	1
31.	Suffix *-able*	0	1
32.	Base words and ending *-er*	0	1
33.	Base words and ending *-ing*	0	1
34.	Base words and ending *-ed*	0	1

Student's Regrouping Multiple-Choice Score/Total Possible Score _____/34

Reading – Part 4: Writing Conventions

35.	Capitalization	0	1
36.	Punctuation	0	1
37.	Punctuation	0	1
38.	Punctuation	0	1
39.	Capitalization	0	1
40.	Punctuation	0	1

Student's Reading Total Score/Total Possible Score _____/44

*L = literal   I = inferential   C = critical analysis

Regrouping (Reading – Parts 1–3) percentage: _____ ÷ 34 = _____ × 100 = _____%

                              (student's score)   (percentage score)

Reading – Parts 1–4 percentage score: _____ ÷ 44 = _____ × 100 = _____%

                        (student's total score)   (percentage score)

Writing – Part 5

Writing Score (Complete one.) _____/6 _____/5 _____/4 _____/3

Notes/Observations:

Evaluation Chart: Grade 2 — End-of-Year Benchmark Test

Student Name _____ Date _____

Reading – Parts 1–4						
Item	Tested Skill	Item Type*	Score (circle one)	Item	Tested Skill	Score (circle one)
Reading – Part 1: Comprehension				28.	Context clues: multiple-meaning words	0 1
1.	Literary element: character	I	0 1	29.	Context clues: unfamiliar words	0 1
2.	Main idea	I	0 1	30.	Word structure: suffix -*ly*	0 1
3.	Compare and contrast	L	0 1	31.	Context clues: multiple-meaning words	0 1
4.	Sequence	L	0 1	32.	Context clues: unfamiliar words	0 1
5.	Literary element: setting	I	0 1	33.	Context clues: antonyms	0 1
6.	Cause and effect	L	0 1	**Reading – Part 3: Phonics**		
7.	Literary element: plot	I	0 1	34.	Long *i: igh*	0 1
8.	Literary element: theme	C	0 1	35.	Vowel diphthong *ou, ow* /ou/	0 1
9.	Main idea	I	0 1	36.	Vowel patterns: *ew* /oo/ (*moon*)	0 1
10.	Fact and opinion	C	0 1	37.	Consonant pattern *gh* /f/	0 1
11.	Main idea	I	0 1	38.	Consonant pattern *ph* /f/	0 1
12.	Draw conclusions	I	0 1	39.	Long *e: ee, ea*	0 1
13.	Compare and contrast	L	0 1	40.	Vowel diphthong *oi, oy* /oi/	0 1
14.	Author's purpose	C	0 1	41.	Long *o:* CVCe, *oa*	0 1
15.	Draw conclusions	I	0 1	42.	Base words and ending -*ing*	0 1
16.	Facts and details	L	0 1	43.	Syllables: multisyllabic words, VCCV + suffix	0 1
A.	Constructed-response item		0 1 2	44.	Comparative ending -*er*	0 1
17.	Author's purpose	C	0 1	45.	Ending -*ed*	0 1
18.	Draw conclusions	I	0 1	46.	Contraction '*s*	0 1
19.	Literary element: setting	L	0 1	47.	Suffix -*ness*	0 1
20.	Cause and effect	I	0 1	48.	Contraction '*ll*	0 1
21.	Cause and effect	I	0 1	49.	Silent consonant *kn*	0 1
22.	Compare and contrast	L	0 1	50.	Prefix *mid-*	0 1
23.	Sequence	I	0 1	51.	Silent consonant *wr*	0 1
24.	Cause and effect	I	0 1	**Reading – Part 4: Writing Conventions**		
B.	Constructed-response item		0 1 2	52.	Verbs	0 1
Reading – Part 2: Vocabulary				53.	Pronouns	0 1
25.	Context clues: unfamiliar words		0 1	54.	Adjectives	0 1
26.	Word structure: compound words		0 1	55.	Verbs	0 1
27.	Context clues: antonyms		0 1	56.	Verbs	0 1

Reading – Part 4: Writing Conventions (continued)						
57.	Punctuation	0	1	59.	Punctuation	0　1
58.	Punctuation	0	1	60.	Punctuation	0　1
Student's Reading Total Score/Total Possible Score					_____/64	

Reading – Parts 1–4 percentage score: _____ ÷ 64 = _____ × 100 = _____%

　　　　　　　　　　　　　　　　　(student's total score)　　　　　　　　　　　　　　(percentage score)

Writing – Part 5

Writing Score (Complete one.)　_____/6　_____/5　_____/4　_____/3

Notes/Observations:

Monitor Progress Passages

from
Second Grade Teacher's Editions

Name _____

Read the Sentences

1. Sad Sam Willis had bad luck up in the country.

2. Our friend Hank got sick yet did not zip up.

3. Nick was up in front, but Justin sat in back.

4. Will that beautiful duck get wet muck on its head?

5. Somewhere Tess got ink in her hot pink jacket pocket.

6. Did someone pack ham in the big red picnic basket?

| MONITOR PROGRESS | • Fluency
• Short vowels and consonants
• High-frequency words | |

Name _____

Read the Story

The New Friend

    Jack walked slowly home from school. "Why   7
did we have to move here?" he grumbled.   15

    Jack's third day at his new school had been the   25
same as the other days. No one said anything to   35
Jack. Everyone else had friends. Jack did not. He   44
wished for a friend to eat lunch with. On his way   55
home, the lonely boy stared at his feet as he walked.   66
A girl yelled when Jack almost ran into her.   75

    The girl looked at him. "My name is Ming. I saw   86
you in school. Do you live on this block?"   95

    Jack was surprised that she had talked to him.   104
"Yes," he said. "My house is around the corner."   113

    The girl nodded her head. "I live on the next   123
street. I'm meeting some friends to play soccer.   131
Want to come?"   134

    "Sure!" Jack said. Maybe he'd make some   141
friends after all.   144

MONITOR PROGRESS
- Check Fluency
- Character and Setting

Read the Sentences

1. Can the nice woman escape in time?

2. Six fat mice live in a fuzz pile at his gate.

3. Miss Ring will work at home until it is quite late.

4. Did Mom invite Jane to move back home?

5. Dustin will ride everywhere on his bike in his cape.

6. Pete can run five huge machines on his job.

7. Jake will use red pencil to make his world map.

MONITOR PROGRESS
- Fluency
- Long Vowels VCe
- High-frequency words

Exploring Space • **81e**

Name _____

Read the Story

Going into Space

    Do you want to go to new places? Do you like   11
fast rides? If you said yes to all these things, then   22
you can go into space. Some people who went into   32
space began planning for it when they were your   41
age. You can too.   45

    You must go to school for a long time. You will   56
need to know math. You will learn about our Sun.   66
You will learn about other stars too.   73

    What else must you know before going into   81
space? You will need to know how machines in   90
space work. What if something breaks? You must   98
know what to do. Maybe you will take some mice   108
with you. Then you can see how they do in space.   119

    Who knows? One day you might even take a   128
space walk. What a trip that would be!   136

MONITOR PROGRESS
• Check Fluency
• Main Idea and Details

Read the Sentences

1. Father will set the huge crate in his pick-up truck.

2. The black bear can nap in its still, safe den.

3. Big Jon swung his ax straight at the wide trunk.

4. Mike couldn't make himself stop.

5. Bess did love the splendid spring sun!

6. Will Dad help Nick build his big race track?

7. Mother kept us at home and inside until five.

MONITOR PROGRESS
- Fluency
- Consonant blends
- High-frequency words

Henry and Mudge • **113e**

Name _____

Read the Story

A World in the City

Grace and Trent were twins who lived in a   9
skyscraper in a big city. One day their mother's   18
sister, Fran, came to visit.   23

"How is school going?" she asked.   29

"We are reading about exploring the world,"   36
Grace said. "We learned about stars."   42

"Grace and I can't explore the world," Trent said.   51
"We live in the city! What can we explore here?"   61

Fran said, "Well, we have trees here. This place   70
has birds to watch and the sky too. Flowers grow in   81
the park out front, but best of all, we have a giant   93
lake!" She went over to a wide window. "Tell me   103
what you can see from here."   109

"I see the sun and some small clouds. I see   119
birds flying above the lake too," said Grace.   127

"Oh, I get it!" Trent yelled. "We can explore the   137
world that is right outside our window!"   144

MONITOR PROGRESS
- Check Fluency
- Character and Setting

Read the Sentences

1. Zeke rubbed his eyes in the blazing sun and dust.

2. Spike is getting himself a full glass and drinking it.

3. Five animals jumped the fence on his land and escaped.

4. Dad races to his bus stop early and stands in line.

5. Grace dived in the water, rose up, and winked at us.

6. Glen has invited us swimming, but it is not warm.

MONITOR PROGRESS
- Fluency
- Inflected Endings
- High-frequency words

Name _____

Read the Story

A Walk in the Woods

Take a walk in the woods and explore nature.   9
The woods have many kinds of trees. Look at the   19
bark on a tree. It might be smooth. It might have   30
bumps. Bark protects the tree like your skin   38
protects you. Branches have many leaves. The   45
leaves make food to help the tree grow.   53

Now close your eyes and listen. Something is   61
moving in the trees. Look up into a tree's branches.   71
Birds and other animals live in the trees.   79

Squirrels live in trees. They build their nests   87
there. A squirrel has thick fur and a long tail. It eats   99
nuts, fruit, and seeds. A squirrel has sharp teeth to   109
help it break open nuts and seeds.   116

Look at the bottom of the tree. Ants, worms, and   126
other small animals live here. Each tree in the   135
woods has another world for you to explore.   143

MONITOR PROGRESS
• Check Fluency
• Main Idea and Details

Name _____

Read the Sentences

1. Brad and Justin learn that fish makes a fine lunch.

2. His big white dog has gone to chase cats and fetch sticks.

3. King Mitchell sat on his rich throne and ruled very well.

4. Seth will shake fresh spice on his plate, though it is hot.

5. Place nice, wide chicken pieces in that sandwich.

6. Chuck is fishing in Glass Pond together with Len.

7. Kate thinks sleds are quite thrilling and rides them often.

MONITOR PROGRESS
- Fluency
- Consonant Digraphs
- High-frequency Words

Name _____

Read the Story

Little Bear

Characters:	Little Bear	White Bird

5

(Little Bear looks up at a beautiful, huge tree.)   14

Little Bear: Mom said I can learn to go up there. I   26

think I can do it, but I must get the right branch.   38

(A white bird flies into the tree.)   45

Little Bear: I wish I could fly into the tree like you.   57

White Bird: Bears climb trees. You just have to try!   67

(Little Bear tries to climb up and tumbles down.)   76

Little Bear: I'm too short! I can't climb this tree!   86

White Bird: You must try, try, and try again.   95

Little Bear: I'll just grit my teeth and do it.   105

(Little Bear tries climbing the tree but keeps falling.)   114

Little Bear: I'll try one last time. I'll grab the trunk   125

with my claws. I'll hold on with my feet. I'll reach for   137

the branch. There! I did it! I learned how to climb a   149

tree!   150

MONITOR PROGRESS
• Check Fluency
• Facts and Details

Name _____

Read the Sentences

1. His family dwells on that farm in the north land.

2. I heard a large spotted cat roar in its cage.

3. Pull on this cord hard and then stop.

4. Listen as Kate informs us which chore we must do.

5. Will did not break his arm, but it is sore.

6. Barb helped Chan in his garden not once but twice.

MONITOR PROGRESS
- Fluency
- *r*-Controlled *ar, or, ore, oar*
- High-frequency words

Name _____

Read the Story

Bart's Problem

Kim sat on the grass with her book.	8
"Will you help me pick corn?" asked Dad.	16
"Yes, I will help you do that," said Kim.	25
"It will rain soon," said Dad. "So we must	34
be quick!"	36
"I can work fast," said Kim. "May I ride Bart to	47
the field?"	49
That is not a good idea," said Dad.	57
"But Bart is a fast horse," said Kim. "He is our	68
best horse."	70
"I do not think that is wise," said Dad.	79
"But Bart can get me there before it rains,"	88
said Kim.	90
Dad smiled. "I do not think Bart will be a help,"	101
he said. "Bart has a bad habit. He likes to eat corn!"	113
"Oh!" said Kim. "I forgot about that!"	120

MONITOR PROGRESS
- Check Fluency
- Cause and Effect

Name _____

Read the Sentences

1. I'm glad that they'll win second place.

2. "It's great fun!" Bart yells as he's jumping on his bed.

3. It certainly wasn't the best race that she's run.

4. Mom doesn't laugh when we haven't picked up.

5. That's the worst lime punch you'll drink.

6. I'm not an artist, and Brett isn't either.

7. Carl can't help thinking you're smart and she's nice.

MONITOR PROGRESS
- Fluency
- Contractions
- High-frequency words

Name _____

Read the Story

Mark Can't Skate

    Mark put on his skates and stepped on the ice.   10
"This is not going to work," he said to Jack. "I'll   21
never learn to skate."   25

    "You have to let go of the rail," said Jack.   35

    "I'll fall if I let go. I am too scared," said Mark.   47
Then Mark's sister skated past him. "She's such a   56
good skater," he said.   60

    "Let go of the rail!" she called.   67

    Next, Mark saw a lady helping other skaters.   75
"Who's that?" Mark asked.   79

    "She's a skating teacher," said Jack. "I'm sure   87
she'll help you. Let's ask her."   93

    The skating teacher came over to Mark. "First you   102
have to let go of the rail," she said.   111

    Mark tried to be brave. He let go and began to   122
skate around the ice. He did fall, but it wasn't bad.   133
"I'm skating!" he said. "I guess I can't hold on to   144
things that can't help me!"   149

MONITOR PROGRESS   • Check Fluency   • Author's Purpose

Name _____

Read the Sentences

1. The girl raced on hot sand toward the surf.

2. Did Kirk get enough bread and milk at supper?

3. Which word did Kim note first on her list?

4. While a bird chirped above his head, Luke slept.

5. Dan penned his whole horse herd in that third corral.

6. Herman fixed that chipped curb just a short time ago.

MONITOR PROGRESS
- Fluency
- *r*-controlled *er, ir, ur*
- High-frequency words

Name _____

Read the Story

The Biggest Birds

Ostriches are very big birds. A male ostrich can   9
weigh as much as 330 pounds. He may grow to be   20
9 feet tall. These birds do not fly. But they sure can   32
run! They can run up to 45 miles per hour. That helps   44
them get away from their enemies. Ostriches also   52
use their strong legs to kick their enemies.   60

Some ostriches live in large herds. There might   68
be 100 or more birds in a herd. Others live in small   80
groups. Each group has a male and female leader.   89
The female is called the "main hen." An ostrich hen   99
lays a very large egg. The egg weighs almost three   109
pounds. How big is that? It is about the size of a   121
football.   122

Ostriches like to eat plants. But they are willing   131
to eat other things. So they sometimes eat small   140
animals, as well. These birds live a long time. They   150
can live between 30 and 40 years.   157

MONITOR PROGRESS
• Check Fluency
• Facts and Details

Name _____

Read the Sentences

1. People sat on park benches and ate sandwiches.

2. I shall get nice dishes and glasses for Mom and Dad.

3. The red roses and pink pansies had a pleasant smell.

4. When foxes scared them, five smart bunnies hid.

5. Mike bought bunches of grapes for his picnic with us.

6. Her sign read that Kate is selling puppies and kittens.

7. Thunder probably woke up her fillies and mules.

MONITOR PROGRESS
- Fluency
- Plurals with -s, -es, -ies
- High-frequency words

Name _____

Read the Story

Animal Wishes

Owl asked her friends to gather around. Summer   8
had almost arrived, and she wanted to hear their   17
wishes. "Bees, what is your wish?" asked Owl.   25
"We wish for lots of flowers," said the bees.   34
"Please tell us why," said Owl.   40
"The flowers will help us make honey for other   49
animals," said the bees.   53
"That is a good wish," said Owl.   60
Then the turtles told Owl their wish. "We wish   69
for lots of rain," they said.   75
"Please tell us why," said Owl.   81
"The rain will fill the ponds and lakes," said the   91
turtles. "Then all the animals will have water to   100
drink and places to swim."   105
"That is a fine wish," said Owl.   112
Then the birds told Owl their wish. "We wish   121
for lots of berry bushes. Then we will have   130
berries to eat, and we will chirp all day. The   140
other animals like to hear birds chirp."   147
"I like that wish," said Owl.   153
Finally, one little bird asked Owl what she   161
wished for. "I wish that all of your wishes come   171
true!" said Owl.   174
"Thank you, Owl! We love you!" cried all   182
the animals.   184

MONITOR
PROGRESS

• Check Fluency
• Cause and Effect

Name _____

Read the Sentences

1. Everybody felt bad that Jay did not stay with us.

2. Luke waited at the train stop for one more minute.

3. I promise I'll wipe that basin after playing with Jane.

4. His red apron is on a nail behind that huge desk.

5. Fern brought in her mail and paper.

6. This main door is not locked on Thursday.

7. Ray is sorry that he didn't pay his gas bill.

MONITOR PROGRESS
- Fluency
- Vowel patterns *a, ai, ay*
- High-frequency words

One Good Turn • **345e**

Name _____

Read the Story

The Ant and the Grasshopper

Long ago, there lived an ant and a grasshopper.   9
The ant worked hard. Each summer morning, he   17
woke up early. Then he gathered food for winter.   26
The grasshopper, however, slept late each   32
morning. Then he played all day long. Often, the   41
grasshopper invited the ant to play. But the ant   50
always refused. "I must gather food for winter,"   58
he said.   60
    The grasshopper always made fun of him. "You   68
are silly to worry about winter," said the grasshopper.   77
"Today is such a pretty day!"   83
    Soon fall came. The ant worked even harder.   91
But the grasshopper kept on playing. "Winter is   99
coming," warned the ant. But the grasshopper   106
ignored him.   108
    Then winter arrived with a big snowstorm. The   116
ant rested in his cozy home. He had plenty of   126
food. However, the grasshopper was cold and   133
hungry. So he went to see the ant. "May I have   144
some food?" he asked.   148
    "I am sorry," said the ant. "I do not have   158
enough for both of us. You played all summer   167
while I worked. Perhaps you have learned a   175
lesson."   176

MONITOR PROGRESS   • Check Fluency
• Compare and Contrast

Name _____

Read the Sentences

1. Please watch for facts and details when reading.

2. Which eager team won that relay race?

3. That quaint village borders a deep, rocky stream.

4. Jenny cleaned her dirty soccer shoe.

5. Steven will plant bean seeds in science class.

6. We guess that the teacup in this sink is clean.

7. Ask that pretty lady when she'll be finished.

MONITOR PROGRESS
- Fluency
- Vowel patterns *e, ee, ea, y*
- High-frequency words

Pearl and Wagner • **381e**

Name _____

Read the Story

Sailing the Sea

A friend asked me if I would like to go sailing on   12
the sea. I was eager to go. My dream was to see at   25
least one whale.   28

We made many plans for our trip. We shopped   37
for enough food to last a week. We would be fixing   48
all our meals on a little stove inside the boat. We   59
rolled up our sleeping bags so they would take up   69
little room inside the tiny boat. Then we looked at a   80
map of the sea and planned where we would go.   90

At last, we were ready to set sail. A light wind   101
filled our sails. We took off at an easy speed. Sea   112
birds screamed as they flew by us. Seals jumped   120
off rocks. They looked for food in the deep water.   131

Each day on the sea was a joy. Then on our   142
last day, it happened. Three whales leaped out of   154
the water in front of us. My dream had come true.   162

MONITOR PROGRESS
- Check Fluency
- Author's Purpose

Name _____

Read the Sentences

1. Take it slow and use this moment to locate an answer.

2. Coach Ray told Bob to wash his cut elbow.

3. His picture of an old, groaning goat made us grin.

4. Snow is piled up way past the first row of windows at school.

5. Her parents own that nice hotel on North Road.

6. Company just came, so bring over loads of games!

7. That faraway yellow glow on the dark lake is a lamp on her boat.

MONITOR PROGRESS
- Fluency
- Vowel patterns *o, oa, ow*
- High-frequency words

Dear Juno • **417e**

Name _____

Read the Story

Goby the Goat

There once was an old goat named Goby. He had   10
spent his whole life eating grass. Goby roamed from   19
field to field to find the best grass to eat. One day,   31
Goby stopped eating. He had had so much grass that   41
he could not eat another bite.   47

Logan was Goby's owner. Logan was afraid his goat   56
was sick. So Logan took Goby to the vet. The vet told   68
Logan to give Goby other food.   74

Sometimes Logan gave Goby oats in a bowl. Other   83
times he would throw him a tomato or potato. He even   94
tried giving him fruit. Goby just groaned and turned up   104
his nose.   106

One day, Logan gave his goat most of his toast. It   117
had butter and jam on it. Goby tasted it. From then on,   129
Goby ate only toast with butter and jam.   137

MONITOR PROGRESS
• Check Fluency
• Draw Conclusions

Read the Sentences

1. I believe that meatloaf is best on homemade bread.

2. That blackbird just caught bugs on this riverbank.

3. Trent finally got a skateboard for his birthday.

4. Mom has been on five seacoasts during her lifetime.

5. Whatever can this postcard from Granddad mean?

6. Today we had sunshine after three short rainstorms.

7. Jo and her playmate will meet at lunchtime tomorrow.

MONITOR PROGRESS
- Fluency
- Compound words
- High-frequency words

Name _____

Read the Story

Snowstorm Fun

    Sometimes when there is a big snowstorm,   7
school is called off. School is great, but I like having   18
fun on a snow day more than working at school.   28

    Mom calls a babysitter on snow days. I like it   38
best when my grandmother gets that call. That's   46
because Grandma loves baking!   50

    Grandma and I make homemade bread   56
together. I stir everything. We take the small ball of   66
dough and put it in a warm place where it will rise to   79
twice its size. Then it will be ready to bake. We   90
work so hard that I get hot and my face turns red.   102

    Now it's time to go outside. I wear a coat and   112
hat because I don't want to get too cold. Soon   123
snowflakes cover my coat. I build a giant snowman.   132
The cold turns my face red again. Grandma calls   141
me inside. The kitchen feels warm. I eat the hot   151
bread we made. Yum!   155

MONITOR PROGRESS
- Check Fluency
- Compare and Contrast

Name _____

Read the Sentences

1. Each wildcat hides alone behind grass or rocks.

2. Dad will buy three neckties and more items.

3. Her daughters made three pies for the bake sale
   on Friday.

4. Half the streetlights came on at twilight.

5. Lightning is flashing over many homes and highways.

6. Spiders make webs with their own silky fiber.

7. His youngest girl wore a tiny yellow nylon jacket.

MONITOR PROGRESS
- Fluency
- Vowel patterns *i, ie, igh, y*
- High-frequency words

Rosa and Blanca • **479e**

Name _____

Read the Story

A Tiger at Night

Tiger woke up from a nap. "I'm hungry," he   9
thought. "I should find some food tonight."   16

Tiger spied a wild pig and thought that the pig   26
would make a yummy dinner. Then Tiger decided   34
the pig was too far away, and he did not feel like   46
running after her. "I'll rest now and look for food   56
later."   57

Tiger didn't know it, but the wild pig had seen   67
him, too. She was a kind pig. "I'd better tell my   78
friends that the sly tiger is looking for his dinner."   88
But she was too frightened to go, and she cried.   98

A tiny bird flew out from behind a tree and said,   109
"You hide. I'll fly through the forest and tell the other 120
animals." The other animals were sure that the bird   129
did not lie to them. They hid out of sight.   139

After Tiger woke up, he was hungry and started   148
to hunt. The night was silent. Tiger could not find   158
one animal. He thought, "Why didn't I run after that   168
wild pig when I saw it?" So Tiger went hungry that   179
night.   180

MONITOR PROGRESS
• Check Fluency
• Sequence

Read the Sentences

1. My clothes got wetter and messier as more rain fell.

2. Ed spent three hours hiking the steepest, driest trail.

3. David will start saving money for a bigger bike later.

4. My closest neighbor jogs on the safest path.

5. Only Sunday will be sunnier and hotter than Friday.

6. The tiniest but bravest girl had a question for her king.

7. Mike taught his older dog the silliest trick.

MONITOR PROGRESS
- Fluency
- Comparative endings *-er, -est*
- High-frequency words

A Weed Is a Flower • **517e**

Name _____

Read the Story

The Longest Hike

Come hike the Appalachian Trail! This mountain 7

trail is among the longest hiking trails in the country. 17

It is 2,175 miles long and runs from Maine to 27

Georgia. Most people come for the day. Their hikes 36

are shorter than others. But every year a few 45

thousand people plan much longer trips. They hike 53

the whole trail, which takes from five to seven 62

months to do. 65

One of the nicest surprises of hiking is seeing 74

the wildlife. Many kinds of animals such as deer, 83

moose, and raccoons live in these mountains. 90

These are wild animals. The safest plan is to look at 101

them with your sharpest eyes from a distance. Do 110

not step any closer to them. 116

What is the prettiest time of year here? Many 125

people think it's the fall. The red, yellow, and 134

orange leaves on the trees seem brighter here 142

than in other places. The air seems fresher, too. 151

But I believe that the trail is beautiful all year long. 162

Come take a hike and see. 168

MONITOR PROGRESS
• Check Fluency
• Fact and Opinion

Read the Sentences

1. Jean will read us a fable about a brave eagle.

2. Kim broke up her puzzle that was on the table.

3. We will paddle this boat in a circle on the lake.

4. Tim fed his gentle horse oats in the stable.

5. Did Meg tumble right in the middle of her race?

6. Don't think that it is simple to play a bugle.

Name _____

Read the Story

Jingle and Jangle

    Jingle and Jangle were two horses. Jingle lived   8
on a ranch on the north side of a fence, and Jangle   20
lived on the south side. When they were little, they   30
liked to race along the fence and eat green apples   40
that fell on each side of the fence.   48

    One day Jingle left the stable and trotted to the   58
fence. Jangle was not there. Where could he be?   67
The next day, Jingle trotted to the fence under the   77
apple tree. Jangle still was not there. Jingle nibbled on   87
some apples, but it was no fun without Jangle.   96

    A week later, Jingle's owner put her in a trailer and   107
drove her to another ranch. This would be Jingle's new   117
home. She would never see Jangle again. Then she   126
looked around the barn. There was Jangle munching   134
some oats. They had been sold to the same rancher!   144

MONITOR PROGRESS • Check Fluency • Draw Conclusions

Read the Sentences

1. Mark put the cookbook on the table and opened it.

2. That shed is full of chopped wood for the fireplace.

3. Hang your wool cap and winter coat on the hook.

4. Linda took her pet bulldog to play in the park.

5. Fred looked for a bright red jacket with a hood.

6. We planted five pink rosebushes by the brook.

MONITOR PROGRESS
- Fluency
- Vowel patterns *oo, u*

Name _____

Read the Story

Beth's Garden

    Last summer Beth planted a garden in her yard.   9
She wanted to grow her own beans and beets.   18
When they grew, Beth's family could cook them and   27
eat them.   29

    First, Beth dug up the soil. Next, she planted seeds.   39
She planted five rows of beans at one end of the   50
garden. At the other end, she planted two rows of   60
beets. Then she put soil on top of the seeds and used   72
a hose to water them.   77

    About two weeks later, Beth saw little plants come   86
up out of the soil. She kept them moist and pulled the   98
weeds. She was able to harvest the beans and   107
beets later in the summer. They were so good!   116

MONITOR PROGRESS
- Check Fluency
- Sequence

Read the Sentences

1. A little brown mouse ran down that tiny hole.

2. Roy fished for lake trout to broil for dinner.

3. Joy looked south and spotted storm clouds in the sky.

4. That loud noise sounded like thunder!

5. Ann enjoys drinking soy milk with her sirloin.

6. She spilled powder on her pink gown with purple flowers.

MONITOR PROGRESS
- Fluency
- Diphthongs *ou, ow, oi, oy*

Name _____

Read the Story

All About Corn

Did you know that corn was served at the first   10
Thanksgiving? But people have been eating it longer   18
than that. Kernels that are almost 4,000 years old   27
have been found in caves.   32

Today people still enjoy eating corn. It is the best   42
grain that can be grown. Some animals eat corn, too.   52

Corn comes in many colors. The kernels can look   61
yellow, white, red, or blue. I think white corn is the   72
sweetest. If you took a bite, you would love it!   82

How can you cook corn? Look in a cookbook to   92
find many ways to cook sweet corn. You can cook it in   104
water and eat it right off the cob. You can make corn   116
bread or creamed corn. You might try cooking cobs in   126
foil over a wood fire when you camp. Pull the leaves   137
back and dig in. That's the best way to eat corn. But   149
don't forget popcorn. Everybody likes popcorn!   155

MONITOR PROGRESS
• Check Fluency
• Fact and Opinion

Name _____

Read the Sentences

1. His boyhood was filled with daydreams of cowboys and horses.

2. Grace will bring baskets of oatmeal muffins for our bake sale.

3. The snowplow cleaned our playground when the winter storm ended.

4. We need plenty of space to download music we like.

5. The flavors and odors at the cookout made me lick my lips.

6. The baby held her stuffed rabbit made of pink velvet.

MONITOR PROGRESS
• Fluency
• Syllable Patterns

Name _____

Read the Story

Roy the Cowboy

Roy was a cowboy. He had one problem. He   9
could not eat much of the food that the other cowboys   20
ate. So, he ate soybeans.   25

In the morning, Roy ate fried soybeans. He had   34
boiled soybeans for lunch and mashed soybeans for 42
dinner. For snacks, he ate dry roasted soybeans.   50

One cowboy asked, "Roy, why do you eat so many   60
soybeans?"   61

"Well, I do not eat meat. I enjoy eating soybeans. 71
They are good for you, and they don't spoil in my   82
saddlebag."   83

But one day Roy did get tired of eating soybeans. 93
He wanted something else. So he tried oatmeal.   101

At first Roy liked the oatmeal. Then all Roy ate   111
was oatmeal, until he couldn't eat another bite.   119

Now Roy eats soybeans one day. The next day,   128
he eats oatmeal—just for something different.   135

MONITOR PROGRESS
- Check Fluency
- Plot and Theme

Name _____

Read the Sentences

1. A few baby raccoons scooted down our road.

2. Some papers came unglued and stuck to his new suit.

3. Her scout troop is due home soon.

4. This apple is too juicy to eat without drooling.

5. Bright blue flowers grew next to the swimming pool.

6. Is it true that a screwy goose got loose?

MONITOR PROGRESS
- Fluency
- Vowel Digraphs *oo, ue, ew, ui*

The First Tortilla • **187e**

Name _____

Read the Story

Sue and the Blue Moon

My friend Sue moved far away, so I only get to see   12
her once in awhile. When Sue visited last week, we   22
talked about things we were learning in school. I told   32
her about the moon.   36

"When there is a full moon, we can see the whole   47
side of the moon. Do you know what a blue moon is?"   59
She had never heard of it.   65

I told her, "The moon is never really blue. When   75
there are two full moons in one month, the second   85
one is called a blue moon. If there is a blue moon,   97
you will not see one again for another two years.   107
That's what 'once in a blue moon' means. It is   117
something that happens only once in a while."   125

Sue said, "I guess you could call us 'blue moon   135
friends.' We only see each other once in a while." So   146
now I call Sue my "blue moon friend."   154

MONITOR PROGRESS
• Check Fluency
• Plot and Theme

Read the Sentences

1. The bus driver slowly pulled up safely to our stop.

2. Firefighters find face masks helpful if they put them on correctly.

3. A dreadful thunderclap suddenly woke the campers.

4. The hopeful sailor quickly jumped in the lifeboat.

5. That foolish rider did not hold on tightly to his horse.

6. The boyish actor looked sheepish when he forgot his lines.

MONITOR PROGRESS
- Fluency
- Suffixes *-ly, -ful, -er, -or, -ish*

Fire Fighter! • **221e**

Name _____

Read the Story

Happy Campers at Bat

    The Happy Campers had a good baseball team.   8
Their coach had trained them well. Emma was the   17
pitcher. She had a good arm for throwing. Megan   26
was the catcher. She was great at getting runners   35
out at home plate. The team gladly played every   44
day so they would be the best.   51

    Today was the last game of the summer. It was   61
the last inning. There were two outs. If the Happy   71
Campers won, they would be champs. Emma threw   79
a fastball. The batter swung. It was a home run. The   90
game was over. The Happy Campers had lost.   98

    Emma sadly walked off the field. She thought her   107
friends would be upset. But good friends are helpful   116
to each other. The players gathered around her.   124

    "It's all right," said Megan sweetly. "You did your   133
best. Maybe next year we'll be the champs."   141

MONITOR PROGRESS
- Check Fluency
- Fact and Opinion

Read the Sentences

1. Kris is unhappy that she must rewrite her paper.

2. Mom dislikes seeing my room in a state of disorder.

3. Is Zack unable to be at the pregame meeting?

4. Our town must repave this road and replace those dead trees.

5. I think that it is unwise to displease your teacher.

6. My mom and dad prepaid our preteen babysitter to stay with us.

Name _____

Read the Story

The Fishing Trip

    It was early morning when Kim and Luke got   9
into the boat. A gentle breeze was blowing across   18
the water. It was a perfect day to go fishing. Uncle   29
Ted rowed the boat to the middle of the lake. He   40
took out a can of worms and helped the boys bait   51
their hooks. Then they waited for the fish to bite.   61

    The boat rocked gently. Soon both boys were   69
asleep. All of a sudden, the pole in Luke's hand   79
jerked. He quickly opened his eyes. A fish was   88
tugging on his line.   92

    Uncle Ted helped Luke reel the fish in. It was a   103
small one. Luke held the fish while Uncle Ted took   113
his picture. Then Luke gently took the hook out of   123
the fish's mouth. He carefully lowered the fish into   132
the water.   134

    "Maybe I'll catch you again when you're bigger,"   142
said Luke. "But for now, you're free."   149

MONITOR PROGRESS
• Check Fluency
• Cause and Effect

Name _____

Read the Sentences

1. The dog gnashed its teeth and snarled at the lamb.

2. After knitting a scarf, Loren began making a large wrap.

3. I wriggled under that fence and wrenched my back.

4. Andy used a sharp thumbtack to put up his sign.

5. The brave knight bowed and knelt before his queen.

6. Did Kitty know that her cat went out on a limb?

MONITOR PROGRESS
- Fluency
- Consonant patterns *kn, wr, gn, mb*

Bad Dog, Dodger! • **287e**

Name _____

Read the Story

Needles or Knots

Grace was sitting on the floor playing with her   9
cat. Her grandmother was knitting. "Grandma, I   16
want a hobby. How do you get a hobby?"   25

"Well, first you find something you enjoy. Then   33
you learn how to do it well. I learned to knit a long   46
time ago. Now knitting is my hobby," Grandma said.   55

"But you are so good at it. I always do everything   66
wrong when I try." Grace wrapped some yarn around   75
her fingers and tied it in knots. The cat climbed on   86
Grace's knee and batted at the yarn.   93

Grace thought of the pretty designs that Grandma   101
made. "I could never knit like you do," she said.   111

"It takes practice. You can't learn just by wishing,"   120
said Grandma. "If you want to learn, I'll teach you."   130

Grace thought about what her grandma said and   138
knew what to do. She picked up some knitting   147
needles and said, "I'm ready to start."   154

287f Responsibility • Unit 5 • Week 3

MONITOR PROGRESS
- Check Fluency
- Plot and Theme

Name _____

Read the Sentences

1. I think that singer will win the big trophy.

2. My pal Chuck laughs at all the jokes I tell.

3. The princess had more than enough rings.

4. My mom keeps my photograph in her gold locket.

5. Our classroom party rang with the sound of laughter.

6. Did those pesky gophers wreck our garden?

MONITOR PROGRESS
- Fluency
- Consonant patterns *ph, gh, ck, ng*

Horace and Morris • **323e**

Name _____

Read the Story

A Bear, an Elephant, and a Gopher

Our teacher asked us to dress up like an animal   10
and give a report. I chose to be a bear. My friend   22
Phil wanted to be an elephant, and Ralph decided   31
to be a gopher.   35

Ralph called me on the phone and asked me   44
what sounds gophers make. I said I did not know   54
and told Ralph to read about gophers.   61

On the big day, our teacher took photos of us in   72
our animal suits. My suit was tough to make, but it   83
looked good enough. Phil's suit was very cool. He   92
used sandpaper to make the elephant skin feel rough.   101

After Ralph read his report, he began to cough.   110
He coughed so much that he had to get some water.   121

After school, Ralph told me that he still didn't   130
know what sounds gophers made. I said, "Well, I   139
know one thing. Gophers sure do cough a lot!" We   149
laughed all the way home.   154

MONITOR PROGRESS
• Check Fluency
• Character and Setting

Name _____

Read the Sentences

1. We saw a big red hawk soar high above us.

2. I will add just three pinches of salt to my sauce.

3. The author scrawled her name on the title page.

4. Let's head home now because the mall is closing.

5. Her dance partner taught Jean how to waltz very well.

6. Jane read *Jack and the Beanstalk* to her little daughter.

MONITOR PROGRESS
- Fluency
- Vowel patterns *aw, au, au(gh), al*

The Signmaker's Assistant • **357e**

Name _____

Read the Story

Pies to Go

Every summer the town of Woodson had a	8
contest to see who could make the best pies. The	18
people baked from dawn to dusk. They used lots	27
of fresh fruit and sugar. They added secret spices.	36
Some even served homemade ice cream with their	44
pies. Judges walked from table to table and ate a	54
piece of each pie. Then they picked the winner.	63
One year some hungry blackbirds smelled the	70
pies. The fruit was just what they wanted! They flew	80
in and grabbed whole pies off the tables. The people	90
were at a meeting and did not see them. But a little	102
boy caught the birds in the act.	109
When the people came back, they all blamed each	118
other for stealing their pies. The little boy yelled out,	128
"It's not your fault. I saw the blackbirds do it!"	138
From then on, the town always had a "Bird	147
Watch." No one's pies were ever stolen again.	155

MONITOR PROGRESS
• Check Fluency
• Main Idea and Details

Name _____

Read the Sentences

1. Mark pitches baseballs harder than his friend Jeff.

2. The first player grabbed a bat and raised it up high.

3. See how the ball flies past the speediest player!

4. Sandy is racing for the ball, but it is curving away.

5. We clapped for each player who tried his or her best.

6. That team is happiest when it is winning.

MONITOR PROGRESS
- Fluency
- Inflected Endings

Name _____

Read the Story

Luke and Carlos

Luke and Carlos are best friends. They're the   8
same in many ways but different in other ways.   17

They have always lived on the same street. They   26
are both in the second grade. They each have an   36
older sister and a younger brother. They often ride   45
their bikes together.   48

While Luke and Carlos are the same in many   57
ways, they are different. Luke belongs to a soccer   66
team. He would rather play soccer than any other   75
sport. Carlos is on a baseball team. He is the best   86
player on the team. Carlos says that he does not like   97
soccer. Luke says he does not want to play baseball.   107

The boys would like to play a sport together. But   117
they don't know if they would like the same sport.   127

Luke says, "We would like to try playing basketball   136
on the same team. We're both ready to try it this year.   148
I hope it works out."   153

MONITOR PROGRESS
• Check Fluency
• Compare and Contrast

Name _____

Read the Sentences

1. Mrs. Hines and Ms. Hood sell greeting cards in that store.

2. The last Thurs. in Nov. will be a holiday for us.

3. My house at the corner of Hawk St. and Ray Rd. is thirty feet tall.

4. On Jun. 14 and Jul. 4, people fly the Stars and Stripes.

5. In Dec., Mr. Camp took photos of the White House.

6. Dr. Lott will visit my class in Oct. to talk about health.

MONITOR PROGRESS
- Fluency
- Abbreviations

Red, White, and Blue • **425e**

Name _____

Read the Story

The Grand Canyon

    The Grand Canyon is in Arizona. It is 277 miles long   11
and one mile deep. A river flows through the bottom   21
of the canyon. Many, many years ago this river cut   31
through the rock and made the canyon.   38

    There are many amazing colors of rocks on the   47
steep walls of the canyon. You can see pink, red, and   58
orange rocks.   60

    The Grand Canyon contains different kinds of   67
plants and animals. Willow trees grow near the river.   76
Cactus plants grow in the sand. Foxes, deer, bobcats,   85
and rabbits can be found in many places.   93

    Today, people who visit the canyon like to go   102
down to the river. They can hike along the sloping trail.   113
Some people think it is easier to ride a mule though.   124
By riding a mule, they won't have any worries about   134
tripping. When people get to the bottom of the canyon,   144
they can take a raft trip.   150

- Check Fluency
- Author's Purpose

Name _____

Read the Sentences

1. I took this picture at the train station downtown.

2. This section of the light fixture is slightly cracked.

3. Jill will visit three nature parks on her vacation.

4. We must use caution when we walk in that pasture.

5. Randy liked the sculpture that his companion made.

6. To take away three thousand from one million, you must know subtraction.

MONITOR PROGRESS
- Fluency
- Final Syllables *-tion, -ture, -ion*

Birthday Basket for Tía • **457e**

Name _____

Read the Story

Tim's Pictures

Tim likes to take pictures. His mother lets him use   10
her new camera if he is very careful. The camera lets   21
him look at the pictures right after he takes them.   31
If Tim does not like a photo, he can remove it.   42

Tim likes taking pictures of all creatures, large or   51
small. Sometimes he can capture the moment of an   60
animal in motion. These action pictures are great.   68
Once he got a picture of a bird with its wings out.   80

Of course, he must use caution. He never gets too   90
close to an animal that may sting or bite him. Once he   102
thought he was taking a picture of some ladybugs.   111
When he saw the photo, there was a snake under a   122
plant. That's one reason he must be careful.   130

Taking photos is what Tim likes to do. He collects   140
his pictures in a book. Now and then he looks at them   152
and thinks about his future.   157

MONITOR PROGRESS
• Check Fluency
• Draw Conclusions

Name _____

Read the Sentences

1. That pot of beef stew is tasteless but harmless.

2. This campfire makes the cool, cloudless night quite enjoyable.

3. Jake will be more flexible and feel less soreness if he exercises.

4. She is likable because of her kindness when we need help.

5. That cattle herd is excitable at the loudness of the storm.

6. The stillness of this lifeless train station makes us feel creepy.

MONITOR PROGRESS
- Fluency
- Suffixes *-ness, -less, -able, -ible*

Cowboys • **495e**

Name _____

Read the Story

Maggie's Wish

Maggie wished she had a dog. Her mom said she   10
couldn't have one because dogs were too much   18
trouble. Maggie knew it was useless to keep asking.   27

One rainy night, Maggie heard scratching at the   35
door. There in the darkness sat a little dog with big,   46
sad eyes. Maggie took the helpless dog into the   55
warm house. She dried off the dog because it was   65
soaking wet.   67

"May we keep the dog?" Maggie asked. "I think   76
it's homeless."   78

"You have to try to find its owner first," said Mom.   89

The little dog was quiet as it slept in a cozy corner   101
on a blanket. The next day, Maggie put an ad in the   113
paper. No one claimed the dog.   119

Maggie's mom let her keep the dog because   127
Maggie showed it such kindness. Maggie loved her   135
priceless little dog.   138

MONITOR PROGRESS
- Check Fluency
- Sequence

Name _____

Read the Sentences

1. I misspelled that word on the midweek test.

2. Chen misread the name of the nonfiction book.

3. In midwinter we will need nonskid tires for our car.

4. Please do not misbehave or talk nonstop during her speech.

5. Mr. Dean misplaced the microphone before the meeting started.

6. The waiter misunderstood Mark when he asked for a nonplastic cup.

Name _____

Read the Story

The Layers of a Rain Forest

    Most rain forests are found where it is hot and wet   11
all year. The hot, wet climate helps the trees grow very   22
tall. Because the trees are so tall, a rain forest has four   34
layers, or parts. Different animals live in each part.   43

    The top part of a rain forest is the emergent layer.   54
The branches from the tallest trees reach for the   63
sunlight. Hawks and eagles build their nests here.   71

    The second part is the canopy. The branches of   80
different trees spread out and touch each other. This   89
layer of the rain forest still gets sun. Most rain forest   100
animals, such as monkeys and parrots, live here.   108

    The third part is the understory. The trees are   117
shorter because there isn't much sunlight. It is dark   126
and cool here. Frogs and spiders call this layer home.   136

    The lowest part of the rain forest is the forest   146
floor. Bushes with flowers grow here. Larger   153
animals, like wild pigs and jaguars, hunt for food.   162

MONITOR
PROGRESS
• Check Fluency
• Facts and Details

Assessment Charts and Student Progress Report
from
First Stop Second Grade

Fluency Progress Chart, Grade 2

Name _____

WCPM

	1	2	3	4	5	6	7	8	9	10	11	12	13	14	15	16	17	18	19	20	21	22	23	24	25	26	27	28	29	30	31	32	33	34	35	36
125																																				
120																																				
115																																				
110																																				
105																																				
100																																				
95																																				
90																																				
85																																				
80																																				
75																																				
70																																				
65																																				
60																																				
55																																				
50																																				
45																																				
40																																				
35																																				
30																																				

Timed Reading/Week

Name _____

Sentence Reading Chart

USE WITH GRADE 2 UNIT 1

	Phonics		High-Frequency		Reteach	Reassess: Words Correct
	Total Words	Words Correct	Total Words	Words Correct	✔	
Week 1 *The Twin Club*						
Short Vowels; /e/ea	4					
High-Frequency Words			2			
Week 2 *Exploring Space with an Astronaut*						
Long Vowels (vowel_e); /s/c, /j/g, /z/s	4					
High-Frequency Words			2			
Week 3 *Henry and Mudge and the Starry Night*						
Consonant Blends	4					
High-Frequency Words			2			
Week 4 *A Walk in the Desert*						
Inflected Endings -s, -ed, -ing	4					
High-Frequency Words			2			
Week 5 *The Strongest One*						
Consonant Digraphs	4					
High-Frequency Words			2			
Unit Scores	20		10			

- **RECORD SCORES** Use this chart to record scores for the Day 5 Sentence Reading Assessment.

- **RETEACH PHONICS SKILLS** If the child is unable to read all the tested phonics words, then reteach the phonics skills using the Reteach lessons in *First Stop*.

- **PRACTICE HIGH-FREQUENCY WORDS** If the child is unable to read all the tested high-frequency words, then provide additional practice for the week's words.

- **REASSESS** Use two different sentences for reassessment.

Name _____

Sentence Reading Chart

USE WITH GRADE 2 UNIT 2

	Phonics		High-Frequency		Reteach	Reassess: Words Correct
	Total Words	Words Correct	Total Words	Words Correct	✔	
Week 1 *Tara and Tiree, Fearless Friends*						
r-Controlled *ar, or, ore, oar*	4					
High-Frequency Words			2			
Week 2 *Abraham Lincoln*						
Contractions *n't, 's, 'll, 'm*	4					
High-Frequency Words			2			
Week 3 *Scarcity*						
r-Controlled *er, ir, ur*	4					
High-Frequency Words			2			
Week 4 *The Bremen Town Musicians*						
Plurals *-s, -es, -ies*	4					
High-Frequency Words			2			
Week 5 *One Good Turn Deserves Another*						
Long *a: a, ai, ay*	4					
High-Frequency Words			2			
Unit Scores	20		10			

- **RECORD SCORES** Use this chart to record scores for the Day 5 Sentence Reading Assessment.
- **RETEACH PHONICS SKILLS** If the child is unable to read all the tested phonics words, then reteach the phonics skills using the Reteach lessons in *First Stop*.
- **PRACTICE HIGH-FREQUENCY WORDS** If the child is unable to read all the tested high-frequency words, then provide additional practice for the week's words.
- **REASSESS** Use two different sentences for reassessment.

Name _____

Sentence Reading Chart

	Phonics		High-Frequency		Reteach	Reassess: Words Correct
	Total Words	Words Correct	Total Words	Words Correct	✔	
Week 1 *Pearl and Wagner: Two Good Friends*						
Long *e: e, ee, ea, y*	4					
High-Frequency Words			2			
Week 2 *Dear Juno*						
Long *o: o, oa, ow*	4					
High-Frequency Words			2			
Week 3 *Anansi Goes Fishing*						
Compound Words	4					
High-Frequency Words			2			
Week 4 *Rosa and Blanca*						
Long *i: i, ie, igh, y*	4					
High-Frequency Words			2			
Week 5 *A Weed Is a Flower*						
Comparative Endings *-er, -est*	4					
High-Frequency Words			2			
Unit Scores	20		10			

- **RECORD SCORES** Use this chart to record scores for the Day 5 Sentence Reading Assessment.

- **RETEACH PHONICS SKILLS** If the child is unable to read all the tested phonics words, then reteach the phonics skills using the Reteach lessons in *First Stop*.

- **PRACTICE HIGH-FREQUENCY WORDS** If the child is unable to read all the tested high-frequency words, then provide additional practice for the week's words.

- **REASSESS** Use two different sentences for reassessment.

Name _____

Sentence Reading Chart

USE WITH GRADE 2 UNIT 4

	Phonics		Selection Vocabulary		Reteach	Reassess: Words Correct
	Total Words	Words Correct	Total Words	Words Correct	✔	
Week 1 *A Froggy Fable*						
Syllables C + *le*	4					
Selection Vocabulary			2			
Week 2 *Life Cycle of a Pumpkin*						
Vowels *oo, u*	4					
Selection Vocabulary			2			
Week 3 *Soil*						
Diphthongs /ou/*ou, ow,* /oi/*oi, oy*	4					
Selection Vocabulary			2			
Week 4 *The Night the Moon Fell*						
Syllable Patterns CVC, CV	4					
Selection Vocabulary			2			
Week 5 *The First Tortilla*						
Vowels *oo, ue, ew, ui*	4					
Selection Vocabulary			2			
Unit Scores	20		10			

- **RECORD SCORES** Use this chart to record scores for the Day 5 Sentence Reading Assessment.

- **RETEACH PHONICS SKILLS** If the child is unable to read all the tested phonics words, then reteach the phonics skills using the Reteach lessons in *First Stop*.

- **PRACTICE LESSON VOCABULARY** If the child is unable to read all the tested vocabulary words, then provide additional practice for the week's words.

- **REASSESS** Use two different sentences for reassessment.

Name _____

Sentence Reading Chart

USE WITH GRADE 2 UNIT 5

	Phonics		Selection Vocabulary		Reteach	Reassess: Words Correct
	Total Words	Words Correct	Total Words	Words Correct	✔	
Week 1 *Firefighter!*						
Suffixes -*ly*, -*ful*, -*er*, -*or*, -*ish*	4					
Selection Vocabulary			2			
Week 2 *Carl the Complainer*						
Prefixes *un*-, *re*-, *pre*-, *dis*-	4					
Selection Vocabulary			2			
Week 3 *Bad Dog, Dodger!*						
Silent Consonants *kn*, *wr*, *gn*, *mb*	4					
Selection Vocabulary			2			
Week 4 *Horace and Morris but mostly Dolores*						
/f/*ph*, *gh*	4					
Selection Vocabulary			2			
Week 5 *The Signmaker's Assistant*						
Vowels *aw*, *au*, *augh*, *al*	4					
Selection Vocabulary			2			
Unit Scores	20		10			

- **RECORD SCORES** Use this chart to record scores for the Day 5 Sentence Reading Assessment.

- **RETEACH PHONICS SKILLS** If the child is unable to read all the tested phonics words, then reteach the phonics skills using the Reteach lessons in *First Stop*.

- **PRACTICE LESSON VOCABULARY** If the child is unable to read all the tested vocabulary words, then provide additional practice for the week's words.

- **REASSESS** Use two different sentences for reassessment.

Name _____

Sentence Reading Chart

USE WITH GRADE 2 UNIT 6

	Phonics		Selection Vocabulary		Reteach	Reassess: Words Correct
	Total Words	Words Correct	Total Words	Words Correct	✔	
Week 1 *Just Like Josh Gibson*						
Inflected Endings	4					
Selection Vocabulary			2			
Week 2 *Red, White and Blue: The Story of the American Flag*						
Abbreviations	4					
Selection Vocabulary			2			
Week 3 *A Birthday Basket for Tía*						
Syllables *-tion, -ture, -ion*	4					
Selection Vocabulary			2			
Week 4 *Cowboys*						
Suffixes *-ness, -less, -able, -ible*	4					
Selection Vocabulary			2			
Week 5 *Grace For President*						
Prefixes *mis-, micro-, mid-, non-*	4					
Selection Vocabulary			2			
Unit Scores	20		10			

- **RECORD SCORES** Use this chart to record scores for the Day 5 Sentence Reading Assessment.

- **RETEACH PHONICS SKILLS** If the child is unable to read all the tested phonics words, then reteach the phonics skills using the Reteach lessons in *First Stop*.

- **PRACTICE LESSON VOCABULARY** If the child is unable to read all the tested vocabulary words, then provide additional practice for the week's words.

- **REASSESS** Use two different sentences for reassessment.

Student Progress Report: Grade 2

Name _____

This chart lists the skills taught in this program. Record your child's progress toward mastery of the skills covered in this school year here. Use the chart below to track the coverage of these skills.

Skill	Date	Date	Date	Date	Date
Distinguish features of a sentence.					
Decode multisyllabic words by applying letter-sound correspondences of single letters.					
Decode words with consonant blends.					
Decode words with consonant digraph.					
Decode words with vowel digraphs and diphthongs.					
Use common syllable patterns to decode words with closed syllables.					
Use common syllable patterns to decode words with open syllables.					
Use common syllable patterns to decode words with final stable syllables.					
Use common syllable patterns to decode words with a silent "e" at the end.					
Use common syllable patterns to decode words with r-controlled vowels.					
Use common syllable patterns to decode words with vowel digraphs and diphthongs.					
Decode words with common spelling patterns.					
Read words with common prefixes and suffixes.					
Identify and read abbreviations.					
Identify and read contractions.					

Skill	Date	Date	Date	Date	Date
Identify and read at least 300 high-frequency words from a commonly used list.					
Monitor accuracy of decoding.					
Use ideas to make and confirm predictions.					
Ask relevant questions, clarify text, locate facts and details about texts, and support answers with evidence.					
Establish a purpose for reading and monitor comprehension.					
Read aloud grade-level appropriate text with fluency and comprehension.					

Skill	Date	Date	Date
Use prefixes and suffixes to determine the meaning of words.			
Use context to determine the meaning of unfamiliar words or multiple-meaning words.			
Identify and use antonyms and synonyms.			
Alphabetize a series of words and use a dictionary or a glossary to find words.			
Identify themes in well-known fables, legends, myths, or stories.			
Compare the characters, settings, and plots in traditional and contemporary folktales.			
Describe how rhyme, rhythm, and repetition create images in poetry.			
Identify the elements of dialogue and use them in informal plays.			

Skill	Date	Date	Date
Describe similarities and differences in the plots and settings of works by the same author.			
Describe main characters in works of fiction, including their traits, motivations, and feelings.			
Distinguish between fiction and nonfiction.			
Recognize that some words and phrases have literal and non-literal meanings.			
Read independently for a sustained period of time and paraphrase texts.			
Identify the topic and explain the author's purpose for writing.			
Students should be able to identify the main idea in a text and distinguish it from the topic.			
Locate the facts that are clearly stated in a text.			
Describe the order of events or ideas in a text.			
Use text features to locate specific information.			
Follow written multi-step directions.			
Use graphic features to interpret text.			
Recognize different purposes of media.			
Describe techniques that are used to create media messages.			
Identify the conventions of writing for different kinds of media and the Internet.			

Skill	Date	Date	Date
Plan a first draft by generating ideas for writing.			
Develop drafts and put ideas in order through sentences.			
Revise drafts by adding or deleting words, phrases, or sentences.			
Edit drafts for grammar, punctuation, and spelling using a teacher-developed rubric.			
Publish and share writing with others.			
Write brief stories that include a beginning, middle, and end.			
Write short poems that convey sensory details.			
Write brief nonfiction compositions about topics of interest to them.			
Write short letters.			
Write brief comments on literary or informational texts.			
Write persuasively on issues that are important to the student.			
Understand and use verbs (past, present, and future) in when reading, writing, and speaking.			
Understand and use nouns (singular/plural, common/ proper) when reading, writing, and speaking.			
Understand and use adjectives when reading, writing, and speaking.			
Understand and use adverbs when reading, writing, and speaking.			

Skill	Date	Date	Date
Understand and use prepositions and prepositional phrases when reading, writing, and speaking.			
Understand and use pronouns when reading, writing, and speaking.			
Understand and use time-order transition words when reading, writing, and speaking.			
Use complete sentences with correct subject-verb agreement.			
Distinguish among declarative and interrogative sentences.			
Write legibly and leave appropriate margins for readability.			
Use capitalization for proper nouns.			
Use capitalization for months and days of the week.			
Use capitalization for the salutation and closing of a letter.			
Recognize and use ending punctuation in sentences.			
Recognize and use apostrophes and contractions.			
Recognize and use apostrophes and possessives.			
Match sounds to letters to construct unknown words.			
Spell words with complex consonants.			
Spell words with r-controlled vowels.			
Spell words with long vowels.			
Spell words with vowel digraphs and diphthongs.			
Spell high-frequency words from a commonly used list.			

Skill	Date	Date	Date
Spell base words with inflectional endings.			
Spell simple contractions.			
Use resources to find correct spellings.			
Generate topics for research and ask questions about the topics.			
Determine relevant sources to use to answer questions.			
Gather evidence from sources and experts.			
Use text features in reference works to locate information.			
Record basic information in simple visual formats.			
Revise the topic as a result of answers to initial research questions.			
Create a visual display to show the results of research.			
Listen attentively and ask relevant questions.			
Follow, restate, and give oral instructions.			
Share information and ideas about the topic and speak at an appropriate pace.			
Follow rules for discussion.			
Set a purpose for reading.			
Ask literal questions of text.			
Monitor and adjust comprehension.			

Skill	Date	Date	Date
Make inferences about text using textual evidence to support understanding.			
Retell important events in stories in logical order.			
Make connections to own experiences, to ideas in other texts, and to the larger community.			

Third Grade Formal Assessment Tools

Forms from Third Grade Baseline Group Test Teacher's Manual

Phonemic Awareness Scoring Sheet

Student's Name _____ Date _____

Directions: Follow the instructions for scoring as given for each section below. Record notes and observations in the box at the bottom. Count up the total number correct, and record the results of this assessment on the Evaluation Chart for Grade 3.

Element	Points
Segmentation/Blending of Phonemes:	Underline each correct sound/blend that the student says. All sounds in a word must be identified to score 1 point for each word. (Maximum: 3 points)
1. /b/ /l/ /a/ /s/ /t/	
2. /s/ /p/ /e/ /n/ /d/	
3. /p/ /u/ /p/ /ē/ /z/	
	Underline and score 1 point for each word that the student says correctly. (Maximum: 3 points)
4. club	
5. great	
6. print	
Syllabification:	Underline the number of syllables if the student answers correctly. Score 1 point for each word. (Maximum: 3 points)
7. 3	
8. 4	
9. 4	
	Underline the word if the student answers correctly. Each word is worth 1 point. (Maximum: 3 points)
10. president	
11. information	
12. impossible	

Rhyming Words:	Underline the word if the student answers correctly. Each word is worth 1 point. (Maximum: 3 points)
13. twice	
14. part	
15. patch	
PHONEMIC AWARENESS TOTAL:	_____ **(Maximum: 15 points)**

Notes and Observations:

Grade 3 Baseline Test Evaluation Chart

Student's Name _____ Date _____

Teacher's Name _____ Class _____

SUBTEST Skills/Item Numbers			Subtest Percentages	SUBTEST Skills/Item Numbers			Subtest Percentages
Phonics _____/10 Correct				**Reading Comprehension** _____/20 Correct			
1.	0	1	1=10%	1.	0	1	1=5%
2.	0	1	2=20%	2.	0	1	2=10%
3.	0	1	3=30%	3.	0	1	3=15%
4.	0	1	4=40%	4.	0	1	4=20%
5.	0	1	5=50%	5.	0	1	5=25%
6.	0	1	6=60%	6.	0	1	6=30%
7.	0	1	7=70%	7.	0	1	7=35%
8.	0	1	8=80%	8.	0	1	8=40%
9.	0	1	9=90%	9.	0	1	9=45%
10.	0	1	10=100%	10.	0	1	10=50%
				11.	0	1	11=55%
Vocabulary _____/15 Correct				12.	0	1	12=60%
				13.	0	1	13=65%
1.	0	1	1=7%	14.	0	1	14=70%
2.	0	1	2=13%	15.	0	1	15=75%
3.	0	1	3=20%	16.	0	1	16=80%
4.	0	1	4=27%	17.	0	1	17=85%
5.	0	1	5=33%	18.	0	1	18=90%
6.	0	1	6=40%	19.	0	1	19=95%
7.	0	1	7=47%	20.	0	1	20=100%
8.	0	1	8=53%				
9.	0	1	9=60%	**Phonemic Awareness** _____/15 Correct			
10.	0	1	10=67%				
11.	0	1	11=73%	**Total Test** _____/60 Correct			
12.	0	1	12=80%				
13.	0	1	13=87%	**Fluency** _____			
14.	0	1	14=93%				
15.	0	1	15=100%	**Alternate Baseline Test** _____/61 Correct			

Total # Correct	Total Percentage	Total # Correct	Total Percentage	Total # Correct	Total Percentage	Total # Correct	Total Percentage
1	2%	16	27%	31	52%	46	77%
2	3%	17	28%	32	53%	47	78%
3	5%	18	30%	33	55%	48	80%
4	7%	19	32%	34	57%	49	82%
5	8%	20	33%	35	58%	50	83%
6	10%	21	35%	36	60%	51	85%
7	12%	22	37%	37	62%	52	87%
8	13%	23	38%	38	63%	53	88%
9	15%	24	40%	39	65%	54	90%
10	17%	25	42%	40	67%	55	92%
11	18%	26	43%	41	68%	56	93%
12	20%	27	45%	42	70%	57	95%
13	22%	28	47%	43	72%	58	97%
14	23%	29	48%	44	73%	59	98%
15	25%	30	50%	45	75%	60	100%

Initial Placement: Strategic Intervention   On-Level   Advanced

Fluency Forms

Reading Fluency Progress Chart

Student's Name	Unit 1		Unit 2		Unit 3		Unit 4		Unit 5		Unit 6	
	Date	WCPM	Date	WCPM	Date	WCPM	Date	WCPM	Date	WCPM	Date	WCPM
1.												
2.												
3.												
4.												
5.												
6.												
7.												
8.												
9.												
10.												
11.												
12.												
13.												
14.												
15.												
16.												
17.												
18.												
19.												
20.												
21.												
22.												
23.												
24.												
25.												
26.												
27.												
28.												
29.												
30.												
31.												
32.												
33.												
34.												
35.												

Fluency Progress Chart, Grade 3

Name ____________________

WCPM

145																																				
140																																				
135																																				
130																																				
125																																				
120																																				
115																																				
110																																				
105																																				
100																																				
95																																				
90																																				
85																																				
80																																				
75																																				
70																																				
65																																				
60																																				
55																																				
50																																				
	1	2	3	4	5	6	7	8	9	10	11	12	13	14	15	16	17	18	19	20	21	22	23	24	25	26	27	28	29	30	31	32	33	34	35	36

Timed Reading/Week

REPRODUCIBLE

Forms from Third Grade Weekly Tests Teacher's Manual

Scott Foresman *Reading Street*
Class Weekly Test Progress Chart—Grade 3

Teacher's Name: _____

Student Name	Weekly Test Total Score																													
	1	2	3	4	5	6	7	8	9	10	11	12	13	14	15	16	17	18	19	20	21	22	23	24	25	26	27	28	29	30
1																														
2																														
3																														
4																														
5																														
6																														
7																														
8																														
9																														
10																														
11																														
12																														
13																														
14																														
15																														
16																														
17																														
18																														
19																														
20																														
21																														
22																														
23																														
24																														
25																														
26																														
27																														
28																														
29																														
30																														

Scott Foresman *Reading Street*
Student Weekly Test Progress Chart—Grade 3

Student Name: _____

Test	Vocabulary	Phonics/Word Analysis	Comprehension	Multiple-Choice Total	Writing	TOTAL
Weekly Test 1	/7	/5	/8	/20		
Weekly Test 2	/7	/5	/8	/20		
Weekly Test 3	/6	/6	/8	/20		
Weekly Test 4	/6	/6	/8	/20		
Weekly Test 5	/7	/5	/8	/20		
Weekly Test 6	/7	/5	/8	/20		
Weekly Test 7	/7	/5	/8	/20		
Weekly Test 8	/6	/6	/8	/20		
Weekly Test 9	/7	/5	/8	/20		
Weekly Test 10	/7	/5	/8	/20		
Weekly Test 11	/7	/5	/8	/20		
Weekly Test 12	/6	/6	/8	/20		
Weekly Test 13	/7	/5	/8	/20		
Weekly Test 14	/7	/5	/8	/20		
Weekly Test 15	/7	/5	/8	/20		
Weekly Test 16	/7	/5	/8	/20		
Weekly Test 17	/7	/5	/8	/20		
Weekly Test 18	/7	/5	/8	/20		
Weekly Test 19	/7	/5	/8	/20		
Weekly Test 20	/7	/5	/8	/20		
Weekly Test 21	/7	/5	/8	/20		
Weekly Test 22	/7	/5	/8	/20		
Weekly Test 23	/7	/5	/8	/20		
Weekly Test 24	/7	/5	/8	/20		
Weekly Test 25	/7	/5	/8	/20		
Weekly Test 26	/7	/5	/8	/20		
Weekly Test 27	/7	/5	/8	/20		
Weekly Test 28	/7	/5	/8	/20		
Weekly Test 29	/7	/5	/8	/20		
Weekly Test 30	/7	/5	/8	/20		

Comprehension Target Skill Coverage

How can the Weekly Tests predict student success on Unit Benchmark Tests?

Each Unit Benchmark Test, as well as assessing overall student reading ability, concentrates on two skills taught and/or reviewed during the unit by including several questions on those skills. In order to ensure that comprehension target skill can be accurately learned and then tested, students learn each target skill through a combination of being taught and reviewing the skill multiple times before testing occurs. The charts below show the units/weeks where the target comprehension skills are taught and where they are tested on Weekly Tests. Based on the student's number of correct answers for each tested target skill, the teacher will know whether a student has gained the necessary skill knowledge before the Unit Test is given. A low score on the Weekly Tests probably indicates a need for closer review of the student's performance and perhaps additional instruction. It is important to understand that these tests provide only one look at the student's progress and should be interpreted in conjunction with other assessments and the teacher's observation.

Using the Comprehension Target Skill Coverage Chart

To score target skill knowledge, use the Comprehension Target Skill Coverage Chart.

1. Make a copy of the appropriate Comprehension Target Skill Coverage chart for each student.

2. To score, circle the number of correct answers the student had for that skill on the appropriate Weekly Test.

3. Using the total number of correct answers for a skill, check the appropriate box under *Student Trend* to indicate whether or not the student has acquired the target skill knowledge. We recommend 90% correct as the criterion for skill acquisition at this level. Add any notes or observations that may be helpful to you and the student in later instruction.

Grade 3 — Comprehension Target Skill Coverage Chart

Student Name _____

Unit 1 Tested Skills	Weekly Test Locations	Number Correct	Student Trend
Literary Elements: Character/Theme	Weekly Test 1	0 1 2 3 4	_____ Skill knowledge acquired _____ Skill needs further review
	Weekly Test 2	0 1	
	Weekly Test 3	0 1	
Sequence	Weekly Test 2	0 1 2 3 4 5	_____ Skill knowledge acquired _____ Skill needs further review
	Weekly Test 3	0 1 2 3 4 5	
	Weekly Test 5	0 1	

Unit 2 Tested Skills	Weekly Test Locations	Number Correct	Student Trend
Compare and Contrast	Weekly Test 4	0 1 2 3 4 5	_____ Skill knowledge acquired _____ Skill needs further review
	Weekly Test 6	0 1	
	Weekly Test 7	0 1 2 3 4 5	
	Weekly Test 8	0 1	
	Weekly Test 9	0 1	
Main Idea and Supporting Details	Weekly Test 5	0 1	_____ Skill knowledge acquired _____ Skill needs further review
	Weekly Test 6	0 1 2 3 4 5 6 7	
	Weekly Test 8	0 1	
	Weekly Test 10	0 1 2 3 4 5	

Grade 3 — Comprehension Target Skill Coverage Chart

Student Name _____

Unit 3 Tested Skills	Weekly Test Locations	Number Correct	Student Trend
Draw Conclusions	Weekly Test 1	0 1 2	
	Weekly Test 2	0 1 2	
	Weekly Test 3	0 1	
	Weekly Test 4	0 1	
	Weekly Test 8	0 1 2 3 4 5	
	Weekly Test 10	0 1	
	Weekly Test 11	0 1 2 3 4 5	
	Weekly Test 12	0 1	
	Weekly Test 13	0 1	
	Weekly Test 14	0 1	_____ Skill knowledge acquired
	Weekly Test 15	0 1	_____ Skill needs further review
Author's Purpose	Weekly Test 4	0 1	
	Weekly Test 5	0 1 2 3 4 5	
	Weekly Test 9	0 1 2 3 4 5	
	Weekly Test 11	0 1	_____ Skill knowledge acquired
	Weekly Test 13	0 1	_____ Skill needs further review

Grade 3 — Comprehension Target Skill Coverage Chart

Student Name _____

Unit 4 Tested Skills	Weekly Test Locations	Number Correct	Student Trend
Generalize	Weekly Test 9	0 1	
	Weekly Test 14	0 1 2 3 4 5	
	Weekly Test 15	0 1	_____ Skill knowledge acquired
	Weekly Test 16	0 1 2 3 4 5	
	Weekly Test 19	0 1	_____ Skill needs further review
Fact and Opinion	Weekly Test 4	0 1	
	Weekly Test 9	0 1	
	Weekly Test 15	0 1	_____ Skill knowledge acquired
	Weekly Test 18	0 1 2 3 4 5	
	Weekly Test 19	0 1 2 3 4 5	_____ Skill needs further review

Grade 3 — Comprehension Target Skill Coverage Chart

Student Name _____

Unit 5 Tested Skills	Weekly Test Locations	Number Correct	Student Trend
Main Idea and Supporting Details	Weekly Test 5	0 1	
	Weekly Test 6	0 1 2 3 4 5 6 7	
	Weekly Test 8	0 1	
	Weekly Test 10	0 1 2 3 4 5	
	Weekly Test 11	0 1	
	Weekly Test 16	0 1	
	Weekly Test 17	0 1	
	Weekly Test 18	0 1	_____ Skill knowledge acquired
	Weekly Test 22	0 1 2 3 4 5	
	Weekly Test 25	0 1	_____ Skill needs further review
Compare and Contrast	Weekly Test 4	0 1 2 3 4 5	
	Weekly Test 6	0 1	
	Weekly Test 7	0 1 2 3 4 5	
	Weekly Test 8	0 1	
	Weekly Test 9	0 1	
	Weekly Test 12	0 1	
	Weekly Test 14	0 1	
	Weekly Test 21	0 1 2 3 4 5	
	Weekly Test 22	0 1	_____ Skill knowledge acquired
	Weekly Test 23	0 1	
	Weekly Test 24	0 1	_____ Skill needs further review

Grade 3 — Comprehension Target Skill Coverage Chart

Student Name _____

Unit 6 Tested Skills	Weekly Test Locations	Number Correct	Student Trend
Literary Elements: Plot/Theme	Weekly Test 1	0 1 2	
	Weekly Test 2	0 1	
	Weekly Test 7	0 1	
	Weekly Test 12	0 1	
	Weekly Test 27	0 1 2	____ Skill knowledge acquired
	Weekly Test 29	0 1 2 3 4 5	____ Skill needs further review
	Weekly Test 30	0 1	
Cause and Effect	Weekly Test 5	0 1	
	Weekly Test 7	0 1	
	Weekly Test 8	0 1	
	Weekly Test 10	0 1	
	Weekly Test 12	0 1	
	Weekly Test 15	0 1 2 3 4 5	
	Weekly Test 18	0 1	
	Weekly Test 20	0 1 2 3 4 5	
	Weekly Test 21	0 1	
	Weekly Test 22	0 1	
	Weekly Test 25	0 1	____ Skill knowledge acquired
	Weekly Test 27	0 1 2 3 4 5	____ Skill needs further review
	Weekly Test 29	0 1	

Weekly Test Item Analysis—Grade 3

TEST	SECTION	ITEMS	SKILL
Weekly Test 1	**Vocabulary**	1–7	Understand and use new vocabulary
	Phonics	8–12	Short vowels; Syllables VC/CV
		13, 14, 16, 18, 20	◉ Literary elements: Character, setting, theme
		15	R Literary element: Plot
		17, 19	Draw Conclusions
	Written Response	Look Back and Write	Respond to literature
Weekly Test 2	**Vocabulary**	1–7	Understand and use new vocabulary
	Word Analysis	8–12	Plurals -s, -es, -ies
	Comprehension	14–18	◉ Sequence of events
		13, 19	Draw conclusions
		20	R Literary element: Theme
	Written Response	Look Back and Write	Respond to literature

Weekly Test Item Analysis—Grade 3

TEST	SECTION	ITEMS	SKILL
Weekly Test 3	**Vocabulary**	1–6	Understand and use new vocabulary
	Word Analysis	7–12	Base words and endings (*-ed, -ing, -er, -est*)
	Comprehension	13, 15, 16, 18, 20	◉ Sequence of events
		17, 19	Literary element: Character, Draw conclusions
		14	**R** Literary elements: Character and theme
	Written Response	Look Back and Write	Respond to literature
Weekly Test 4	**Vocabulary**	1–6	Understand and use new vocabulary
	Phonics	7–12	Vowel digraphs (*ee, ea; ai, ay; oa, ow*)
	Comprehension	14–18	◉ Compare and contrast
		13, 19	Author's purpose, Draw conclusions
		20	**R** Fact and opinion
	Written Response	Look Back and Write	Respond to literature
Weekly Test 5	**Vocabulary**	1–7	Understand and use new vocabulary
	Phonics	8–12	Vowel diphthongs (/ou/ spelled *ou, ow*; /oi/ spelled *oi, oy*)
	Comprehension	14–16, 18, 19	◉ Author's purpose
		13, 20	Cause and effect, Main idea and details
		17	**R** Sequence of events
	Written Response	Look Back and Write	Respond to literature

Weekly Test Item Analysis—Grade 3

TEST	SECTION	ITEMS	SKILL
Weekly Test 6	**Vocabulary**	1–7	Understand and use new vocabulary
	Phonics	8–12	Syllables V/CV, VC/V
	Comprehension	13–17, 19, 20	◉ Main idea and details
		18	**R** Compare and contrast
	Written Response	Look Back and Write	Respond to literature
Weekly Test 7	**Vocabulary**	1–7	Understand and use new vocabulary
	Word Analysis	8–12	Final syllable -*le*
	Comprehension	13, 16–18, 19	◉ Compare and contrast
		15, 20	Cause and effect, Literary element: Character
		14	**R** Literary element: Plot
	Written Response	Look Back and Write	Respond to literature
Weekly Test 8	**Vocabulary**	1–6	Understand and use new vocabulary
	Word Analysis	7–12	Compound words
	Comprehension	13–15, 17, 20	◉ Draw conclusions
		16, 19	Cause and effect, Compare and contrast
		18	**R** Main idea and details
	Written Response	Look Back and Write	Respond to literature

Weekly Test Item Analysis—Grade 3

TEST	SECTION	ITEMS	SKILL
Weekly Test 9	**Vocabulary**	1–7	Understand and use new vocabulary
	Phonics	8–12	Consonant blends (*squ, spl, thr, str*)
	Comprehension	13–15, 19, 20	◉ Author's purpose
		16, 18	Fact and opinion, Generalize
		17	**R** Compare and contrast
	Written Response	Look Back and Write	Respond to literature
Weekly Test 10	**Vocabulary**	1–7	Understand and use new vocabulary
	Phonics	8–12	Consonant digraphs (/sh/, /th/, /f/, /ch/, /ng/)
	Comprehension	13–15, 18, 20	◉ Main idea and details
		16, 17	Cause and effect, Sequence of events
		19	**R** Draw conclusions
	Written Response	Look Back and Write	Respond to literature
Weekly Test 11	**Vocabulary**	1–7	Understand and use new vocabulary
	Word Analysis	8–12	Contractions
	Comprehension	13–16, 20	◉ Draw conclusions
		18, 19	Main idea and details Graphic sources
		17	**R** Author's purpose
	Written Response	Look Back and Write	Respond to literature

Weekly Test Item Analysis—Grade 3

TEST	SECTION	ITEMS	SKILL
Weekly Test 12	**Vocabulary**	1–6	Understand and use new vocabulary
	Word Analysis	7–12	Prefixes (*un-, re-, mis-dis, non-*)
	Comprehension	14–18	◎ Literary elements: Character, setting, and plot
		19, 20	Draw conclusions, Cause and effect
		13	**R** Compare and contrast
	Written Response	Look Back and Write	Respond to literature
Weekly Test 13	**Vocabulary**	1–7	Understand and use new vocabulary
	Phonics	8–12	Spellings of /j/, /s/, /k/ (*g* /j/, *c* /s/, *k* /k/, *ck* /k/, *ch* /k/)
	Comprehension	14–16, 18, 20	◎ Graphic sources
		17,19	Sequence of events, Draw conclusions
		13	**R** Author's purpose
	Written Response	Look Back and Write	Respond to literature
Weekly Test 14	**Vocabulary**	1–7	Understand and use new vocabulary
	Phonics	8–12	Suffixes (*-ly, -ful, -ness, -less, -able, -ible*)
	Comprehension	13, 15, 17, 18, 20	◎ Generalize
		14, 16	Compare and contrast, Literary element: Setting
		19	**R** Draw conclusions
	Written Response	Look Back and Write	Respond to literature

Weekly Test Item Analysis—Grade 3

TEST	SECTION	ITEMS	SKILL
Weekly Test 15	**Vocabulary**	1–7	Understand and use new vocabulary
	Phonics	8–12	Consonant patterns *wr, kn, gn, st, mb*
	Comprehension	13–15, 17, 18	◉ Cause and effect
		19, 20	Fact and opinion, Draw conclusions
		16	R Generalize
	Written Response	Look Back and Write	Respond to literature
Weekly Test 16	**Vocabulary**	1–7	Understand and use new vocabulary
	Phonics	8–12	Irregular plurals
	Comprehension	13, 14, 16, 18, 19	◉ Generalize
		15, 17	Sequence of events, Main idea and details
		20	R Graphic sources
	Written Response	Look Back and Write	Respond to literature
Weekly Test 17	**Vocabulary**	1–7	Understand and use new vocabulary
	Phonics	8–12	Vowels: r-controlled (/er/ spelled *ir, er, ur, ear, or,* and *ar, or, ore, oar*)
	Comprehension	13–17	◉ Graphic sources
		19, 20	Draw conclusions
		18	R Main idea and details
	Written Response	Look Back and Write	Respond to literature

Weekly Test Item Analysis—Grade 3

TEST	SECTION	ITEMS	SKILL
Weekly Test 18	**Vocabulary**	1–7	Understand and use new vocabulary
	Word Analysis	8–12	Prefixes (*pre-, mid-, over-, out-, bi-, de-*)
	Comprehension	13, 15–18	◉ Fact and opinion
		19, 20	Main idea and details, Draw conclusions
		14	**R** Cause and effect
	Written Response	Look Back and Write	Respond to literature
Weekly Test 19	**Vocabulary**	1–7	Understand and use new vocabulary
	Word Analysis	8–12	Suffixes (*-er, -or, -ess, -ist*)
	Comprehension	13–17	◉ Fact and opinion
		19, 20	Draw conclusions
		18	**R** Generalize
	Written Response	Look Back and Write	Respond to literature
Weekly Test 20	**Vocabulary**	1–7	Understand and use new vocabulary
	Word Analysis	8–12	Syllables VCCCV
	Comprehension	13, 15, 16, 18, 19	◉ Cause and effect
		14, 17	Visualize
		17	Sequence
		20	**R** Draw conclusions
	Written Response	Look Back and Write	Respond to literature

Weekly Test Item Analysis—Grade 3

TEST	SECTION	ITEMS	SKILL
Weekly Test 21	**Vocabulary**	1–7	Understand and use new vocabulary
	Phonics	8–12	Syllable pattern CV/VC
	Comprehension	13, 14, 15, 16, 19	◎ Compare and contrast
		17, 20	Draw conclusions
		18	R Cause and effect
	Written Response	Look Back and Write	Respond to literature
Weekly Test 22	**Vocabulary**	1–7	Understand and use new vocabulary
	Phonics	8–12	Homophones
	Comprehension	13, 14, 16, 17, 20	◎ Main idea and details
		18, 19	Cause and effect, Draw conclusions
		15	R Compare and contrast
	Written Response	Look Back and Write	Respond to literature
Weekly Test 23	**Vocabulary**	1–7	Understand and use new vocabulary
	Phonics	8–12	Vowel patterns *a, au, aw, al, augh, ough*
	Comprehension	14, 15, 17, 19, 20	◎ Sequence of events
		18	Compare and contrast
		13, 16	R Draw conclusions
	Written Response	Look Back and Write	Respond to literature

Weekly Test Item Analysis—Grade 3

TEST	SECTION	ITEMS	SKILL
Weekly Test 24	**Vocabulary**	1–7	Understand and use new vocabulary
	Phonics	8–12	Vowel patterns *ei, eigh*
	Comprehension	13, 14, 17, 19, 20	⊙ Draw conclusions
		15, 18	Compare and contrast, Sequence of events
		16	**R** Sequence of events
	Written Response	Look Back and Write	Respond to literature
Weekly Test 25	**Vocabulary**	1–7	Understand and use new vocabulary
	Word Analysis	8–12	Suffixes (*-y, -ish, -hood, -ment*)
	Comprehension	13–16, 20	⊙ Author's purpose
		18, 19	Main idea and details, Cause and effect
		17	**R** Draw conclusions
	Written Response	Look Back and Write	Respond to literature
Weekly Test 26	**Vocabulary**	1–7	Understand and use new vocabulary
	Phonics	8–12	Vowel sounds in *moon* and *foot* (*oo, ew, ue, ui,* and *oo, u*)
	Comprehension	14, 16, 17, 19, 20	⊙ Fact and opinion
		13, 18	Main idea and details, Generalize
		15	**R** Author's purpose
	Written Response	Look Back and Write	Respond to literature

Weekly Test Item Analysis—Grade 3

TEST	SECTION	ITEMS	SKILL
Weekly Test 27	**Vocabulary**	1–7	Understand and use new vocabulary
	Phonics	8–12	Schwa spelled with *a, e, i, o, u* and *y*
	Comprehension	13, 15–17, 19	◉ Cause and effect
		14, 18	Literary element: Plot
		20	**R** Literary element: Theme
	Written Response	Look Back and Write	Respond to literature
Weekly Test 28	**Vocabulary**	1–7	Understand and use new vocabulary
	Phonics	8–12	Final syllables (*-tion, -ion, -ture, -ive, -ize*)
	Comprehension	15–18, 20	◉ Graphic sources
		14, 19	Compare and contrast, Follow multi-step instructions
		13	**R** Fact and opinion
	Written Response	Look Back and Write	Respond to literature

Weekly Test Item Analysis—Grade 3

TEST	SECTION	ITEMS	SKILL
Weekly Test 29	**Vocabulary**	1–7	Understand and use new vocabulary
	Word Analysis	8–12	Prefixes *im-, in-*
	Comprehension	13–17	◎ Literary elements: Plot and theme
		18, 19	Draw conclusions
		20	**R** Cause and effect
	Written Response	Look Back and Write	Respond to literature
Weekly Test 30	**Vocabulary**	1–7	Understand and use new vocabulary
	Word Analysis	8–12	Related words
	Comprehension	13–17	◎ Generalize
		18, 19	Draw conclusions, Literary element: Character
		20	**R** Literary elements: Plot and theme
	Written Response	Look Back and Write	Respond to literature

Forms from Grade 3 Unit and End-of-Year Benchmark Tests
Teacher's Manual

CLASS RECORD CHART

Grade 3 Unit Benchmark Tests

Teacher Name _____ **Class** _____

Student Name	Unit 1		Unit 2		Unit 3		Unit 4		Unit 5		Unit 6	
	Pt 1–4	Pt 5	Pt 1–4	Pt 5	Pt 1–4	Pt 5	Pt 1–4	Pt 5	Pt 1–4	Pt 5	Pt 1–4	Pt 5
1.												
2.												
3.												
4.												
5.												
6.												
7.												
8.												
9.												
10.												
11.												
12.												
13.												
14.												
15.												
16.												
17.												
18.												
19.												
20.												
21.												
22.												
23.												
24.												
25.												
26.												
27.												
28.												
29.												
30.												

Evaluation Chart: Grade 3 — Unit 1 Benchmark Test

Student Name _____ **Date** _____

Reading – Parts 1–4			
Item	**Tested Skill**	**Item Type***	**Score** (circle one)
Reading – Part 1: Comprehension			
1.	Literary elements: setting	L	0 1
2.	Literary elements: character	I	0 1
3.	Literary elements: character	I	0 1
4.	Sequence	I	0 1
5.	Sequence	L	0 1
6.	Draw conclusions	C	0 1
7.	Sequence	L	0 1
8.	Literary elements: character	I	0 1
9.	Literary elements: theme	C	0 1
A.	Constructed-response text-to-self connection		0 1 2
10.	Literary elements: character	I	0 1
11.	Draw conclusions	C	0 1
12.	Sequence	L	0 1
13.	Literary elements: character	I	0 1
14.	Draw conclusions	I	0 1
15.	Sequence	I	0 1
16.	Sequence	L	0 1
17.	Literary elements: theme	C	0 1
18.	Literary elements: theme	C	0 1
B.	Constructed-response text-to-text connection		0 1 2
Reading – Part 2: Vocabulary			
19.	Word structure: suffixes		0 1
20.	Word structure: suffixes		0 1
21.	Word structure: compound words		0 1
22.	Context clues: multiple-meaning words		0 1
23.	Dictionary/glossary: unknown words		0 1
24.	Word structure: prefixes		0 1
Reading – Part 3: Phonics			
25.	Medial consonants: VCCV		0 1
26.	Plural nouns: *-ies*		0 1
27.	Base words and endings: *-ed*		0 1
28.	Vowel digraphs: *ai*		0 1

	Reading – Part 3: Phonics (continued)		
29.	Vowel diphthongs: /ou/ spelled *ou, ow*	0	1
30.	Short vowels	0	1
31.	Plural nouns: *-es*	0	1
32.	Base words and endings: *-er*	0	1
33.	Vowel digraphs: *ea*	0	1
34.	Vowel diphthongs: /oi/ spelled *oi, oy*	0	1
	Reading – Part 4: Writing Conventions		
35.	Declarative and interrogative sentences	0	1
36.	Subjects and predicates	0	1
37.	Subjects and predicates	0	1
38.	Declarative and interrogative sentences	0	1
39.	Imperative and exclamatory sentences	0	1
40.	Compound sentences	0	1
	Student's Reading Total Score/Total Possible Score _____		**/44**

*L = literal   I = inferential   C = critical analysis

Reading – Parts 1–4 percentage score: _____ ÷ 44 = _____ × 100 = _____%

(student's total score)   (percentage score)

Writing – Part 5

Writing Score (complete one) _____/6 _____/5 _____/4 _____/3

Notes/Observations:

Evaluation Chart: Grade 3 — Unit 2 Benchmark Test

Student Name _____ **Date** _____

	Reading – Parts 1–4		
Item	**Tested Skill**	**Item Type***	**Score** (circle one)
Reading – Part 1: Comprehension			
1.	Literary elements: character	I	0 1
2.	Literary elements: setting	C	0 1
3.	Literary elements: character	I	0 1
4.	Compare and contrast	I	0 1
5.	Compare and contrast	I	0 1
6.	Draw conclusions	C	0 1
7.	Sequence	L	0 1
8.	Literary elements: theme	I	0 1
9.	Compare and contrast	I	0 1
A.	Constructed-response text-to-world connection		0 1 2
10.	Main idea and details	I	0 1
11.	Main idea and details	I	0 1
12.	Main idea and details	I	0 1
13.	Main idea and details	L	0 1
14.	Compare and contrast	L	0 1
15.	Main idea and details	I	0 1
16.	Sequence	L	0 1
17.	Draw conclusions	I	0 1
18.	Author's purpose	C	0 1
B.	Constructed-response text-to-text connection		0 1 2
Reading – Part 2: Vocabulary			
19.	Context clues: synonyms		0 1
20.	Context clues: synonyms		0 1
21.	Context clues: antonyms		0 1
22.	Context clues: synonyms		0 1
23.	Context clues: antonyms		0 1
24.	Context clues: unfamiliar words		0 1
Reading – Part 3: Phonics			
25.	Syllables: V/CV		0 1
26.	Compound words		0 1
27.	Syllables: VC/V		0 1
28.	Final syllables: *-le*		0 1

Reading – Part 3: Phonics (continued)

29.	Consonant digraphs: *ph*	0	1
30.	Consonant blends: *str*	0	1
31.	Compound words	0	1
32.	Syllables: VC/V	0	1
33.	Consonant blends: *spl*	0	1
34.	Consonant digraphs: *sh*	0	1
Student's Regrouping Multiple-Choice Score/Total Possible Score			_____ /34

Reading – Part 4: Writing Conventions

35.	Irregular plural nouns	0	1
36.	Singular possessive nouns	0	1
37.	Plural possessive nouns	0	1
38.	Common and proper nouns	0	1
39.	Singular possessive nouns	0	1
40.	Irregular plural nouns	0	1
Student's Reading Total Score/Total Possible Score		_____ /44	

*L = literal   I = inferential   C = critical analysis

Regrouping (Reading – Parts 1–3) percentage: _____ ÷ 34 = _____ × 100 = _____ %
(student's score)   (percentage score)

Reading – Parts 1–4 percentage score: _____ ÷ 44 = _____ × 100 = _____ %
(student's total score)   (percentage score)

Writing – Part 5

Writing Score (complete one) _____ /6 _____ /5 _____ /4 _____ /3

Notes/Observations:

Evaluation Chart: Grade 3 — Unit 3 Benchmark Test

Student Name _____ Date _____

Item	Tested Skill	Item Type*	Score (circle one)		
Reading – Parts 1–4					
Reading – Part 1: Comprehension					
1.	Author's purpose	C	0	1	
2.	Draw conclusions	I	0	1	
3.	Author's purpose	C	0	1	
4.	Draw conclusions	I	0	1	
5.	Sequence	L	0	1	
6.	Draw conclusions	I	0	1	
7.	Draw conclusions	I	0	1	
8.	Compare and contrast	C	0	1	
9.	Literary elements: plot	I	0	1	
A.	Constructed-response text-to-world connection		0	1	2
10.	Cause and effect	L	0	1	
11.	Compare and contrast	I	0	1	
12.	Draw conclusions	I	0	1	
13.	Cause and effect	I	0	1	
14.	Draw conclusions	I	0	1	
15.	Author's purpose	C	0	1	
16.	Main idea and details	I	0	1	
17.	Draw conclusions	I	0	1	
18.	Draw conclusions	C	0	1	
B.	Constructed-response text-to-text connection		0	1	2
Reading – Part 2: Vocabulary					
19.	Word structure: suffixes		0	1	
20.	Compound words		0	1	
21.	Dictionary/glossary: unfamiliar words		0	1	
22.	Dictionary/glossary: unfamiliar words		0	1	
23.	Homonyms		0	1	
24.	Context clues: multiple-meaning words		0	1	
Reading – Part 3: Phonics					
25.	Contractions		0	1	
26.	Prefixes: *re-*		0	1	
27.	Consonant sounds: *c* /k/		0	1	
28.	Suffixes: *-ly*		0	1	

Reading – Part 3: Phonics (continued)			
29.	Consonant patterns: *kn*	0	1
30.	Contractions	0	1
31.	Prefixes: *un-*	0	1
32.	Consonant sounds: *g/j/*	0	1
33.	Suffixes: *-ly*	0	1
34.	Silent consonant: *st*	0	1
Student's Regrouping Multiple-Choice Score/Total Possible Score _____ /34			
Reading – Part 4: Writing Conventions			
35.	Subject-verb agreement	0	1
36.	Subject-verb agreement	0	1
37.	Subject-verb agreement	0	1
38.	Past, present, and future tense verbs	0	1
39.	Past, present, and future tense verbs	0	1
40.	Past, present, and future tense verbs	0	1
Student's Reading Total Score/Total Possible Score _____ /44			

*L = literal   I = inferential   C = critical analysis

Regrouping (Reading – Parts 1–3) percentage: _____ ÷ 34 = _____ × 100 = _____ %
                     (student's score)   (percentage score)

Reading – Parts 1–4 percentage score: _____ ÷ 44 = _____ × 100 = _____ %
                (student's total score)   (percentage score)

Writing – Part 5

Writing Score (complete one)   _____ /6   _____ /5   _____ /4   _____ /3

Notes/Observations:

Evaluation Chart: Grade 3 — Unit 4 Benchmark Test

Student Name _____ **Date** _____

Item	Tested Skill	Item Type*	Score (circle one)
Reading – Parts 1–4			
Reading – Part 1: Comprehension			
1.	Main idea and details	I	0 1
2.	Generalize	I	0 1
3.	Fact and opinion	C	0 1
4.	Generalize	I	0 1
5.	Generalize	I	0 1
6.	Generalize	I	0 1
7.	Main idea and details	I	0 1
8.	Author's purpose	C	0 1
9.	Main idea and details	I	0 1
A.	Constructed-response text-to-world connection		0 1 2
10.	Cause and effect	L	0 1
11.	Cause and effect	I	0 1
12.	Sequence	I	0 1
13.	Fact and opinion	C	0 1
14.	Sequence	L	0 1
15.	Generalize	I	0 1
16.	Fact and opinion	C	0 1
17.	Draw conclusions	I	0 1
18.	Fact and opinion	C	0 1
B.	Constructed-response text-to-text connection		0 1 2
Reading – Part 2: Vocabulary			
19.	Context clues: unfamiliar words		0 1
20.	Context clues: multiple-meaning words		0 1
21.	Word structure: compound words		0 1
22.	Context clues: synonyms		0 1
23.	Context clues: multiple-meaning words		0 1
24.	Context clues: multiple-meaning words		0 1
Reading – Part 3: Phonics			
25.	Plurals -*f* and -*fe* to *v*		0 1
26.	*r*-controlled /er/ spelled *ur*, *er*		0 1
27.	Prefixes: *pre-*		0 1
28.	Suffixes: -*er*		0 1

Reading – Part 3: Phonics (continued)			
29.	Syllable patterns: VCCCV	0	1
30.	Plurals -f and -fe to v	0	1
31.	r-Controlled /er/ spelled er	0	1
32.	Prefixes: out-	0	1
33.	Suffixes: -ist	0	1
34.	Syllable pattern VCCCV	0	1
Student's Regrouping Multiple-Choice Score/Total Possible Score		_____	**/34**
Reading – Part 4: Writing Conventions			
35.	Pronouns	0	1
36.	Pronouns	0	1
37.	Pronouns	0	1
38.	Contractions	0	1
39.	Pronouns	0	1
40.	Prepositions	0	1
Student's Reading Total Score/Total Possible Score		_____	**/44**

*L = literal   I = inferential   C = critical analysis

Regrouping (Reading – Parts 1–3) percentage: _____ ÷ 34 = _____ × 100 = _____%

(student's score)   (percentage score)

Reading – Parts 1–4 percentage score: _____ ÷ 44 = _____ × 100 = _____%

(student's total score)   (percentage score)

Writing – Part 5
Writing Score (complete one) _____/6   _____/5   _____/4   _____/3
Notes/Observations:

Evaluation Chart: Grade 3 — Unit 5 Benchmark Test

Student Name _____ **Date** _____

Item	Tested Skill	Item Type*	Score (circle one)		
Reading – Parts 1–4					
Reading – Part 1: Comprehension					
1.	Main idea and details	L	0	1	
2.	Compare and contrast	L	0	1	
3.	Compare and contrast	I	0	1	
4.	Draw conclusions	I	0	1	
5.	Compare and contrast	L	0	1	
6.	Author's purpose	I	0	1	
7.	Draw conclusions	I	0	1	
8.	Compare and contrast	L	0	1	
9.	Draw conclusions	I	0	1	
A.	Constructed-response text-to-self connection		0	1	2
10.	Fact and opinion	C	0	1	
11.	Cause and effect	I	0	1	
12.	Main idea and details	I	0	1	
13.	Compare and contrast	I	0	1	
14.	Author's purpose	C	0	1	
15.	Main idea and details	I	0	1	
16.	Main idea and details	I	0	1	
17.	Draw conclusions	I	0	1	
18.	Main idea and details	L	0	1	
B.	Constructed-response text-to-text connection		0	1	2
Reading – Part 2: Vocabulary					
19.	Word structure: compound words		0	1	
20.	Context clues: unfamiliar words		0	1	
21.	Context clues: homonyns		0	1	
22.	Context clues: synonyms		0	1	
23.	Context clues: unfamiliar words		0	1	
24.	Context clues: antonyms		0	1	
Reading – Part 3: Phonics					
25.	Syllable patterns: CVVC		0	1	
26.	Homophones		0	1	
27.	Vowel sound in *ball*: -al, -aw		0	1	
28.	Vowel sound in *thought*: -ough, -augh		0	1	

Reading – Part 3: Phonics (continued)			
29.	Suffixes: *-ment*	0	1
30.	Syllable patterns: CVVC	0	1
31.	Homophones	0	1
32.	Vowel sound in *weight*: *a*	0	1
33.	Vowel sound in *taught*: *-augh, -ough*	0	1
34.	Suffixes: *-hood*	0	1
Student's Regrouping Multiple-Choice Score/Total Possible Score _____/34			
Reading – Part 4: Writing Conventions			
35.	Adjectives	0	1
36.	Adjectives and articles	0	1
37.	Comparative and superlative adjectives	0	1
38.	Comparative and superlative adjectives	0	1
39.	Comparative and superlative adjectives	0	1
40.	Conjunctions	0	1
Student's Reading Total Score/Total Possible Score _____/44			

*L = literal   I = inferential   C = critical analysis

Regrouping (Reading – Parts 1–3) percentage: _____ ÷ 34 = _____ × 100 = _____%
(student's score)   (percentage score)

Reading – Parts 1–4 percentage score: _____ ÷ 44 = _____ × 100 = _____%
(student's total score)   (percentage score)

Writing – Part 5

Writing Score (complete one) _____/6 _____/5 _____/4 _____/3

Notes/Observations:

Evaluation Chart: Grade 3 — Unit 6 Benchmark Test

Student Name _____ **Date** _____

Item	Tested Skill	Item Type*	Score (circle one)
Reading – Parts 1–4			
Reading – Part 1: Comprehension			
1.	Cause and effect	L	0 1
2.	Main idea and details	I	0 1
3.	Cause and effect	I	0 1
4.	Draw conclusions	C	0 1
5.	Cause and effect	I	0 1
6.	Draw conclusions	I	0 1
7.	Compare and contrast	C	0 1
8.	Main idea and details	I	0 1
9.	Draw conclusions	I	0 1
A.	Constructed-response text-to-self connection		0 1 2
10.	Sequence	L	0 1
11.	Main idea and details	I	0 1
12.	Literary elements: plot	C	0 1
13.	Literary elements: plot	L	0 1
14.	Literary elements: plot	I	0 1
15.	Literary elements: character	I	0 1
16.	Literary elements: theme	C	0 1
17.	Draw conclusions	I	0 1
18.	Cause and effect	I	0 1
B.	Constructed-response text-to-text connection		0 1 2
Reading – Part 2: Vocabulary			
19.	Context clues: antonyms		0 1
20.	Word structure: prefix *un-*		0 1
21.	Context clues: antonyms		0 1
22.	Context clues: unknown words		0 1
23.	Word structure: suffix *-ful*		0 1
24.	Word structure: prefix *dis-*		0 1
Reading – Part 3: Phonics			
25.	Vowel sounds spelled *oo, ue (tooth/blue)*		0 1
26.	Final syllable: *-tion*		0 1
27.	Unaccented syllables (schwa)		0 1
28.	Prefixes: *im-, in-*		0 1

Reading – Part 3: Phonics (continued)			
29.	Vowel sounds spelled *oo, u* (*cook*)	0	1
30.	Related words	0	1
31.	Prefixes: *im-, in-*	0	1
32.	Multisyllabic words with word parts	0	1
33.	Unaccented syllables (schwa)	0	1
34.	Related words	0	1
Student's Regrouping Multiple-Choice Score/Total Possible Score		_____/34	
Reading – Part 4: Writing Conventions			
35.	Capitalization	0	1
36.	Punctuation	0	1
37.	Combining sentences	0	1
38.	Punctuation	0	1
39.	Punctuation	0	1
40.	Combining sentences	0	1
Student's Reading Total Score/Total Possible Score		_____/44	

*L = literal   I = inferential   C = critical analysis

Regrouping (Reading – Parts 1–3) percentage: _____ ÷ 34 = _____ × 100 = _____%

（student's score）   (percentage score)

Reading – Parts 1–4 percentage score: _____ ÷ 44 = _____ × 100 = _____%

(student's total score)   (percentage score)

Writing – Part 5

Writing Score (complete one) _____/6   _____/5   _____/4   _____/3

Notes/Observations:

Evaluation Chart: Grade 3 — End-of-Year Benchmark Test

Student Name _____ **Date** _____

Reading – Parts 1–4

Item	Tested Skill	Item Type*	Score (circle one)	Item	Tested Skill	Item Type*	Score (circle one)
Reading – Part 1: Comprehension				27.	Fact and opinion	C	0 1
1.	Literary elements: theme	C	0 1	B	Constructed-response text-to-text connection		0 1 2
2.	Draw conclusions	I	0 1	**Reading – Part 2: Vocabulary**			
3.	Main idea and details	I	0 1	28.	Word structure: compound words		0 1
4.	Literary elements: character	I	0 1	29.	Word structure: suffix -*ful*		0 1
5.	Literary elements: plot	I	0 1	30.	Word structure: prefix *dis-*		0 1
6.	Author's purpose	C	0 1	31.	Dictionary/glossary: unfamiliar words		0 1
7.	Sequence	I	0 1	32.	Context clues: antonyms		0 1
8.	Compare and contrast	I	0 1	33.	Context clues: synonyms		0 1
9.	Cause and effect	L	0 1	34.	Context clues: unfamiliar words		0 1
10.	Literary elements: character	I	0 1	35.	Context clues: synonyms		0 1
11.	Draw conclusions	I	0 1	36.	Context clues: homonyms		0 1
12.	Literary elements: character	I	0 1	**Reading – Part 3: Phonics**			
13.	Literary elements: plot	I	0 1	37.	Base words and endings: -*ed*		0 1
14.	Main idea and details	C	0 1	38.	Compound words		0 1
15.	Sequence	L	0 1	39.	Contractions		0 1
16.	Generalize	I	0 1	40.	Base words and endings: -*ing*		0 1
17.	Main idea and details	I	0 1	41.	Vowel sounds spelled *oo, u* (*tooth*)		0 1
18.	Author's purpose	C	0 1	42.	*r*-Controlled /er/ spelled *ir, ear*		0 1
A.	Constructed-response text-to-text connection		0 1 2	43.	Base words with ending -*er* and spelling change		0 1
19.	Fact and opinion	C	0 1	44.	Plurals: -*s*		0 1
20.	Author's purpose	C	0 1	45.	Consonant sound *ck* /k/		0 1
21.	Cause and effect	L	0 1	46.	Long vowel digraphs: *ay, ai*		0 1
22.	Cause and effect	L	0 1	47.	Syllable patterns		0 1
23.	Main idea and details	I	0 1	48.	Vowel sound in *ball*: *aw, au*		0 1
24.	Main idea and details	I	0 1	49.	Suffixes: -*ist*		0 1
25.	Draw conclusions	C	0 1	50.	Consonant digraphs: *ch*		0 1
26.	Compare and contrast	I	0 1	51.	Silent consonants: *wr*		0 1

Reading – Part 4: Writing Conventions							
52.	Quotation marks	0	1	57.	Verbs	0	1
53.	Past, present, and future verb tenses	0	1	58.	Adjectives and articles	0	1
54.	Capitalization	0	1	59.	Subject/verb agreement	0	1
55.	Subject and object pronouns	0	1	60.	Conjunctions and compound sentences	0	1
56.	Possessive pronouns	0	1				
Student's Reading Total Score/Total Possible Score						**_____/64**	

*L = literal   I = inferential   C = critical analysis

Reading – Parts 1–4 percentage score: _____ ÷ 64 = _____ × 100 = _____%
(student's total score)   (percentage score)

Writing – Part 5

Writing Score (complete one) _____/6 _____/5 _____/4 _____/3

Notes/Observations:

Monitor Progress Passages
from
Third Grade Teacher's Editions

Name _____

The Car Puzzle

We went out to dinner for Dustin's birthday. Dustin read his cards 12

and then blew out his candles. After we had cake, we went to the 26

parking lot. The van would not start. "The battery might be dead," said 39

Dustin's mother. 41

"I can offer help if you need it," said a woman who was nearby. 55

"We would love some help!" said Dustin's mother. "We think the 66

battery is dead." 69

"Might I suggest you let me jump it?" the woman asked Dustin's 81

mother. "I'll connect my battery to yours and then start my car, which 94

should start your van." The woman connected the cables. Then she 105

started her car. Our van's engine made a sad chirp, but it did not start. 120

The woman got out and looked confused. Then she snapped her 131

fingers. "Say!" she said. "Have you tried checking the fuel line? Do you 144

have gas?" 146

"I didn't check that!" said Dustin's mother. She found the problem: 157

The car was out of gas. 163

MONITOR PROGRESS • Check Fluency

Charlie McButton **55k**

Josh Learns

Josh shivered by the frozen lake. Jolie, his older cousin, helped him lace up his ice skates. Josh was sure that skating would make him shiver even more. Yet Josh didn't complain. If he did, Jolie might tease him in her gentle way. She already teased him enough to get him to try skating.

At last, Josh's skates were ready. Jolie said, "Okay, young Mr. Texas. Let's see if you can learn to skate in the Iowa cold."

Josh smiled. Brownsville, Texas, was his home. People there did not see much cold, snow, or ice.

Josh stood up. He felt the edges of his skates cut into the lake ice. He felt good until he moved. Then he slipped and started to fall. Jolie caught him!

"Wow! Skating is hard," said Josh.

"It will get easier," said Jolie with a smile.

Jolie led Josh around the lake. She showed him how to move his feet and keep his balance. After a bit, Josh tried it on his own. At first, he skated slowly and fell more than once. But soon Josh could glide a little. He saw why people liked to ice skate.

Josh also noticed something else. He wasn't cold any more. Skating helped to warmed him up.

Later, Josh and Jolie drank hot chocolate. "You did well, young Mr. Texas," said Jolie.

Josh grinned. He did skate well today! And he could not wait to skate again tomorrow.

MONITOR PROGRESS • Literary elements: Character, setting, and theme

Charlie McButton **55m**

Name _____

Blue House

Alice's family has a new house. Last week, they went to buy things   13

for it. First they talked to the carpenter. They asked him to build a bed   28

for Alice. Then, they went to the carpetmaker. Alice picked out rugs for   41

her room. There were plenty of colors. "Hmmm," said Alice. She picked   53

blue.   54

"What color would you like for your room?" Alice's mom asked.   65

"Blue," said Alice. "That will match my rugs. May I have a blue   78

desk too?"   80

"That's fine," Alice's mom said. Alice's room would be all blue!   91

Later, they went to the marketplace. They needed food and supplies   102

for the new house.   106

"What kind of snack would you like?" Alice's mom asked. Alice   117

looked at the cookies. She looked at the candies. She looked at the   130

cherries.   131

"Hmmm," said Alice. Then her eyes got big. "Here's what I want!"   143

she said.   145

Alice's mother laughed. "I should have guessed," she said. "You   155

want the berries that are blue."   161

MONITOR PROGRESS   • Check Fluency

Name _____

Bobblehead Collecting

Two summers ago, my dad gave me my first bobblehead doll. Do you know what that is? It is like a little statue. It has a big head that shakes. The bobblehead was supposed to look like my favorite baseball player. And it did, a little. I really liked it.

Then, my dad gave me a bobblehead doll that was supposed to look like his favorite football player. This one looked just like that player! Too bad I didn't like football much. Still, I kept the doll.

Next, I decided to collect bobbleheads. I bought two used ones in a resale shop. Each bobblehead was a baseball player. They did not cost too much. But I knew I would have to save money to buy more.

After I decided to collect bobbleheads, I lined up mine on my shelf. But then I made a big decision. I only wanted to collect baseball bobbleheads!

But what should I do with my football player bobblehead? That's when my mom had a great idea. She said I should find other kids who collect bobbleheads and see if they want to trade.

That's what I did. In my school, I found kids who collected bobbleheads too. I traded my football player with one of them. I got a great baseball bobblehead in return.

And the best thing about the trade was this. The bobblehead fans in my school started a bobblehead collectors club. I am president of the club. Do you want to join?

MONITOR PROGRESS   • Sequence of Events

Planning A Camping Trip

Are you planning to go camping? Here are some	9
tips. First, go shopping for the proper gear. Are you	19
going with a big group? Then you should buy a bigger	30
tent. You will need a sleeping bag. Many people bring	40
a soft mat because it makes sleeping easier.	48

Are you planning to go camping? Here are some tips. First, go shopping for the proper gear. Are you going with a big group? Then you should buy a bigger tent. You will need a sleeping bag. Many people bring a soft mat because it makes sleeping easier.

Make sure what you are taking to wear is warm. Camping can be cold. If you are worried about freezing, buy heavier clothes that will keep you warm. You can buy thick pants and a warm parka.

You will be making meals, so make sure an adult brings matches to start fires. You may need a gas stove. Bring food from home. That is easier than buying food on the road. Dried foods like pasta are easier to carry. You will be making breakfast, so bring eggs. Frying eggs is easier than you think. Don't be worried about food tasting good. Food always tastes yummier on a camping trip!

Before leaving, make sure you have all your gear. You are sure to have a splendid time.

MONITOR PROGRESS

• Check Fluency

Kumak's Fish **121k**

Bob's Report

Bob had just one huge goal this afternoon. It was to write a school report. The report was due tomorrow. But Bob didn't have an idea for the report! Bob tried to think. What could he write about? Bob just wasn't sure.

Bob switched on TV and flipped through the channels. He didn't think of a report idea, but he did find a show to watch.

After the show, Bob tried again to think of an idea. How about monsters? Bob started drawing. He drew a funny and scary monster. He took a long time to make it perfect.

When Bob finished the drawing, he remembered his report. He could not think of what to write about his drawing, so he gave up on that idea.

Time was running out! How about something about music? Bob turned on his CD player and played some songs. They were so great that he sang along for twenty minutes or so. Then he remembered that he still didn't have a report idea!

How about a report on hamsters as pets? Bob didn't have a pet hamster, so he decided that wasn't a good idea after all.

Now it was suppertime! Bob still didn't have an idea. Then he grinned. At last, he figured it out. His report could be called "How Not to Write a Report." Bob could write about all the things he did when he should have been writing his report.

That is just what Bob wrote about in his report!

MONITOR PROGRESS

• Sequence of Events

Kumak's Fish **121m**

The Laundry Room Fort

Hanna and her friend Dean didn't know what to play.	10
"Let's make a fort!" said Hanna. "How about in the laundry	21
room?"	22
"Sure!" said Dean. They went down the stairs.	30
There were lots of sheets in the laundry room. Dean found	41
a green sheet and three pillows while Hanna found blankets	51
and other items on the shelves. They put the blankets and sheets	63
over the pillows and made a fort with plenty of room.	74
Then they heard a clatter on the stairs. The two children hid	86
in the fort. Suddenly the blanket came off the top of the fort.	99
Mother had spoiled the fort!	104
"Mother, why did you do that?" asked Hanna.	112
"I must do laundry. But look at this!" Mother pointed into the	124
playroom. "This was going to be a surprise, but here is a new	137
set of blocks I've been saving. Why don't you make your fort	149
with those?"	151
Hanna and Dean ran into the playroom and agreed the	161
blocks might make the greatest block fort ever.	169

MONITOR PROGRESS

• Check Fluency

A Big Question

When you ask your parents for something, do they say, "Do you need it or want it?"

That is an important question. Think about your answer carefully. Do you know what is a need, really? And what is a want?

A need is a thing you must have. That means the thing is so important that if you don't get it, you'll be harmed in some way. A good example is water. You need to drink water to stay healthy. You also need good food, clean air, sunlight, exercise, and other things to stay healthy.

A want is a thing you would like to have but something that you could live without. An example of a want is lemonade. You might want it because you like its taste. But you don't need to drink it to stay healthy.

The difference seems simple, but sometimes it can get confusing. For example, what if your friends have new baseball gloves and you don't. You feel terrible and think you really, really need a new glove too. But do you? Can you live without it? You know the answer.

Here's a surprise. Most things that you buy, wish for, or ask for are wants, not needs. That's okay. It means you're already getting your important needs. It means that your parents and other adults make sure you have what you need.

You probably will never get everything that you want. But that's okay—as long as you get everything that you need.

MONITOR PROGRESS   • Compare and contrast

Katie Bakes a Cake

Katie wanted to make a special birthday cake for her friend Joy.   12

Katie saved her allowance and used it to buy the ingredients she   24

needed.   25

"Do you want some help?" asked Mother.   32

"No," said Katie, annoyed. "I can do it."   40

"It's your choice," said Mother. "But I'll be around if you need   52

anything."   53

Katie wanted to make a yellow cake with white frosting. Katie got   65

out the flour and eggs, unwrapped the butter, and found the brown   77

sugar. She mixed the batter and started to pour it into a pan. The pan   92

wobbled dangerously.   94

"Watch out!" said Katie. She reached for the pan as it fell.   106

Mother turned and caught the pan, just in time. Then she held the   119

pan steady while Katie poured. "Thanks, Mother," said Katie.   128

Katie and Mother put the cake in the oven to bake for an hour.   142

It looked great when it came out, and Katie was proud.   153

"Do you want to help me frost the cake?" Katie asked her mother.   166

"Sure," said Mother, smiling at Katie. "That would be great."   176

MONITOR PROGRESS   • Check Fluency

Grandma's Old Collection

Sondra set a huge tin can on the kitchen counter. The can was almost as old as Grandma.

Grandma smiled and thanked Sondra. Then she asked, "Do you know the story about this can?"

"Yes, Grandma," said Sondra. "The can has all the money that you found ever since you were little."

"That's right! And I have found hundreds of dollars in my long life," explained Grandma.

"This all started back when I was eight years old," said Grandma. "I found a nickel on a sidewalk and stuck it in this can. Since then, I have found dimes, quarters, and even twenty-dollar bills. I found another dollar just last week."

Sondra tapped the old can and said, "It's full now."

Grandma said, "Yes, it is. I always felt terrible for the people who lost that money. Even pennies can be important, and no one wants to lose twenty dollars! Yet I could never find a way to return this money to the people who lost it. So I made myself a promise."

"You did?" asked Sondra.

"I promised myself that I would save the money. Then, when I got much older, I would use the money to help others," Grandma said.

"I'm sending this money to those people," Grandma said.

Sondra gave Grandma a big hug. Sondra knew she too would save any money that she found. She wanted to be just like Grandma.

MONITOR PROGRESS • Author's purpose

Birthday for Ducklings

A mother duck may take a few weeks to lay all of her eggs. She   15

sits on them after all the eggs are laid. This way, they will all be born   31

at the same time.   35

She sits calmly on her nest and cuddles her eggs to keep them   49

warm. The mother duck sits and waits for her ducklings to hatch. She   62

gets up from the nest only for food and water.   71

Suddenly, a tiny beak pecks its way out of one egg. The baby   84

ducklings are hatching! A few minutes go by and more beaks peck   96

through their shells. The baby ducks need to dry off after they hatch.   109

The ducklings follow their mother to the river. Each duckling   119

glides into the water. The ducks' webbed feet help them swim. They   131

work like flippers to help the ducks paddle down the river.   142

The ducklings take only a short swim because they can't stay in   154

the water for long. They do not have feathers, and their down is not   168

waterproof.   169

All the ducks preen themselves when they are back on dry land.   181

When they finish, they nap in silence under the bushes nearby.   192

MONITOR PROGRESS • Check Fluency

Name _____

Kangaroos!

What's so interesting about kangaroos? Well, there are many things that you might be familiar with, but other things will surprise you.

First, you may know that kangaroos really do not have four legs like many other animals. They have two arms and two legs. On TV programs, you may have seen kangaroos use those arms to box with humans. Here's what you might not know. When the temperature is high and the day is hot, kangaroos lick their arms to keep cool.

Second, you may know that kangaroos have thick tails, powerful legs, and strong feet. They use these to hop around. Here's what you may not know. The thick tail acts like a third leg. It helps kangaroos keep their balance as they stand.

Third, you may know that female kangaroos have pouches. They look like big pockets. Kangaroos use pouches to carry their babies. Here's what you might not know. A newborn kangaroo is tiny, less than one inch long. Yet it uses its arms to climb into its mother's pouch. It stays there for many weeks. After the baby grows, it climbs in and out of the pouch. When it is seven to ten months old, it leaves the pouch for good.

Fourth, you may know that kangaroos eat plants. They hop around looking for grass and other plants to eat. Here's what you might not know. Although kangaroos do not hunt other animals, they are tough fighters if attacked. Even people should be afraid of wild kangaroos!

MONITOR PROGRESS   • Main Idea and Details

A Great Day

Dear Diary, 2

Today was a great day. It was my birthday. My mother threw a big 16
party for me. The party had a football theme because football is my 29
favorite sport. 31

Many people came to the party, and I got many presents. My 43
favorite gift was a bicycle. Uncle Steve gave it to me. I was really 57
shocked to get it. All the gifts had been piled on the table. I opened 72
them all and said "thank you" to everyone. But Uncle Steve smirked. 84
The sparkle in his eye made me realize that there was another gift 97
to be opened. 100

Behind some crates in the garage, I found the bicycle. It was green 113
with big, fat tires. I could not wait to ride it! 124

Uncle Steve held the seat while I climbed on. I began to pedal 137
slowly. The bike lurched from side to side. I finally got my balance. After 151
a few minutes, I was able to ride a few feet by myself before falling. 166
I was so proud. I will ride my bike every day. Thank you, Uncle Steve! 181

MONITOR PROGRESS   • Check Fluency

I Wanna Iguana **265k**

Purple Milk

Phil was in the kitchen. His older brother Tony had eaten breakfast earlier and had left a dirty cereal bowl on the counter. Phil was neat, but Tony definitely not!

Phil gazed in the bowl and saw purple milk in it! Phil was shocked. Where did Tony get purple milk? Then Phil started to worry. He wondered if the purple milk made Tony ill. He called Tony, but Tony didn't answer. Phil shouted again, and Tony heard this time. Tony also heard the frightened tone in Phil's voice. Tony came into the kitchen and asked. "What's wrong?"

"Look, Tony! You drank purple milk!" Phil said. "Are you okay?"

Tony smiled. "Sit down and relax, Phil. You worry too much," he said.

Phil did worry too much. He even worried about that. Tony never worried. "I'll fix your breakfast," Tony told Phil. "Do you want bananas and cereal?"

Phil shook his head yes. Every morning, he had bananas and cereal. Every morning, Tony tried different things. "I'll have more cereal, too," said Tony.

Tony poured cereal into two clean bowls. In Phil's bowl, he added bananas and milk. In his bowl, he added berries and milk.

"Let's eat," said Tony. "But first look in our bowls."

Phil saw that the milk in his bowl was white. Then he looked in Tony's bowl. There was purple milk again! "It's from the blueberries on my cereal," said Tony. "They make milk turn purple."

Phil laughed at himself. He did worry too much.

MONITOR PROGRESS

• Compare and contrast

Something for Everyone

    Mr. Chen's store sells many interesting items. It is the one place in   13

town where everyone can find something they like. My father likes to go   26

there on Sundays. This is the day that new items are put onto the shelves. I   42

like going because Mr. Chen gives me a free bag of popcorn.   54

    Today it was cold outside as we walked to the store. Enormous bells   67

jingled when we opened the door to go inside.   76

    Mr. Chen was happy to see us. He greeted us with a big smile and   91

pointed to the counter. Boxes of all shapes and sizes were scattered on   104

top. "Jeff, I think I have something you might really enjoy."   115

    "Really?" I said, excitedly. "What is it?"   122

    "Look at this," said Mr. Chen, reaching into a shoebox. He pulled   134

out a very old super-hero comic book.   141

    My eyes lit up. "Wow! What a great addition to my collection."   153

    Mr. Chen smiled and said, "I knew you would like it. I found this   167

while cleaning out some boxes downstairs."   173

    "Wow! Thank you very much."   178

MONITOR PROGRESS   • Check Fluency

The First Airplane

Have you heard of the Wright brothers? They invented the first airplane. They flew it for the first time in 1903. Before that, many others tried to invent an airplane, but they failed. Why then did the Wright Brothers' succeed?

The Wright brothers read the daily newspapers. They read about other inventors and how their attempts had failed. The brothers learned helpful things that way. They learned that other inventors couldn't control their airplanes. So the Wrights made special wings that would help them control their airplane.

The Wrights built a glider with the wings. A glider is similar to an airplane, but without a motor and propeller. The Wrights tested the glider by flying it off hills for a short time. It flew a bit, like a kite would, but it wasn't a real airplane.

Then the Wrights worked on a motor and propeller. A propeller is like a giant fan. It helps to make an airplane fly. The motor turns the propeller. Before the Wrights, no one knew how to make the propeller work properly. The Wrights hoped they could do it.

The brothers tested their airplane at Kitty Hawk, North Carolina. It was near the ocean and soft sand hills. If their airplane crashed, Orville and Wilbur hoped the sand might stop them from getting hurt.

On December 17, 1903, the Wrights tested their airplane. It didn't fly a very great distance, but it did fly. The brothers succeeded in doing what no other inventor had done!

MONITOR PROGRESS

• **Drawing conclusions**

Prudy's Problem **299m**

Name _____

Meet Tom Sawyer

You may have heard of Tom Sawyer. A writer named Mark Twain 12
created him. A book, *The Adventures of Tom Sawyer,* is about the 24
trouble Tom gets into. 28

Tom lived with his Aunt Polly. He was in love with a girl named 42
Becky. His best friend was Huck Finn. Tom was very clever, but he was 56
also lazy. 58

One day Tom skipped school. Aunt Polly punished him by making 69
Tom spend a Saturday painting her fence. Tom was mad. He didn't 81
want to spend a Saturday working. But he was smart. He got local kids 95
to paint the fence for him by telling them how excited he was about 110
it. He said it would be a thrill. The kids even gave him gifts so that he 127
would let them work! 131

Tom causes more trouble later in the story. This time Tom, Huck, 143
and another friend decide to play pirates. They run away to an island. 156
Nobody sees them for a few days. Family and friends think this is 169
strange. Search parties go looking for the boys. The searchers split up 182
and spread out to look all over. 189

Finally the boys return to their families. Everyone is happy to see them. 203

MONITOR PROGRESS   • Check Fluency

Name _____

Garbage!

Most kids know recycling is a good idea. They know that old paper, cans, plastic, and glass can be used to make new products. That helps save the earth! Most kids do not even think of paper, cans, plastic and glass as garbage anymore. It is just stuff to be recycled.

What about other kinds of garbage? Does it all have to add to stinky, smelly landfills? Or can it be recycled too? The answer is a good one. Some garbage, such as leftover vegetables and mowed grass, can be reused to make compost. Many kids already know that. Did you?

Compost is like fertilizer. If you put it in gardens and farmers' fields, it will help things grow.

Perhaps you have seen how this works. When you walk in the woods, you often see and smell piles of dead wet leaves and plants. They smell because they are rotting. That's good! As the plants rot, they turn into compost. Compost leaves *nutrients* in the soil. Nutrients help new plants grow.

Much garbage has nutrients that can help things grow too. Some towns collect certain kinds of garbage and put it in piles. The towns add leaves, some dirt, and other things to the piles. After awhile, the piles change into brown stuff that looks like dirt. This is compost.

Later, the compost is spread on gardens and fields. It helps new plants and foods to grow. So, used the right way, smelly garbage can help grow new food. Cool!

MONITOR PROGRESS

• Author's purpose

Name _____

The Tree House

    My dad and I built a tree house. We studied each tree in our   14

yard to find one that was big enough. We looked for a tree with big,   29

thick branches. My father didn't want to use a tree that was too old or   44

diseased. We finally decided on an oak tree. It was perfect. The trunk   57

was short. I would be able to climb up to the tree house without   71

a ladder.   73

    I went with my dad to buy the wood and other materials we   86

needed. A man at the store used a special machine to cut the wood for   101

us. Dad had tools at home that he used to build the house. They were   116

unsafe for me to touch. Instead, I acted as his assistant. I handed him   130

nails. I also held parts in place while he nailed them together. When   143

there was nothing for me to do, I sat on the ground and watched him   158

work.   159

    The first thing Dad built was a platform. Then he added a floor. The   173

tree house was finished in a few days. Now I have a wonderful place   187

to call my own.   191

MONITOR PROGRESS   • Check Fluency

Yikes! Meat-Eating Plants

"Look out—that wild plant is hungry!"

Have you ever heard those words? Probably not, but if you were as small as an insect, you might. That's because some plants regularly make dinner out of bugs! Some plants even dine on small animals and birds. These plants are meat eaters!

There are different kinds of meat-eating plants. A famous one is the Venus flytrap. It has two leaves that are close to each other. Each leaf has bits of green strings that look like hairs. Insects buzz around and land on the leaves. That's okay, but if an insect touches one of the green strings, the leaves snap shut. The insect is trapped inside!

What happens to the trapped insect? The Venus flytrap slowly covers the bug with juices that turn it into a mushy liquid. This makes the insect easier to use as food. The Venus flytrap feeds on the insect for several days. When that bug is gone, the Venus flytrap opens its leaves and waits for its next meal.

The plants that eat animals and birds are pitcher plants. Their leaves look like tiny milk pitchers. The leaves hold a liquid that usually attracts insects. When an insect stands on the side to get a drink, its finds that the leaf is slippery. It slides into the pitcher and never gets out. Some pitcher plants are so big that even thirsty, small animals drop in for a drink. When they do, they stay a long, long time!

MONITOR PROGRESS
- Author's purpose
- Main Ideas and Details

Amazing Bird Nests **363m**

Name _____

A Giant Garden

    Would you like to see the largest flower garden in the world? You'd   13

probably have to take a plane! The garden is in the Netherlands, a   26

country in Europe. It's called the Keukenhof.   33

    The Keukenhof isn't open all year. It's only open in the spring. It   46

opens at the end of March. Then it closes in the middle of May because   61

the flowers in the garden are bulbs. Most bulbs bloom in the spring.   74

    More than seven million flower bulbs are planted in the Keukenhof   85

every year. When the flowers are blooming, it's an amazing sight.   96

There are flowers everywhere! The beauty takes your breath away!   106

    The Keukenhof has been open for more than fifty years. The garden   118

gets thousands of visitors each spring.   124

    What would you see if you visited the Keukenhof? Let's imagine   135

your visit. You will gaze out upon a rainbow of flowers. You might   148

recognize pink tulips or orange lilies or yellow daffodils. If you're lucky,   160

you'll get a day without any spring showers. Even if it is wet, though,   174

the garden will still be lovely.   180

MONITOR PROGRESS • Check Fluency

Raise a Raisin? **403k**

Name _____

Coyotes

What do you know about coyotes? Did you realize that they might be your neighbors? They probably are, even if you happen to live in a city.

Coyotes are the most amazing animals in America! They are wild dogs, similar to wolves. But unlike wolves, they can live near where people live.

People often think that humans moved into coyote territory. That is sometimes true, but not always. Coyotes originally lived in the Great Plains area. That includes states from North Dakota down to Texas. Now coyotes roam all over the entire United States, except Hawaii. That means coyotes moved into human territory.

In addition, coyotes have proven they can survive almost anywhere, including in big cities and suburbs. Although they like to eat meat, coyotes can eat many things: sandwiches, grass, garbage, and more. That is why they can live just about anywhere.

If a coyote is not the most amazing animal in America, it is certainly one of the smartest! Being smart is one reason coyotes can live around people. Part of being smart means they usually stay away from humans. However, coyotes are starting to show themselves more. That may be because there are more of them. It also may be because coyotes are not as afraid of people as they used to be.

A coyote is not a pet. If you happen to see a coyote once in a while on your street and in a park, remember that it is a wild animal. Stay away!

MONITOR PROGRESS • Draw conclusions

How the Reindeer Got Antlers

When Bear first walked the earth, he possessed antlers, which made   11
Bear very unhappy. He really disliked his antlers because his friends   22
constantly got poked. Once, Bear poked Elk so hard that Elk started to cry.   36

"Bear," Elk sobbed, "I don't understand how you can be so clumsy   48
when antlers are so easy to use!"   55

Bear disagreed because he didn't think it was so easy. When Bear   67
stood up in the forest, his antlers got caught on overhead branches. Bear   80
wanted his antlers to disappear.   85

Then, one night, Bear had an unusual dream in which he met a   98
strange white bear without antlers.   104

"Why don't you have antlers?" Bear asked the white bear.   114

"I had them once," the white bear answered, "but they were so   126
uncomfortable that I gave them away to Deer."   134

Bear woke up happy. Now he knew how to get rid of his antlers.   148
He went to see his friend Reindeer. He held out his antlers.   160

"Reindeer," said Bear, "I have a special gift for you. Please take   172
them."   173

And that is why today bears don't have antlers but reindeer do.   185

MONITOR PROGRESS • Check Fluency

Name _____

Red Leaves

Dan's favorite aunt was nicknamed Aunt Red. She had the loveliest red hair. When Dan was a newborn, Aunt Red sent a special gift, a little tree. The note attached to it said, "May Dan and this tree both grow up to be strong and healthy."

Mom and Dad carefully planted the tree outside Dan's window. It grew as Dan grew. Each autumn, its leaves turned a bright lovely red.

Aunt Red lived far away and didn't get to see the tree's red leaves. Dan didn't see her often either, but he and Aunt Red chatted a lot on the phone. On the last call, Aunt Red had wonderful news. She would visit him on the last weekend of October. That was when the tree's leaves were the brightest red! Dan couldn't wait for Aunt Red to see them.

Then the week before Aunt Red came, wind blew all the bright red leaves off the tree! Now Aunt Red wouldn't see them!

Dan had an idea. On the morning of Aunt Red's visit, he was outside. He had a rake, a stepstool, and tape. He raked up red leaves and taped them on the tree! It took a long time, and he knew that Aunt Red would notice the tape. Still, he wanted her to know how beautiful the tree was.

When Aunt Red arrived, she saw the lovely tree. She knew how hard Dan had worked. She knew that both the tree and Dan were growing up well.

MONITOR PROGRESS

• Literary elements: character, setting, plot

A Mysterious Scene

The clock in the kitchen struck midnight. A book lay open on the   13

table. In the dim light, a cracked teacup could be seen next to the book.   28

Gigantic shadows made the edges of the room impossible to see.   39

These shadows cast patterns on the floor. Next to the gas stove, a bowl   53

of milk sat waiting for a kitten to drink it.   63

The detective shivered as he stepped into the room. It was as if   76

the temperature had suddenly dropped twenty degrees. He took a   86

handkerchief from his pocket and nervously wiped his brow.   95

What had gone on in this room? The detective wasn't sure. He only   108

knew that Mr. Adams was mysteriously missing. The man's jacket still   119

hung on his chair. However, the man himself was nowhere to be found.   132

How long the detective stood there, he wasn't sure. Suddenly, he   143

was startled by a sound. A man was coming into the kitchen. It was   157

Mr. Adams!   159

"I'm sorry about that, Detective," Mr. Adams said. "I had to fix the   172

heat. It must be near freezing in here! Now, what did you want to see   187

me about?"   189

MONITOR PROGRESS   • Check Fluency

Name _____

Weather

Do you watch weather reports on TV? The weather forecasters do more than just predict what the weather will be like today or tomorrow. Do you ever notice that? They also tell you what the weather was like earlier today or yesterday. And sometimes, they tell you what the weather has been like for years and years. For example, they will tell how hot it usually gets in Dallas every August. How do they know?

Weather forecasters know because their computers keep very good records of weather. Every day, the computers record things such as temperatures, how much rain falls, and how much sunshine there is. After years of recordkeeping, forecasters know a lot. They know that in most years, the month of August is very hot.

With all that information, forecasters make charts. Look at this one. It tells how much rain usually falls in the Dallas-Fort Worth area every month. Which month usually has the most rain? Which has the least?

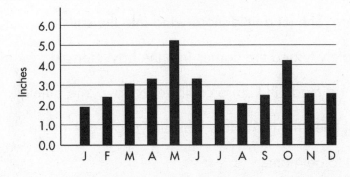

Average Monthly Rainfall

MONITOR
PROGRESS
• Graphic sources

Sailing Home

Claire anxiously scanned the horizon. She was guiding her little old   11

sailboat across the channel and into the bay. Though the water looked   23

calm and peaceful now, she knew a storm was coming.   33

The channel was beautiful, surrounded by tree-covered mountains.   41

Claire loved sailing here. An afternoon spent on her boat always made   53

her cheerful. It was truly the one place where she felt at peace with the   68

world.   69

Suddenly, a strong wind began whipping across the channel. Claire   79

looked anxiously at the big swells it was creating. Her boat was small,   92

perhaps too small for such a big wind. She would be helpless if the   106

wind capsized her boat.   110

Fortunately, it was a tailwind. The boat sped across the channel,   121

surging on the crest of the waves. Claire was almost in the bay now.   135

She would be safe there. She let a little more wind into the sails.   149

Finally, the boat safely turned the corner into the bay. Her old,   161

dependable sailboat had made it! Claire could relax now. She quietly   172

studied the houses that lined the bay. Hers was the yellow one at the   186

end. She couldn't wait to get home.   193

MONITOR PROGRESS

• Check Fluency

Wild Animal Babies

Have you seen TV reports about lonely puppies or kittens that need homes? These pets usually get sent to animal shelters. Volunteers then care for them and find them decent homes.

What about wild animals? What happens when a baby bird falls out of a nest or a baby squirrel is left alone on a front lawn? Special volunteers and animal shelters can aid them too.

But there is a problem with wild animals. At times, people think they're in trouble when they're not. People often see baby birds or baby deer that seem alone. It looks as if their mothers have deserted them. People feel sorry for these babies. At times, they even go get the babies.

Yet the mothers didn't really leave these little critters. Baby birds that seem to be alone in a nest usually aren't in trouble. Their mother is just out getting food. The same thing is true with baby birds hopping on the ground. They aren't really alone. They are just learning to take of themselves. Their mother is nearby.

People also see baby deer alone and think their mothers have deserted them. That's not true! Like mother birds, mother deer are just out looking for baby food!

It is good that people worry about wild animals. It is good that shelters and volunteers can help animals that need it. Yet before people try to help these little animals, they should call animal experts to see if the babies are really in trouble.

MONITOR PROGRESS

• Generalize

Name _____

Hiking?

Hiking on a vacation? Harry was unhappy. Couldn't his family find   11

anything better to do than hike?   17

Still Harry didn't complain. He liked being with Mom, Dad, and his   29

sister, Trish. Maybe after the hike, they could do something exciting, like   41

visit an amusement park!   45

The hike was along a mountain trail in Big Bend National Park. Dad   58

said the trail was exactly six miles long. Harry frowned. He guessed the   71

hike would take forever. There wouldn't be time for anything else!   82

The family walked uphill a bit, but it wasn't too tough. Harry   94

pretended he enjoyed it. He really did enjoy the green trees and   106

colorful flowers alongside the trail. The huge house-size rocks impressed   116

him. Had they dropped from the sky and landed here?   126

Harry looked up. High in the sky, vultures flew in circles. Harry had   139

never seen vultures before!   143

From the mountaintop, the family could see for miles. The Rio   154

Grande River was in the distance. On the other side of it was Mexico,   168

another country!   170

Harry gazed out at the view. "Hiking is fun!" he said aloud.   182

Harry couldn't believe it. Why did he say that? He knew the answer—   195

because hiking was fun!   199

MONITOR PROGRESS   • Fluency

Weeds?

In Texas and other states, more and more people seem to be growing weeds in their yard instead of grass. Why?

The answer is that these people aren't growing weeds. They're growing prairies. People fill their yards with prairie plants for many reasons.

Though prairie plants may look like weeds at some times of the year, they also have beautiful flowers at other times. When a prairie is in full bloom, it becomes a bright garden. The flowers draw many kinds of birds and butterflies. Prairie flowers help these winged critters survive. What had been a boring lawn becomes a lovely, lively place.

But a prairie isn't just beautiful. It is good for land and people. Prairie plants have deep, deep roots. Some reach 15 feet into the earth. Regular lawn roots reach only an inch or so. Why is the difference important? When it rains, prairie-plant roots absorb a lot of water. A lawn's roots do not. If it rains too much, prairie roots can prevent flooding, and that's good for people and houses. Prairie roots also store water, and that's good for all living things on the prairie.

Is there anything wrong with a prairie in a yard? Not really, but it does take work to care for a new prairie. There are often real weeds in a prairie. Those should be removed, just as in a lawn. After the prairie has been around a few years though, it can take care of itself. And it never has to be mowed!

MONITOR PROGRESS

• Cause and effect

Zora the Zebra

Zora was a zebra with only one stripe. Most of the time Zora   13
struggled to hold her head up high. It wasn't easy hearing what the   26
other animals had to say.   31

"A zebra isn't a zebra unless it has at least seven stripes," the other   45
zebras would say.   48

"Zora should change her name to Zero," laughed the mice.   58

"But I would love you if you had *no* stripe," her mother would say.   72

One day, while the other zebras were drinking from the lake, Zora   84
was standing on a hill. She could see them because their stripes stood   97
out against the light ground.   102

Then Zora noticed something terrible. A pack of wolves was glaring   113
down at the zebras.   117

"Oh no, I must warn them!" Zora cried.   125

She quickly ran down the hill.   131

It was clear that the wolves couldn't see Zora because she only had   144
one stripe. Her color blended well with the ground.   153

"Quick, run for your lives!" Zora shouted.   160

At that moment, the wolves came swooping down the hill. The   171
zebras had a head start and ran to safety.   180

That night, the zebras held a party for Zora. They were sorry for the   194
way they had treated her. "Three cheers for Zora!" they yelled.   205

"Now, this is the kind of attention I like," Zora said.   216

MONITOR PROGRESS   • Check Fluency

Wanda's Bad Play

Wanda raced to catch the baseball in the air. But she wasn't fast enough, and the ball bounced in front of her. When she tried to scoop it up after that, she completely missed it. Other kids on her team groaned loudly at Wanda's bad play. The kids often groaned at her bad plays.

Later, Wanda sat next to Coach Johnson. "I'm an awful baseball player. In fact, the truth is I'm an awful athlete," Wanda said.

"Why do you say that?" asked Coach Johnson.

Wanda thought for an instant and said, "I'd say that for six reasons. First, I don't run very fast. Second, I can't tell where a ball is going. Third, I don't catch balls well. Fourth, I don't throw balls well. Fifth, I don't hit well when I bat. Sixth, when I do hit something, it doesn't go far because I'm not strong. There is only one thing I'm good at. I know baseball rules."

"Hmm," said Coach Johnson. "I know something else you're good at, Wanda."

Wanda couldn't guess what it was. She asked, "Making lists?"

"Maybe," answered Coach Johnson with a laugh. "But that's not what I was thinking. You're good at analyzing things. That means you are good at thinking about things and figuring out what's right and wrong."

It was Wanda's turn to say, "Hmmm."

Then she asked, "Coach, does that mean I might make a good scientist?"

"Sure," said Coach Johnson. "Or a baseball coach."

Wanda smiled. She liked that idea!

MONITOR PROGRESS　　• Generalize

Name _____

Ring of Fire

One special area of Earth is known as the Ring of Fire. It is the 15

land areas that surround the Pacific Ocean. The edges of Asia, North 27

America, Central America, and South America are a part of the Ring. 39

This area contains 75 percent of the world's volcanoes. 48

Earth's top layer is made up of plates, or layers of land. These 61

plates move. The largest plate in the world is the Pacific Plate. It is 75

located under the Pacific Ocean. When the plates collide into one 86

another, there can be trouble. The collision may cause an earthquake. 97

Ocean tides may rise very high during earthquakes too. 106

When one plate slides under another plate, melted rock called 116

magma may rise to Earth's surface. This causes volcanoes to erupt. 127

On May 18, 1980, a volcano in Washington called Mount St. Helens 139

erupted. Thousands of animals died because they could not outrun the 150

melted rock rushing from the volcano. 156

Before Mount St. Helens erupted, its peak was 9,677 feet high. 167

After the eruption, its height was 8,363 feet. The volcano lost 1,314 feet 180

when the top of the mountain blew off during the eruption. 191

Scientists are always looking for ways to warn people well ahead of 203

a volcano's eruption or an earthquake. It is important to save lives. 215

MONITOR PROGRESS • Check Fluency

The Texas 8000 Patch

The newest members of the Texas Climbers Club were excited. This morning they were going to hike up Mt. Livermore, the fifth highest mountain in Texas. Mt. Livermore is one of Texas's seven mountains that reach more than 8,000 feet high. The club calls those mountains the Texas 8000.

"When we reach the peak of Mt. Livermore, I'll have only three more of the Texas 8000 left to climb," said Sylvia.

"When you've done that, you'll get a patch exactly like this," said Maria.

Maria pointed to a colorful patch sewn on her hiking vest. The patch had the phrase "Texas 8000" and a picture of a mountaintop on it. Maria is a leader of the club. She has climbed all the Texas 8000 mountains more than once. Like other leaders, she can sign members' cards to show that they have climbed each of the Texas 8000 mountains.

As the group started their hike, Sylvia looked at Maria's Texas 8000 patch one more time. She couldn't wait to get hers!

The Texas 8000: Sylvia's Climbs				
Mountain	**County**	**Height**	**Date Climbed**	**Leader's Name**
Guadalupe Peak	Culberson	8,749 feet	Dec. 15, 2008	Maria Perez
Bush Mountain	Culberson	8,631 feet	Oct. 12, 2007	Maria Perez
Shumard Peak	Culberson	8,615 feet		
Bartlett Peak	Culberson	8,508 feet		
Mt. Livermore	Jeff Davis	8,368 feet		
Hunter Peak	Culberson	8,368 feet	April 26, 2008	David Keltner
El Capitan	Culberson	8,085 feet		

MONITOR PROGRESS • Graphic Sources

Name _____

Mona's Stamp Collection

It was midday when Mona had finished her chores.   9

"Where are you going?" asked her friend Jules.   17

"I'm going to Stone's Stamp Store to see if I can trade this dinosaur   31
stamp for a cartoon stamp," she answered.   38

"Who are you mailing the stamp to?" Jules asked.   47

"No one. I collect stamps," Mona replied.   54

"Why?" Jules said in a puzzled voice.   61

"It's fun to collect stamps. They're small and easy to keep," Mona   73
explained.   74

"Can I come with you?" Jules asked.   81

"Sure," Mona said.   84

Mona and Jules entered the stamp store. There were racks of stamps   96
on overhead shelves. The racks were labeled with names from around   107
the world.   109

"Hi, Mr. Stone. I found this stamp in my attic," Mona started to   122
explain, "and I was wondering if I might trade it for a cartoon stamp."   136

Mr. Stone looked at the stamp carefully. "Do you know what you   148
have here?" he asked.   152

"An old prehistoric dinosaur standing in an overgrown grass field,"   162
Mona answered.   164

"This is a one-of-a-kind stamp. It's worth quite a bit of money,"   176
Mr. Stone explained.   179

"Does this mean I can have the cartoon stamp?" Mona asked.   190

"No, this means you can have a *hundred* cartoon stamps,"   200
Mr. Stone laughed.   203

MONITOR PROGRESS   • Check Fluency

Name _____

Coyotes

What do you know about coyotes? Did you realize that they might be your neighbors? They probably are, even if you happen to live in a city.

Coyotes are the most amazing animals in America! They are wild dogs, similar to wolves. But unlike wolves, they can live near where people live.

People often think that humans moved into coyote territory. That is sometimes true, but not always. Coyotes originally lived in the Great Plains area. That includes states from North Dakota down to Texas. Now coyotes roam all over the entire United States, except Hawaii. That means coyotes moved into human territory.

In addition, coyotes have proven that they can survive almost anywhere, including in big cities and suburbs. Although they like to eat meat, coyotes can eat many things: sandwiches, grass, garbage, and more. That is why they can live just about anywhere.

If a coyote is not the most amazing animal in America, it is certainly one of the smartest! Being smart is one reason coyotes can live around people. Part of being smart means they usually stay away from humans. However, coyotes are starting to show themselves more. That may be because there are more of them. It also may be because coyotes are not as afraid of people as they used to be.

A coyote is not a pet. If you happen to see a coyote once in a while on your street and in a park, remember that it is a wild animal. Stay away!

MONITOR PROGRESS • Fact and Opinion

The Duck Olympics

Henry always dreamed of swimming in the Duck Olympics. He   10
practiced his strokes every day. Sometimes the ocean current was very   21
strong. Once he almost drowned.   26

Jerry was also trying out for the Olympics.   34

"You'll never be able to win because your feet are too small," Jerry   47
told Henry.   49

Henry didn't need to be reminded of his problem.   58

"I'm still going to try," Henry replied.   65

"Why bother? It's a waste of your time," Jerry said.   75

All his life, Henry was always in last place. It was true that his feet   90
were very small for a duck, but why shouldn't he try?   101

Henry's teacher Bert helped Henry improve his strokes.   109

"Keep kicking your feet," he would shout.   116

Henry listened to everything Bert said. Bert had trained many other   127
ducks. One even made it to the Olympics.   135

Henry continued practicing. Another swimmer would have given up   144
a long time ago.   148

When the day of the tryouts came, Henry was nervous. Other ducks   160
had their instructors pushing them too.   166

"On your mark, get ready, swim!" shouted the head duck.   176

Henry moved his feet faster than he ever did before. He zoomed   188
past Jerry and swam straight to the finish line.   197

"You made it to the Olympics!" shouted Bert.   205

Henry quacked for joy.   209

MONITOR PROGRESS   • Check Fluency

Gertrude Ederle **149k**

Bessie Coleman

When the Wright Brothers invented and flew the first airplane in 1903, Bessie Coleman was eight years old. There wasn't TV or radio then, and poor families like Bessie's probably didn't see a newspaper regularly. So it is likely that Bessie didn't know about the Wright Brothers' success immediately.

But when she did finally hear about it, what did Bessie think? Did she realize that she might fly too someday? That idea may have seemed impossible then.

Bessie came from a large, poor Texas family. Both of her parents had been slaves when they were young. Most of her brothers and sisters still worked in cotton fields.

Bessie was smart. She was good at math. She even went to college for a year. In those days, most African Americans didn't get that chance. Did Bessie think about flying while she was in college?

During World War I, two of Bessie's brothers were soldiers. In 1919, they told her about women pilots in France. Their stories gave Bessie a goal. She would become a pilot!

Yet in 1919, no American flying school would teach an African American woman to fly. That didn't stop Bessie. She found a way to get to France, thousands of miles away! There she learned to fly.

When she returned to America, Bessie flew in air shows. She shocked Americans. There was great prejudice against women and African Americans then. At first, many people didn't believe that Bessie was really a pilot. But then they saw her fly!

MONITOR PROGRESS   • Fact and opinion

Gertrude Ederle   **149m**

Name _____

Bats Are Special

Andy and Dora were exploring the valley with their parents when it   12
started to rain.   15

"Let's look for a place to stay dry," Mom said.   25

"There's a cave just over the gully," Dad added.   34

"Aren't bats in caves?" Dora asked in a frightened voice.   44

"You shouldn't be afraid of bats. They're really cool," Andy replied.   55

"How cool can they be? They can't even see!" Dora exclaimed.   66

"Are you kidding? Bats can't see color, but they can see in the dark   80
better than you or me," Andy said. "They also use echoes to help them   94
hunt for insects," Andy added.   99

"What about vampire bats?" Dora asked.   105

"They can be found in Mexico, Central America, and South   115
America," Andy answered. "Unlike Dracula, they only need about   124
2 tablespoons of blood a day. That amount doesn't hurt the animal it   137
takes the blood from," Andy added.   142

"Did you know that the smallest bat weighs less than a penny?"   154
Mom said.   165

"I'd like to see one of those," Dora said excitedly.   166

"You'd have to go to Thailand. They're called bumblebee bats," her   177
father added.   179

"Let's hurry to the cave," Dora said as she scrambled ahead.   190

"I thought you were afraid," Andy shouted.   197

"Not anymore! Bats are too special to be afraid of," Dora laughed.   209

MONITOR PROGRESS   • Check Fluency

Fly, Eagle, Fly! **183k**

Armadillos

Are you curious about armadillos? These weird-looking critters are covered with big, tough scales. They even have scales on their faces and long, skinny tails. The scales look like armor that ancient knights wore. Armadillos need to protect themselves, so they use their armor. They quickly pull their legs under the armor and hide because they are frightened.

What happens when you poke an armadillo hiding in its armor? It usually fakes being dead. But if you scare it enough, it might jump straight up and scare you back.

Most of the day, armadillos live in burrows because they are shy and do not want to be seen. A burrow is a hole or tunnel. Armadillos have sharp claws that help them to dig burrows and to catch food. They also use their claws to fight anything that attacks them. Armadillos will fight only when hiding, jumping, or playing dead doesn't work.

Armadillos come out at night to hunt for dinner. They eat bugs, small animals, and some plants. Some armadillos also eat small worms that live in dead, rotting animals! Yuck! Armadillos have a strong sense of smell, so they use it to find food in the dark night. Rotting animals must be easy to smell.

How big do armadillos grow? The kind found in the United States can be 30 inches long. There are giant armadillos in South America that grow five feet long and can weigh over 60 pounds. That's as big as some dogs!

MONITOR PROGRESS   • Cause and effect

Cinco de Mayo

"What if I forget the dance, Mama?" Carmen said. She looked   11
at her red cotton dress in the mirror and twirled. Her skirt spun in a   26
graceful circle around her feet. Carmen loved to dance; she didn't love   38
an audience.   40

"You'll remember. You and Manuel are a beautiful dancing duo,"   50
Mama said.   52

"Besides," Manuel said, "no one at the festival knows the steps   63
we practiced at the studio. If you make a mistake, smile and keep   76
dancing."   77

Carmen tried to smile. She tried to eat her breakfast cereal, but   89
she was still nervous. They drove to the Cinco de Mayo Festival at the   103
county rodeo grounds. There was a stage across from the stadium.   114
Carmen and Manuel helped their parents unpack the guitar, violin,   124
and audio equipment. Their cousin Maria came to play piano in the   136
family trio.   138

"Carmen, you're as pale as a handkerchief," Maria said. "Are you   149
nervous?"   150

Carmen nodded.   152

"Just think about the rhythm of the music and keeping pace with   164
your brother," Maria said. "The audience won't see a frightened girl.   175
They'll see a graceful *dama*—a young lady—who is proud of her   188
heritage."   189

That afternoon at the performance, Carmen didn't think about the   199
audience or the video cameras. She thought, *This is my family's music.*   211
I am proud to dance with them.   218

MONITOR PROGRESS   • Check Fluency

Cowboy Clothes

Today, folks wear cowboy clothing because they like the style. In the Old West, a cowboy wasn't worried much about fashion. His clothes were practical and aided him in his job. When a cowboy rode a horse and herded cattle, he was outside all day in all kinds of weather. It was incredibly tough work.

These days, you see big-brimmed cowboy hats on a lot of people. An Old West cowboy wore a big-brimmed hat as protection from sun, rain, and snow. The hat also had a bigger top to help keep his head cool. In addition, his hat could be a tool of sorts. It could be a water scooper, a flag, or even a fan.

Cowboy's boots are popular today. They look great and are comfortable. However, a real cowboy wore them because he sat on a saddle on his horse. A saddle has stirrups, which are big rings for a cowboy's feet. The heels of cowboy boots were designed to help a cowboy keep his feet in the stirrups. The design also let him slip his feet out fast if he were to fall off his horse. That way the horse wouldn't drag the cowboy!

People today wear bandanas around their necks. Some people do this because they like the look. But others wear them for the same reasons that a cowboy did. A bandana keeps dust and dirt from going down a shirt. A cowboy also used a bandana to cover his face on dusty trails. We don't see dusty trails much in today's cities!

MONITOR PROGRESS • **Compare and Contrast**

A Day at the Circus

Once upon a time there were eight dwarfs, the usual seven plus   12

Sweepy. Sweepy came to clean the dwarfs' cottage after Snow White   23

left. One Saturday, after a long week of working in the mines, the   36

dwarfs were weak and tired too. They decided to take a long nap and   50

then go to the circus.   55

The dwarfs paid the bus fare to get to the fair grounds where the   69

circus was performing. When they got there, they bought peanuts to   80

nibble and pears for a snack. They ate the snack on the grass outside   94

the circus tent. They were sure to spill plenty of treats on the ground for   109

mice and swallows to eat. Then the dwarfs found their seats, and the   122

circus began.   124

They watched a pair of trapeze artists soar through the air. They   136

watched two high-wire walkers do a difficult dance overhead. The   146

dwarfs clapped until their hands were sore. Everyone had a favorite   157

act. Some liked the lions, jugglers, and horses best. Others liked the   169

acrobats, dogs, and clowns.   173

At the end of the show, the elephants made a parade around the   186

ring, and all the circus performers took a bow. On the way home,   199

Sweepy picked a bouquet of wildflowers for the cottage. It would   210

remind them all of their happy day at the circus.   220

MONITOR PROGRESS   • Check Fluency

Saturdays y domingos **253k**

New Words!

John lived on the sixth floor of a huge Dallas skyscraper. From his balcony, he could see the street below. Today, he watched carefully. His aunt, uncle, and cousins were arriving soon for a visit. They lived in England and seldom traveled to the United States. John had never met them.

"Mom, are you sure they really speak English?" John questioned. "They live in a foreign country."

"Yes, they're citizens of England," Mom answered with a chuckle. "English people speak the English language! But they do use some words differently than we do."

"They do?" asked John.

"Yes, for example, English people call an elevator a *lift*," said Mom.

"That makes sense because an elevator lifts people," said John.

"And they call a car's trunk a *boot*," explained Mom.

That didn't make sense! But before John could say that, he spotted a taxicab down below. "They're here, Mom!" he said.

Mom and John took the elevator down to the ground floor. Then they stood by the building's front door and watched as their English guests got out of the taxicab. John's uncle said to driver, "I'll get the suitcases out of the boot."

Boot! John looked at Mom.

One of John's cousins said, "I'll carry them to the lift."

Lift! John looked again at Mom.

Then John's aunt said to the driver, "We used a bit of petrol getting here from the airport."

"*Petrol* means gasoline," Mom whispered to John.

John smiled. This visit was going to be fun!

MONITOR PROGRESS • Main Idea and Details

Name _____

Stuck at the Airport

June 13, 10:43 am   4

Dear Diary,   6

It's the first day of summer vacation. Am I at the beach with my   20

friends? No, because I am stuck at the airport, waiting for a plane to   34

Grandma's house in Kansas. What normal person goes to Kansas for   45

the summer? All morning Dad has been describing Grandma's delicious   55

cooking. She makes her own sausage. She also makes homemade   65

applesauce. Dad's the one who's homesick for Grandma's house. I think   76

he should go!   79

June 13, 11:19 am   83

Dear Diary,   85

Now it's Mom's turn to talk my ear off. "Call if you get homesick.   99

Wear sunscreen. If there's a tornado warning, go straight for the cellar,"   111

she says. "You will be safe there." I promise that I'll run and hide the   126

minute I feel a raindrop.   131

June 13, 11:52 am   135

Dear Diary,   137

Grandma called and said she was glad she caught me. She told   149

me that her neighbor gave her a straw-colored cocker spaniel puppy.   160

She said he's very active and curious, and he's going to need a lot   174

of attention. Grandma asked if I would please teach him not to dig up   188

the lawn.   190

This is going to be the best summer ever!   199

MONITOR PROGRESS   • Check Fluency

Name _____

Berta Is Lonely

Berta sat on Grandpa's front stoop and gazed around, but she didn't see any kids. In fact, she hadn't seen any kids since she arrived at Grandpa's yesterday.

Berta had been looking forward to this visit to Mexico for a long time. She was really thrilled about seeing her dad's old neighborhood. Some of his childhood friends still lived nearby. She knew she would meet them later. Right now, however, Berta was a little bit bored. She wished there were kids around.

Suddenly, Berta had a brilliant idea. She asked Grandpa if she could stroll up and down the street. Maybe she would meet some kids that way.

Berta took her walk, but it didn't work. She didn't see any kids, and if kids saw her, they didn't come out to say hello. Berta had to try something else.

Then Berta grabbed her dad's old baseball mitt and a ball. She walked down the street again. As she did, Berta tossed the ball up in the air and caught it, over and over. She thought some boy or girl might see her and come out to play catch. That didn't work either.

Next, Berta saw her dad's old soccer ball. She walked down the street again and bounced the ball. She hoped the bouncing sound would get some attention. It did. As she passed a house, a door opened. Three kids came running out. In Spanish, they asked if they could play soccer with her.

Yes! Berta was happy.

MONITOR PROGRESS • Sequence

Name _____

Making Challah

Making challah bread for the Sabbath is a tradition in many Jewish   12

families. The Sabbath is a day of rest. Many families share a special   25

dinner and spend time playing with family members. Challah may be   36

bought at a bakery. But many sons and daughters learn to make it from   50

an old family recipe. Some families have used the same one for many   63

generations.   64

First, the best bread ingredients are sought: flour, yeast, sugar,   74

salt, and eggs. The ingredients are mixed together. They are kneaded,   85

squeezing the dough between flour-covered hands until it is smooth. The   96

dough is left to rise in a warm place. After the first rising, the mixture   111

is punched down and left to rest for a few minutes. Then the dough is   126

separated into three pieces and braided into one long loaf. The bread is   139

set out to rise a second time.   146

Some people put poppy seeds or sesame seeds on top of the loaf.   159

Most people brush the uncooked dough with raw egg to give the crust a   173

glossy brown color when it is done baking.   181

Family recipes for challah may be different, but most families agree   192

that it is important to make bread for your family with loving thoughts.   205

Copyright © by Pearson Education, Inc., or its affiliates. All Rights Reserved.

MONITOR PROGRESS   • Check Fluency

Arnie's Idea

The neighborhood public school was planning an International Fair. Kids and adults would display crafts, jewelry, and costumes from all over the world.

Mrs. Lanning's third graders wanted to do something really special to demonstrate that Americans eat foods from many different countries.

"How about making pizza?" suggested Arnie.

"That isn't such a good idea because pizza is just an Italian-American food," said Tess. "What about other countries?"

"Well, I meant we should bake pizzas in a special way," explained Arnie.

Then Arnie described his idea to the class.

On the evening of the fair, the third grade class had a large, colorful booth. Across the top, a sign said "Pizzas of the World." The class made little pizzas using ideas from all around the world. The Mexican pizza had taco sauce, cheese, and ground beef on it. The Chinese pizza had vegetables and little shrimp. The kids also made Jamaican pizza, German pizza, Indian pizza, Vietnamese pizza, and more.

Mrs. Lanning baked little pizza after pizza in an oven. The third graders served little pizzas to a long line of kids, parents, and teachers. Most people wanted to try more than one kind.

Tess, Arnie, and all the third graders were busy the whole evening of the fair. When it was finally over, the third grade class had no pizza left!

As the class cleaned up, Tess looked at Arnie and said, "Hey Arnie, I told you this wasn't such a good idea."

Then she added, "It was a great idea!"

MONITOR PROGRESS • **Draw conclusions**

Hunting Treasure

"What fine feast have you prepared for the crew's enjoyment?" the   11

Captain asked as he opened the hatch and went down the short flight of   25

steps to the kitchen. He had to bend down to enter the low doorway.   39

"The usual, Sir," I said as cheerfully as possible. *Ruined soup, moldy*   51

apples, and lumpy oatmeal is what I thought. I poured the captain a cup   65

of goat's milk from my pitcher.   71

I had left my childhood home in London to make my livelihood as a   85

cook at sea. I would have been better off living in a garbage dump. I   100

was sleepy and cold the entire voyage. But now it was spring, and our   114

voyage was almost over.   118

"Land ho!" a voice called from aloft.   125

At last! I went up on deck. There was a fair green strip of land   141

before us. The next morning, I set out with my shipmates to explore it.   155

The captain came seeking furs and spices. I had more practical things   166

in mind.   168

I searched the creek sides for green sprouts that are good to eat. I   182

filled my cap full of walnuts from the ground. Then, in an open meadow,   196

I found what I had been dreaming of for months. Fresh strawberries,   208

treasure enough for this ship's cook.   214

MONITOR PROGRESS • Check Fluency

The Last Night

Warren gazed out the upstairs bedroom window into the night. The moon shone brightly and lit up the farmyard. Warren studied the old wooden barn, the towering silo, and the animal pens. He took a deep breath. Through the window screen he could smell the farm. He could smell animals and fields of hay. He loved the summertime smells of this farmland. Then Warren heard a distant train whistling as it rumbled through a rail crossing on its way to the city.

Warren took another deep breath and wondered what his new life would be like. Tomorrow, his family would move into that huge city. Warren was looking forward to it. The city was full of excitement. There were busy people rushing around. There were zoos and museums. There were baseball parks and football stadiums. There were interesting things to do and interesting people to meet. City living would be a great adventure.

Yet Warren felt sad tonight. He knew he would miss this old farm. He would miss the sounds of roosters in the morning, of cows waiting to be milked, of pigs snorting as the gobbled down their food.

Warren wondered if he would ever again ride on a tractor or climb in a hayloft. He wondered if his mom and dad would be happy working in the city. City work would have to be easier than farming!

Warren leaned closer to the window and to the farm outside of it. Would he be happy in the city?

MONITOR PROGRESS

• Author's purpose

Me and Uncle Romie **359m**

Name _____

Grace's Place

Grace's class was putting on a play about famous places in the   12
United States. Each student was to choose his or her favorite place   24
and dress up to look like that place. Grace didn't know which place to   38
choose.   39

Her friend Nora was very tall. She was going to be the Washington   52
Monument. She was going to get a white suit and make a pointy white   66
hat with paper and glue. Grace couldn't think of anything as good as   79
that.   80

Grace had only a few days left to choose her place. She still had   94
no idea what to be. Grace went into her room and looked around.   107
She saw a crown from when she had dressed up as a princess. Then   121
she saw a flashlight that she had bought for camp. She looked in her   135
closet and saw a green dress that her mom had made her. She saw her   150
notebook on her desk.   154

Grace got an idea! She got all of the things together.   165

On the night of the play, all of Grace's friends showed up as   178
different famous places. There was a Mount Rushmore, a Craters of   189
the Moon, a White House, and of course the Washington Monument.   200
Grace unveiled her outfit last.   205

Grace's green dress became a gown. Her flashlight became a   215
torch, and her notebook became a tablet. She put the crown on top of   229
her head.   231

Grace was the Statue of Liberty!   237

MONITOR PROGRESS • Check Fluency

The Pony Express

Through much of American history, there wasn't an easy way to deliver mail around the country. There were no telephones, email, or televisions. It took a long time for information to get from one place to another.

By the 1850s, the telegraph started to be used. It allowed printed messages to be sent from place to place. Telegraph wires stretched across distant parts of America, but it took many, many years to get poles and wires up all over. In 1860, the Pony Express began to carry messages to some places where telegraph lines did not yet reach.

How did the Pony Express work? Horses and riders made up the Pony Express. The horses carried saddlebags filled with mail. A rider and horse started at one station and raced to the next. Then a new rider and horse would take the saddlebag and ride to the next station farther away.

The Pony Express could carry mail from Missouri to California in about 10 days. The route used was about 1,800 miles long. There were more than 150 stations along the way.

Pony Express riders were the bravest of all Americans alive in those days. Riders traveled alone on dangerous trails. They raced through icy rivers and along high cliffs. And Pony Express horses were America's fastest. They had to be in order to get the mail across those long distances.

In America's history, the Pony Express was one of the most important methods ever of getting and sending information.

MONITOR PROGRESS

• Fact and opinion

Statue of Liberty **393m**

The Secret Recipe

When it's chilly out, I like to bake. My favorite recipe is a cookie   14
recipe that came from my aunt. When she is free, she travels. My aunt   28
says she found the recipe on one of her travels in a foreign country. She   43
bought a book that had the recipe.   50

When my aunt got home from that trip, she tried the cookie recipe.   63
It is very odd. Besides the other ingredients, she had to use a gallon   77
of milk. The recipe made more than seven dozen cookies. The cookies   89
baked for a long time in the oven. After a while, my aunt felt foolish.   104
Could this be right? When the cookies were done, though, we all loved   117
them.   118

Now, my family makes the cookies every year. We all have different   130
kinds of shapes we like to make. My brother likes animals. He makes   143
cats, dogs, bears, and tigers. Sometimes he makes so many animals he   155
could have his own circus. My cousin likes to make stars. She also likes   169
the color pink, so she colors all the stars pink. My younger cousin likes   183
to make dinosaurs. I like to make circles. I use the bottom of a plastic   198
drinking glass to get a perfect circle shape.   206

All of our friends like the cookies. They think they are the best treats   220
ever. My family laughs. We all know the secret. The famous cookies   232
have vinegar in them!   236

MONITOR PROGRESS   • Check Fluency

Mr. Kang **429k**

Yosuke Returns

There are amazing stories of real lost pets and how they returned to their owners. For example, here's the entertaining tale of a parrot named Yosuke.

Yosuke lived with a Japanese family in a town near Tokyo. From his birth, Yosuke was raised as a pet. His human family took excellent care of him. Like many intelligent parrots, Yosuke was taught to repeat words and phrases. Yosuke could recite his name and address among other things.

One day Yosuke escaped from his cage. That probably wasn't too unusual, but he escaped from his family's house as well. Yosuke had flown to freedom!

The family searched, but couldn't find their Yosuke. How long could he survive without being fed and cared for?

Is a lost parrot happy to be free? There is no way to know what a parrot thinks. But most pet parrots don't have the skills to survive alone. They may not live very long once they have escaped. However, some birds figure out how to stay alive.

Yosuke was gone for two weeks when police noticed a gray parrot on the roof of a house. When they rescued the parrot, they didn't know it could talk. It said nothing to them. The police did know that the parrot needed help. They took it to a vet.

Once the parrot got a little care, it must have felt better. It started talking. It told the vet its name and address. It was Yosuke! Soon Yosuke was back home again.

MONITOR PROGRESS

• Cause and effect

Mr. Kang **429m**

Tips for Taking Great Travel Pictures

One of our freedoms is the freedom to travel, and it is fun to take   15
pictures when you do. They will help you remember your trips. For   27
your next trip, you can take great pictures too. Just follow these easy   40
directions.   41

At times, a close-up shot is best. Let's say you are taking a picture   55
of a sculpture. Use the zoom feature on your camera. That will let you   69
capture small details. The zoom also works well for taking shots of   81
nature. Use it to snap a picture of a native plant or a single tree.   96

Sometimes you may want to take a picture of something in motion.   108
You must be fast to take an action picture. Frame your picture first. Make   122
sure you are very still. Then use a fast shutter speed. If you do this, you   138
can take good shots of nature or people in motion.   148

You might want to take shots of the people you meet. Let's say you   162
are at a local celebration. Always ask before taking your shot. You may   175
think you are just being social. However, others might think you are   187
rude. Even if a person encourages you to take pictures, still ask. Then   200
you will not make anyone angry.   206

Follow these rules. If you do, you will take great pictures. You will   219
be able to look at them and remember your trip.   229

MONITOR PROGRESS

• Check Fluency

Talking Walls **459k**

Name _____

A Small Town Votes

There was an election in the town of Smithson. Voters had to decide whether or not to approve a new highway that would go through town.

Some citizens wanted the highway because it would make travel around Smithson easier. Many also thought the highway would aid the town's businesses.

Other citizens did not want the highway because they were afraid it would mean too much traffic in their local neighborhood. Many of these citizens were also concerned about the expense of building a new highway.

The voting took place on a Tuesday in April. The chart and map show how people voted and where the new highway would go.

	East Smithson	West Smithson
Number of citizens	345	388
Number of yes votes	250	156
Number of no votes	95	232

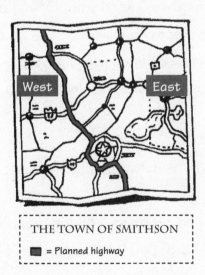

THE TOWN OF SMITHSON

■ = Planned highway

Name _____

The Case of the Missing Crystal

When Ned walked into the dining room, he gasped. A crystal 11
candlestick had disappeared! Who could have taken it? Ned wasn't 21
sure, but he was determined to find out. 29

Ned went to see Rosa. "Rosa," Ned asked, "Do you know where 41
the crystal candlestick is?" 45

"No, I sure don't, but I'll help you look for it," Rosa replied. 58

"I think some immature person has stolen it!" Ned told her 69
impatiently. "My goal is to catch the thief. I've already started an 81
informal list of possible suspects." 86

"Wow, that was fast!" Rosa smiled at Ned. She was unaware that 98
she was the only person on the list so far. 108

Rosa followed Ned on his journey through the house. In the garage 120
they saw broken crystal on the floor. 127

"Wow, I hope no one hurt themselves," Rosa said. "We'd better tell 139
Mom so that she can scoop up the pieces." 148

Ned wasn't paying attention. He was impolitely studying a muddy 158
patch in the corner. "This is an incredible clue," he muttered to himself. 171

"The thief was Rusty," he said. 177

Rusty was their dog. 181

"That's impossible!" Rosa cried. "Why would Rusty take a 190
candlestick?" 191

"I don't know," Ned said. "But he grabbed it off the table and ran 205
outside. Then he came back in and dropped it in the garage. I found a 220
muddy paw print that proves it!" 226

MONITOR PROGRESS • Check Fluency

Two Bad Ants **493k**

A Field Trip

As the bus pulled up to City Museum, Mr. Latham said to the seated third graders, "Now don't forget the rules for our field trip. Always stay with your assigned partner. For the first hour, feel free to visit the dinosaur exhibit and the Texas history room. Don't go to other exhibits until after we meet again at 10 o'clock."

Mr. Latham, the kids, and a few parents walked into the museum together. "I can enjoy dinosaurs and history," said Rich to his partner Felix. "But I'd really like to see the racecar exhibit."

"Me too," agreed Felix.

Rich and Felix didn't realize it, but Mr. Latham heard what they said. He knew they were good kids, yet he wondered if they might break the rules and sneak into the racecar exhibit. For the next hour, Mr. Latham had many students to watch, but now and then he checked to see where Rich and Felix were.

For 45 minutes, Rich and Felix roamed around the dinosaur exhibit. They really enjoyed it. Then they walked to the history room. They passed the big open doorway that led to the racecar exhibit. They peeked in a bit, but didn't go in. Instead, they walked into the history room and studied a model fort. Mr. Latham was proud of them.

At 10 o'clock, the class met. "Now we'll go to a different exhibit," said Mr. Latham. "Rich and Felix, will you pick one?"

"The racecar exhibit!" they both said.

Mr. Latham just smiled.

MONITOR PROGRESS

• Literary elements: Plot and theme

Two Bad Ants **493m**

Liz's Great-Grandfather

Liz sat and watched TV with Gramps, her great-grandfather. He had 11

lived a long time and now needed help doing simple things like getting 24

dressed or eating. He felt bad about that, yet didn't complain. He 36

always said, "In my life, I've seen worse days." 45

Liz and Gramps watched a television program about World War II. 56

When Gramps was a young adult, he was a soldier and fought in that 70

war. Even now, Gramps didn't enjoy talking about it, but Liz knew that 83

he had survived many tough battles. 89

Now the program showed a battle. A voice on TV explained how 101

horrible the battle was and why it was so important in history. Gramps 114

pointed to the TV and said, "I was there." 123

Liz watched the program closely. She didn't understand all of it. Still 135

she could tell that the battle was terrible. Liz thought about how Gramps 148

always said, "I've seen worse days." She knew now that those days 160

were during the war. 164

As the program ended, the voice on TV said that the battle helped 177

America win the war. It helped keep Americans free. Liz looked at 189

Gramps. He had tears in his eyes. So did she. 199

MONITOR PROGRESS • Check Fluency

Name _____

A History Mystery

Sometimes history is a mystery! Take, for example, the famous story of Molly Pitcher. She was known as a Revolutionary War hero, but who was she really?

In the Revolutionary War, American colonies fought against Great Britain. America didn't have a big army, but Great Britain did. Could America win the war and become an independent country? Many Americans thought battling for that freedom was worth the risk.

In those days, only men were allowed to be soldiers. Women wanted to fight but were denied the opportunity. Some women did heroic things anyway. Molly Pitcher was certainly one of those women.

Molly Pitcher's husband was a soldier in charge of a huge gun called a cannon. In battles, cannons fire shell after shell. They would get so hot! They had to be cooled off. Molly Pitcher carried water to cool off cannons during battle. That was dangerous work!

During one battle, Molly Pitcher's husband was wounded. He couldn't fire his cannon. So Molly Pitcher did. She helped the American soldiers. She became a hero.

Here's the mystery. The wounded soldier's name was William Hays, and his wife's name was Mary. Where did Molly Pitcher come from? Molly was a nickname for Mary. And Mary carried pitchers of water to cool cannons. So Mary Hays became Molly Pitcher.

Some people say that Mary Hays wasn't Molly Pitcher. Several other women might have been Molly Pitcher. Which one? That's the mystery. But this isn't: Many women helped America win the Revolutionary War!

MONITOR PROGRESS • Generalizing

Atlantis **531m**

Assessment Charts and Student Progress Report

from

First Stop Third Grade

Fluency Progress Chart, Grade 3

Name _____

WCPM	1	2	3	4	5	6	7	8	9	10	11	12	13	14	15	16	17	18	19	20	21	22	23	24	25	26	27	28	29	30	31	32	33	34	35	36
145																																				
140																																				
135																																				
130																																				
125																																				
120																																				
115																																				
110																																				
105																																				
100																																				
95																																				
90																																				
85																																				
80																																				
75																																				
70																																				
65																																				
60																																				
55																																				
50																																				

Timed Reading/Week

Name _____

Sentence Reading Chart

	Phonics		Selection Vocabulary		Reteach ✔	Reassess: Words Correct
	Total Words	Words Correct	Total Words	Words Correct		
Week 1 *When Charlie McButton Lost Power*						
Short Vowels; Syllables VC/CV	4					
Selection Vocabulary			2			
Week 2 *What About Me?*						
Plurals -s, -es, -ies	4					
Selection Vocabulary			2			
Week 3 *Kumak's Fish*						
Base Words and Endings -ed, -ing; -er, -est	4					
Selection Vocabulary			2			
Week 4 *Supermarket*						
Long Vowel Digraphs	4					
Selection Vocabulary			2			
Week 5 *My Rows and Piles of Coins*						
Vowel Diphthongs	4					
Selection Vocabulary			2			
Unit Scores	20		10			

- **RECORD SCORES** Use this chart to record scores for the Day 5 Sentence Reading Assessment.

- **RETEACH PHONICS SKILLS** If the child is unable to read all the tested phonics words, then reteach the phonics skills using the Reteach lessons in *First Stop*.

- **PRACTICE SELECTION VOCABULARY** If the child is unable to read all the tested selection vocabulary, then provide additional practice for the week's words. See pp. 55o, 81o, 107p, 139o, and 171b in the Teacher's Edition.

- **REASSESS** Use two different sentences for reassessment.

Sentence Reading Chart

USE WITH GRADE 3 UNIT 2

	Phonics		Selection Vocabulary		Reteach	Reassess: Words Correct
	Total Words	Words Correct	Total Words	Words Correct	✔	
Week 1 *Penguin Chick*						
Syllables V/CV and VC/V	4					
Selection Vocabulary			2			
Week 2 *I Wanna Iguana*						
Syllables C + *le*	4					
Selection Vocabulary			2			
Week 3 *Prudy's Problem*						
Compound Words	4					
Selection Vocabulary			2			
Week 4 *Tops and Bottoms*						
Consonant Blends	4					
Selection Vocabulary			2			
Week 5 *Amazing Bird Nests*						
Consonant Digraphs	4					
Selection Vocabulary			2			
Unit Scores	20		10			

- **RECORD SCORES** Use this chart to record scores for the Day 5 Sentence Reading Assessment.

- **RETEACH PHONICS SKILLS** If the child is unable to read all the tested phonics words, then reteach the phonics skills using the Reteach lessons in *First Stop*.

- **PRACTICE SELECTION VOCABULARY** If the child is unable to read all the tested selection vocabulary, then provide additional practice for the week's words. See pp. 199o, 225o, 253o, 281p, and 309b in the Teacher's Edition.

- **REASSESS** Use two different sentences for reassessment.

Name _____

Sentence Reading Chart

USE WITH GRADE 3 UNIT 3

	Phonics		Selection Vocabulary		Reteach	Reassess: Words Correct
	Total Words	Words Correct	Total Words	Words Correct	✔	
Week 1 *How do you Raise a Raisin*						
Contractions	4					
Selection Vocabulary			2			
Week 2 *Pushing Up The Sky*						
Prefixes	4					
Selection Vocabulary			2			
Week 3 *Seeing Stars*						
Spellings of /j/, /s/, /k/	4					
Selection Vocabulary			2			
Week 4 *A Symphony of Whales*						
Suffixes	4					
Selection Vocabulary			2			
Week 5 *Around One Cactus: Owls, Bats and Leaping Rats*						
Silent Consonants	4					
Selection Vocabulary			2			
Unit Scores	20		10			

- **RECORD SCORES** Use this chart to record scores for the Day 5 Sentence Reading Assessment.

- **RETEACH PHONICS SKILLS** If the child is unable to read all the tested phonics words, then reteach the phonics skills using the Reteach lessons in *First Stop*.

- **PRACTICE SELECTION VOCABULARY** If the child is unable to read all the tested selection vocabulary, then provide additional practice for the week's words. See pp. 337o, 365o, 387p, 415o, and 445b in the Teacher's Edition.

- **REASSESS** Use two different sentences for reassessment.

Sentence Reading Chart

USE WITH GRADE 3 UNIT 4

	Phonics		Selection Vocabulary		Reteach	Reassess: Words Correct
	Total Words	Words Correct	Total Words	Words Correct	✔	
Week 1 *The Man who Invented Basketball: James Naismith and His Amazing Game*						
Plurals	4					
Selection Vocabulary			2			
Week 2 *Hottest, Coldest, Highest, Deepest*						
r-Controlled /er/	4					
Selection Vocabulary			2			
Week 3 *Rocks in His Head*						
Prefixes	4					
Selection Vocabulary			2			
Week 4 *Gertrude Ederle*						
Suffixes	4					
Selection Vocabulary			2			
Week 5 *Fly, Eagle, Fly!*						
Syllables VC/CCV, VCC/CV	4					
Selection Vocabulary			2			
Unit Scores	20		10			

- **RECORD SCORES** Use this chart to record scores for the Day 5 Sentence Reading Assessment.

- **RETEACH PHONICS SKILLS** If the child is unable to read all the tested phonics words, then reteach the phonics skills using the Reteach lessons in *First Stop*.

- **PRACTICE SELECTION VOCABULARY** If the child is unable to read all the tested selection vocabulary, then provide additional practice for the week's words. See pp. 51p, 77o, 101o, 129o and 161b in the Teacher's Edition.

- **REASSESS** Use two different sentences for reassessment.

Sentence Reading Chart

USE WITH GRADE 3 UNIT 5

	Phonics		Selection Vocabulary		Reteach	Reassess: Words Correct
	Total Words	Words Correct	Total Words	Words Correct	✔	
Week 1 *Suki's Kimono*						
Syllables CV/VC	4					
Selection Vocabulary			2			
Week 2 *I Love Saturdays y domingos*						
Homophones	4					
Selection Vocabulary			2			
Week 3 *Good-bye, 382 Shin Dang Dong*						
Vowel Sound in *ball*: a, au, aw, al, augh, ough	4					
Selection Vocabulary			2			
Week 4 *Jalapeño Bagels*						
Vowel Patterns: *ei, eigh*	4					
Selection Vocabulary			2			
Week 5 *Me and Uncle Romie*						
Suffixes	4					
Selection Vocabulary			2			
Unit Scores	20		10			

- **RECORD SCORES** Use this chart to record scores for the Day 5 Sentence Reading Assessment.

- **RETEACH PHONICS SKILLS** If the child is unable to read all the tested phonics words, then reteach the phonics skills using the Reteach lessons in *First Stop*.

- **PRACTICE SELECTION VOCABULARY** If the child is unable to read all the tested selection vocabulary, then provide additional practice for the week's words. See pp. 189o, 215p, 243p, 269o, and 307b in the Teacher's Edition.

- **REASSESS** Use two different sentences for reassessment.

Sentence Reading Chart

USE WITH GRADE 3 UNIT 6

	Phonics		Selection Vocabulary		Reteach	Reassess: Words Correct
	Total Words	Words Correct	Total Words	Words Correct	✔	
Week 1 *Statue of Liberty*						
Vowel Sounds in *tooth* and *cook*	4					
Selection Vocabulary			2			
Week 2 *Happy Birthday Mr. Kang*						
Unaccented Syllables (schwa)	4					
Selection Vocabulary			2			
Week 3 *Talking Walls*						
Syllables *-tion, -sion, -ion, -ture, -ive, -ize*	4					
Selection Vocabulary			2			
Week 4 *Two Bad Ants*						
Prefixes	4					
Selection Vocabulary			2			
Week 5 *Atlantis*						
Related Words	4					
Selection Vocabulary			2			
Unit Scores	20		10			

- **RECORD SCORES** Use this chart to record scores for the Day 5 Sentence Reading Assessment.

- **RETEACH PHONICS SKILLS** If the child is unable to read all the tested phonics words, then reteach the phonics skills using the Reteach lessons in *First Stop*.

- **PRACTICE SELECTION VOCABULARY** If the child is unable to read all the tested selection vocabulary, then provide additional practice for the week's words. See pp. 331p, 361o, 385p, 413p, and 447b in the Teacher's Edition.

- **REASSESS** Use two different sentences for reassessment.

Student Progress Report: Grade 3

Name _____

This chart lists the skills taught in this program. On this reproducible chart, record your student's progress toward mastery of the skills covered in this school year here. Use the chart below to track the coverage of these skills.

Skill	Date	Date	Date
Read aloud written words in which the final "e" has been dropped in order to add a word ending.			
Read aloud words in which the final consonant is doubled when adding a word ending.			
Read aloud words in which the final "y" has been changed to "i" in order to add a word ending.			
Read aloud written words in which common suffixes or prefixes are added to the beginning or end of the words.			
Read aloud words with common spelling patterns.			
Read aloud words with closed syllable patterns.			
Read aloud words with open syllable patterns.			
Read aloud words with final stable-syllable patterns.			
Read aloud words with r-controlled vowels.			
Read aloud words with vowel combinations.			
Read aloud words with common spelling patterns.			
Read aloud contractions.			
Monitor reading accuracy.			
Use ideas from text features to make and confirm predictions.			

Skill	Date	Date	Date
Ask relevant questions, clarify what's read, and find facts and details about stories and other texts. Support answers with evidence.			
Understand a variety of texts by establishing a purpose for reading and checking comprehension. Make corrections and adjustments when that understanding breaks down.			
Smoothly read aloud and understand grade-level texts.			
Understand the meaning of common prefixes and common suffixes, and understand how they affect the root word.			
Figure out unfamiliar words or words with multiple meanings based on context.			
Identify and use antonyms, synonyms, words with multiple meanings, and words that are pronounced the same but differ in meaning.			
Identify and apply playful uses of language.			
Alphabetize a series of words to the third letter. Use a dictionary or a glossary to determine the meanings, syllable patterns, and pronunciation of unknown words.			
Paraphrase the themes and supporting details of fables, legends, myths, or stories.			
Compare and contrast the settings in myths and folktales.			
Describe different forms of poetry and how they create images in the reader's mind.			

Skill	Date	Date	Date
Explain how the elements of plot and character are presented through dialogue.			
Sequence and summarize the main events in the plot and explain their influence on future events.			
Describe how characters relate to each other and the changes they undergo.			
Identify whether the narrator or speaker of a story is first or third person.			
Explain the difference in point of view between a biography and autobiography.			
Identify language that creates visual images in a readers mind and appeals to the senses.			
Read quietly to oneself for long periods of time and produce evidence of reading. Explain in one's own words the meaning of what is read, and the order in which events occurred.			
Identify the topic and locate the author's purposes for writing the text.			
Identify the details or facts that support the main idea.			
Analyze, make inferences, and draw conclusions from the facts presented in the text and support those conclusions with evidence.			
Identify cause-and-effect relationships among ideas in texts.			

Skill	Date	Date	Date
Use text features to find information, and to make and verify predictions about the contents of the text.			
Identify what the author is trying to persuade the reader to think or do.			
Follow and explain a set of written multi-step directions.			
Understand how to look for and use information found in graphics.			
Understand how communication changes when moving from one type of media to another.			
Explain how various techniques in media are used to affect the message being delivered.			
Compare how different writing styles are used to communicate different kinds of information on the Internet.			
Plan a first draft and choose the appropriate genre for communicating ideas to an audience. Generate ideas through a range of strategies.			
Develop drafts and organize ideas into paragraphs.			
Revise drafts to make them clear and well organized for their audience. Include simple and compound sentences.			
Edit drafts for grammar, mechanics, and spelling using a teacher-developed rubric.			
Publish work for an audience.			
Write literary texts that are imaginative, build to an ending, and contain details about the characters and setting.			

Skill	Date	Date	Date
Use sensory details and the conventions of poetry.			
Write about important personal experiences.			
Establish a central idea in a topic sentence.			
Include supporting sentences with simple facts, details, and explanations.			
Write compositions that contain a concluding statement.			
Write essays tailored for a specific audience and purpose.			
Write responses to stories, poems, and nonfiction essays using evidence from the text to show understanding.			
Write persuasive essays for specific audiences on specific issues. Include personal opinions and use supporting details.			
Use and understand verbs.			
Use and understand nouns.			
Use and understand adjectives.			
Use and understand adverbs.			
Use and understand prepositions and prepositional phrases.			
Use and understand possessive pronouns.			
Use and understand conjunctions.			
Use and understand time and sequence transition-words.			
Form the complete subject and verb in a sentence.			

Skill	Date	Date	Date
Show agreement between subjects and verbs in simple and compound sentences.			
Print or write in script with spacing between words.			
Correctly capitalize geographical names and places.			
Correctly capitalize historical periods.			
Correctly capitalize official titles of people.			
Recognize and correctly use apostrophes in contractions and possessives.			
Recognize and correctly use commas in series and dates.			
Use correct mechanics and indent paragraphs.			
Use knowledge of letter sounds, word parts, how words break into syllables, and syllable patterns to spell.			
Develop a plan for gathering relevant information about the major research question.			
Spell words that double their final consonant when adding an ending.			
Spell words that drop their final "e" when adding an ending.			
Spell words that change their final "y" to "i" when adding an ending.			
Spell words that double their final consonant when adding an ending.			
Spell words that use complex combinations of consonants.			
Spell words that form vowel sounds from more than one letter.			

Skill	Date	Date	Date
Spell frequently used words and compound words from a common list.			
Spell words with common syllable constructions.			
Spell one-syllable words that sound the same but are spelled differently.			
Spell complex contractions.			
Use knowledge of spelling, and print and online dictionaries, to find the correct spellings of words.			
Develop research topics based on interests or the results of brainstorming sessions.			
Narrow topic and generate questions about it.			
Follow a research plan that includes the use of surveys, visiting places, and interviewing people.			
Collect information from experts, encyclopedias, and online searches.			
Use visual sources for information.			
Skim and scan text features.			
Take notes and organize information.			
Identify the author, title, publisher, and publication year of sources.			
Understand the difference between paraphrasing information and committing plagiarism. Identify why it is important to use reliable sources.			
Make research questions more specific based on the information collected from expert sources.			

Skill	Date	Date	Date
Draw conclusions about a topic in a brief written report, including a works-cited page showing author, title, publisher, and publication year for each source used.			
Listen closely to speakers, ask relevant questions, and make relevant comments.			
Give instructions that involve following directions, and retell instructions in one's own words.			
Speak clearly about a topic, make eye contact, have appropriate speaking rate, volume, and clarity to communicate ideas effectively.			
Work together with other students. Participate in discussions led by teachers and other students, ask and answer questions, and offer suggestions that build upon the ideas of others.			
Establish purposes for reading selected texts based upon own or others' desired outcome to enhance comprehension.			
Ask literal, interpretive, and evaluative questions of a text.			
Monitor and adjust comprehension using a variety of strategies.			
Make inferences about a text and use evidence from the text to support understanding.			
Summarize information in a text, maintaining meaning and logical order.			
Make connections between literary and informational texts with similar ideas and provide evidence from the text.			